Korean Grammar *in Use* Beginning

Korean Grammar

in Use Beginning

Written by	Ahn Jean-myung, Lee Kyung-ah, Han Hoo-young
Translated by	Chad Walker
First Published	February, 2010
21th Printing	October, 2022
Publisher	Chung Kyudo
Editors	Lee Suk-hee, Oh Ju-young, Oh Jeong-min
Design	Bae Young-eun, Son Hye-jung, Cho Hwa-youn, ELIM
Illustrator	Wishingstar
Voice Actors	Jeong Ma-ri, Kim Sung-gon, Mathew Rutledge

DARAKWON Published by Darakwon, Inc.
Darakwon Bldg., 211 Munbal-ro, Paju-si,
Gyeonggi-do, 10881 Republic of Korea
Tel: 02-736-2031 Fax: 02-732-2037
(Marketing Dept. ext.: 250~252 Editorial Dept. ext.: 420~426)

Price : 21,000 won (Free MP3 Download)

ISBN: 978-89-5995-198-7 18710
978-89-277-3118-4 (set)

http://www.darakwon.co.kr
http://koreanbooks.darakwon.co.kr

Visit the Darakwon homepage to learn about our other publications and promotions and to download the contents of the CD in MP3 format.

Korean Grammar *in Use* Beginning

Ahn Jean-myung, Lee Kyung-ah, Han Hoo-young

Preface

한국어를 가르치면서 학생들로부터 한국어가 어렵다는 이야기를 많이 듣습니다. 한국어는 다른 외국어와는 달리 어미와 조사가 상당히 많고 복잡하여 한국어를 오래 배운 고급 학습자들도 문법·문형을 종종 틀리는 것을 보게 됩니다. 의미는 비슷한데 뉘앙스에서 조금 차이가 나 어색하게 사용하거나 의미는 맞게 사용했는데 제약이 있어 비문을 만들기도 합니다. 그래서 학생들로부터 문법을 따로 공부할 수 있는 책이 있느냐는 질문들을 많이 받아 왔습니다. 1급부터 배운 수많은 문법들을 한눈에 볼 수 있는 책, 한국어의 비슷비슷한 문법들이 어떻게 다른지 설명하고 있는 책을 구하고 싶어 했습니다. 그러나 외국인을 위한 한국어 교재는 대부분 통합 교재이고 외국인 학습자들이 쉽게 한국어 문법만을 공부할 수 있는 책은 찾아볼 수 없었습니다. 그래서 문법 공부를 심도 있게 하고 싶은 학생들은 한국인을 대상으로 하는 책을 보는 경우도 있지만 이러한 책들은 복잡한 문법 설명과 예문으로 한국인조차 이해하기가 쉽지 않은 실정입니다. 이런 학생들의 상황에 대해 교사로서 항상 미안하고 안타까운 마음이 들었습니다.

본 교재는 이러한 마음에서 출발하였습니다. 본 교재에서는 한국의 대학 기관과 학원에서 가르치고 있는 교재의 1~2급에 나오는 문법들을 정리하여 초급 한국어 문법을 한눈에 볼 수 있게 하였습니다. 쓰임과 의미가 비슷한 문법들을 서로 비교해 놓아 학습자들이 혼동하는 문법 항목들을 쉽게 찾아볼 수 있도록 하였습니다. 이를 통해 학생들은 의미가 비슷한 문법 항목들을 정리할 수 있는 동시에 한 가지 상황에 대해 다르게 표현하는 것을 배울 수 있을 것입니다. 또한 문법의 뜻은 알아도 문법적인 제약을 모르고 사용해 어색한 문장을 만드는 경우가 많기 때문에 '문법적인 주의'를 요하는 부분도 책에 첨가하였습니다.

그동안 한국어 문법을 어려워했던 많은 학생들이 이 책을 통하여 한국어 문법에 좀 더 쉽게 접근할 수 있었으면 합니다. 더불어 본 교재를 공부하면서 학생들이 한국어를 좀 더 자연스럽고 다양하며, 정확하게 구사할 수 있게 되기를 바랍니다. 또한 학생들 못지않게 한국어 문법을 가르치는 것에 어려움이 많은 교사들 역시 이 책을 통해 수많은 문법 사항을 정리하고 비교하는 데 도움을 받을 수 있기를 진심으로 바랍니다.

끝으로 사명감을 가지고 좋은 한국어 교재 편찬에 열심을 다하는 다락원의 한국어출판부 편집진께 감사의 말을 전하고 싶습니다. 여러 가지 쉽지 않은 일이 많이 있었을 텐데 본 교재가 나오기까지 꼼꼼하게 신경을 써 주신 것에 감사를 드립니다. 또한 이 책의 번역을 맡아 주신 채드 워커 씨와 책에 대해 여러 가지 조언을 해 준 학생들과 친구들에게도 고마움을 전합니다.

저자 일동

We often hear from students that the Korean language is difficult to learn. Compared to other languages, Korean is unique in having a large number of complex endings and particles, and even advanced learners frequently make mistakes in grammar and sentence patterns. In some cases, differences in the nuances between two patterns with similar meanings result in awkward sentences, while in other cases, restrictions on usage can render otherwise correctly constructed sentences ungrammatical. For this reason students have often asked us if there isn't a book available that specifically focuses on Korean grammar. They want a book in which they can find all the grammar they've studied from their introductory Korean classes that also describes the differences between similar grammatical constructions. However, most Korean language materials for foreigners are designed in an integrated format, and thus it has been difficult to locate books from which students can easily study strictly grammar. This has resulted in those students seeking a more in-depth understanding of grammar resorting to grammar books written for native Korean speakers, but often the explanations in such books are so complex that even Korean speakers have difficulty understanding them. As instructors of Korean, we felt this regrettable state of affairs needed to be addressed.

The idea for this book began from such observations. *Korean Grammar In Use* collects the grammar points normally taught in Levels 1 and 2 at most university affiliated and private language institutes. We have attempted to make it easy for learners to locate those grammar patterns that learners find the most confusing by providing comparisons of patterns similar in meaning and usage. In this way, learners can not only clarify the differences between similar patterns but can also study how they are used differently depending on the situation. Further, because it is often the case that learners' awkward constructions result from knowing the correct meaning of a certain grammatical pattern but not its grammatical restrictions, we have added a 'Grammar Note' section to draw attention to such points.

It is our hope that through this book, students who have until now felt Korean grammar to be difficult will discover it to be much more easily accessible. Furthermore, we hope this book will allow students to have a richer, more natural-sounding, and more accurate command of Korean. Similarly, we sincerely hope that teachers of Korean will find this book helpful in the difficult job of clarifying and comparing the many aspects of Korean grammar.

Lastly, we would like to express our gratitude to the editors in the Korean Editorial Department at Darakwon, Inc. for their strong sense of duty and dedication to the editing and publishing of Korean language materials. We thank all of those involved for their tireless attention to detail throughout the long and difficult process leading up to this book's publication. Finally, we wish to extend our thanks to Chad Walker for translating the text and to all of our students and other individuals for their continuous support and advice.

The Authors

How to Use This Book

소제목 (예) N 때, A/V-(으)ㄹ 때

'N'은 '명사', 'A'는 '형용사', 'V'는 '동사'를 가리키고, 'A/V-(으)ㄹ 때'로 표기될 경우, 형용사와 동사와만 결합하는 것을 의미한다. 종종 동사만 결합되는 것에 형용사를 결합하기도 하여 오류를 만들기도 하는데, 그러한 것들을 틀리지 않게 하기 위해 결합 정보를 표시한 것이다.

도입 예문

목표 문법 학습 전 그림과 함께 제시된 문장 속에서 먼저 목표 문법의 의미를 추측할 수 있는 부분이다. 목표 문법이 잘 드러나면서 실생활에서 사용하는 문장으로 구성되었고, 대화의 맥락을 함축하여 제시된 그림을 통해 어렵게 느끼는 문법에 보다 쉽게 접근할 수 있다.

Grammar Focus

문법에 대한 일반적인 지식과 문법적 제약을 학습하는 부분으로 문법 사용 시 범하는 오류를 줄일 수 있다. 학생들이 틀리기 쉬운 활용 방법이 자주 사용하는 품사(명사, 동사, 형용사)와 함께 표로 제시되었다.

- ○는 맞다는 것을 의미하고, ×는 틀리다는 것을 의미한다.

03 못 V-아/어요 (V-지 못해요)

Track 029

저는 수영을 **못해요**.
(= 저는 **수영하지 못해요**.)
I can't swim.

오늘은 술을 **못 마셔요**.
(= 오늘은 술을 **마시지 못해요**.)
I can't drink today.

저는 노래를 **못 불러요**.
(= 저는 노래를 **부르지 못해요**.)
I can't sing.

Grammar Focus

This pattern expresses the subject's lack of ability to do something or the fact that something does not go according to one's wish or hope due to some external factor. It corresponds to the English 'cannot' and is formed by adding 못 in front of a verb or **-지 못해요** to the end of a verb stem.

(See also Unit 6. Ability and Possibility 01 V-(으)ㄹ 수 있다/없다)

못 + 가다 → 못 가요　　　가다 + **-지 못해요** → 가지 못해요
못 + 요리하다 → 요리 못해요 (○)　못 요리해요 (×)

Base Form	못 -아/어요	-지 못해요
타다	못 타요	타지 못해요
읽다	못 읽어요	읽지 못해요
숙제하다	숙제 못해요	숙제하지 못해요
*쓰다	못 써요	쓰지 못해요
*듣다	못 들어요	듣지 못해요

* Irregular form

2. Negative Expressions 65

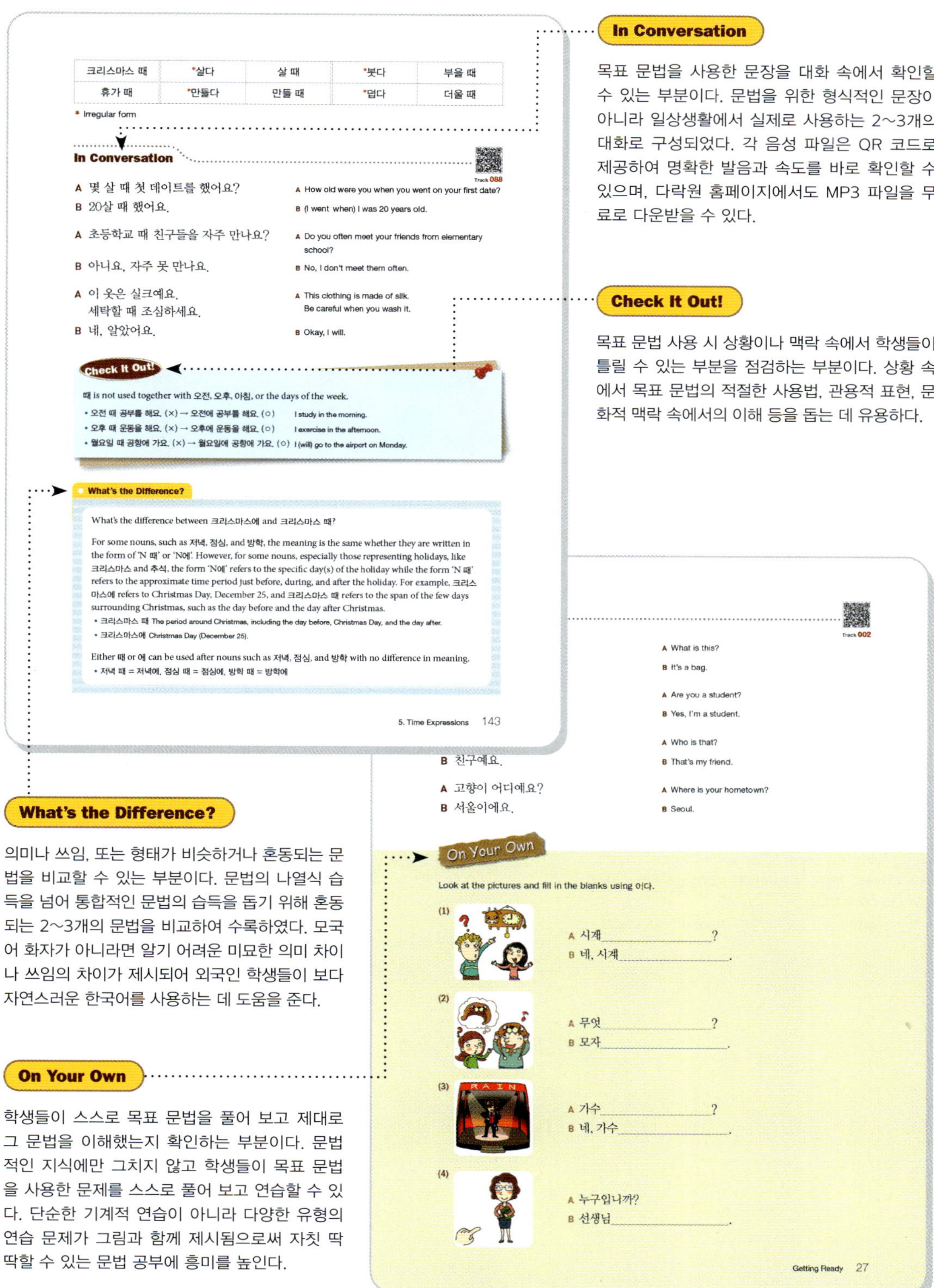

크리스마스 때	*살다	살 때	*붓다	부을 때
휴가 때	*만들다	만들 때	*덥다	더울 때

* Irregular form

In Conversation

Track 088

A 몇 살 때 첫 데이트를 했어요?
B 20살 때 했어요.

A 초등학교 때 친구들을 자주 만나요?
B 아니요, 자주 못 만나요.

A 이 옷은 실크예요.
세탁할 때 조심하세요.
B 네, 알았어요.

A How old were you when you went on your first date?
B (I went when) I was 20 years old.

A Do you often meet your friends from elementary school?
B No, I don't meet them often.

A This clothing is made of silk.
Be careful when you wash it.
B Okay, I will.

Check It Out!

때 is not used together with 오전, 오후, 아침, or the days of the week.

- 오전 때 공부를 해요. (×) → 오전에 공부를 해요. (○) I study in the morning.
- 오후 때 운동을 해요. (×) → 오후에 운동을 해요. (○) I exercise in the afternoon.
- 월요일 때 공항에 가요. (×) → 월요일에 공항에 가요. (○) I (will) go to the airport on Monday.

What's the Difference?

What's the difference between 크리스마스에 and 크리스마스 때?

For some nouns, such as 저녁, 점심, and 방학, the meaning is the same whether they are written in the form of 'N 때' or 'N에'. However, for some nouns, especially those representing holidays, like 크리스마스 and 추석, the form 'N에' refers to the specific day(s) of the holiday while the form 'N 때' refers to the approximate time period just before, during, and after the holiday. For example, 크리스마스에 refers to Christmas Day, December 25, and 크리스마스 때 refers to the span of the few days surrounding Christmas, such as the day before and the day after Christmas.

- 크리스마스 때 The period around Christmas, including the day before, Christmas Day, and the day after.
- 크리스마스에 Christmas Day (December 25).

Either 때 or 에 can be used after nouns such as 저녁, 점심, and 방학 with no difference in meaning.

- 저녁 때 = 저녁에, 점심 때 = 점심에, 방학 때 = 방학에

5. Time Expressions 143

Track 002

B 친구예요.

A 고향이 어디예요?
B 서울이에요.

A What is this?
B It's a bag.

A Are you a student?
B Yes, I'm a student.

A Who is that?
B That's my friend.

A Where is your hometown?
B Seoul.

On Your Own

Look at the pictures and fill in the blanks using 이다.

(1) A 시계________?
B 네, 시계________.

(2) A 무엇________?
B 모자________.

(3) A 가수________?
B 네, 가수________.

(4) A 누구입니까?
B 선생님________.

Getting Ready 27

In Conversation

목표 문법을 사용한 문장을 대화 속에서 확인할 수 있는 부분이다. 문법을 위한 형식적인 문장이 아니라 일상생활에서 실제로 사용하는 2~3개의 대화로 구성되었다. 각 음성 파일은 QR 코드로 제공하여 명확한 발음과 속도를 바로 확인할 수 있으며, 다락원 홈페이지에서도 MP3 파일을 무료로 다운받을 수 있다.

Check It Out!

목표 문법 사용 시 상황이나 맥락 속에서 학생들이 틀릴 수 있는 부분을 점검하는 부분이다. 상황 속에서 목표 문법의 적절한 사용법, 관용적 표현, 문화적 맥락 속에서의 이해 등을 돕는 데 유용하다.

What's the Difference?

의미나 쓰임, 또는 형태가 비슷하거나 혼동되는 문법을 비교할 수 있는 부분이다. 문법의 나열식 습득을 넘어 통합적인 문법의 습득을 돕기 위해 혼동되는 2~3개의 문법을 비교하여 수록하였다. 모국어 화자가 아니라면 알기 어려운 미묘한 의미 차이나 쓰임의 차이가 제시되어 외국인 학생들이 보다 자연스러운 한국어를 사용하는 데 도움을 준다.

On Your Own

학생들이 스스로 목표 문법을 풀어 보고 제대로 그 문법을 이해했는지 확인하는 부분이다. 문법적인 지식에만 그치지 않고 학생들이 목표 문법을 사용한 문제를 스스로 풀어 보고 연습할 수 있다. 단순한 기계적 연습이 아니라 다양한 유형의 연습 문제가 그림과 함께 제시됨으로써 자칫 딱딱할 수 있는 문법 공부에 흥미를 높인다.

How to Use This Book

Grammar Entry (e.g.) N때, A/V-(으)ㄹ 때

The abbreviation 'N' represents 'Noun', 'A' represents 'Adjective' and 'V' represents 'Verb'. For example, 'A/V-(으)ㄹ 때', indicates that the expression attaches to adjectives and verbs only. Sometimes an adjective can attach to a place where normally verbs are attached, and because this can be a cause of grammatical errors among learners, we have added informative notes to the grammatical explanations when necessary.

Introductory Sentences

At the beginning of each chapter, introductory sentences are presented along with illustrations to give the learner a chance to infer the meaning of the target grammar to be introduced in the chapter. These sentences introduce the target grammar points as they are used in real-life situations, incorporating context through the use of accompanying illustrations and allowing the learner to more easily grasp the meaning of the underlying grammar.

Grammar Focus

Grammar focus points are included to help the learner decrease grammatical mistakes by providing information on both the general aspects and grammatical restrictions of Korean. These are presented in table form along with the parts of speech (nouns, verbs, adjectives, etc.) for which conjugation rules can be confusing.

• '○' means "correct", '×' means "incorrect".

03 못 V-아/어요 (V-지 못해요)

Track 029

저는 수영을 못해요.
(= 저는 수영하지 못해요.)
I can't swim.

오늘은 술을 못 마셔요.
(= 오늘은 술을 마시지 못해요.)
I can't drink today.

저는 노래를 못 불러요.
(= 저는 노래를 부르지 못해요.)
I can't sing.

Grammar Focus

This pattern expresses the subject's lack of ability to do something or the fact that something does not go according to one's wish or hope due to some external factor. It corresponds to the English 'cannot' and is formed by adding 못 in front of a verb or -지 못해요 to the end of a verb stem.

(See also Unit 6. Ability and Possibility 01 V-(으)ㄹ 수 있다/없다)

못 + 가다 → 못 가요　　가다 + -지 못해요 → 가지 못해요
못 + 요리하다 → 요리 못해요 (○)　못 요리해요 (×)

Base Form	못 -아/어요	-지 못해요
타다	못 타요	타지 못해요
읽다	못 읽어요	읽지 못해요
숙제하다	숙제 못해요	숙제하지 못해요
*쓰다	못 써요	쓰지 못해요
*듣다	못 들어요	듣지 못해요

* Irregular form

2. Negative Expressions 65

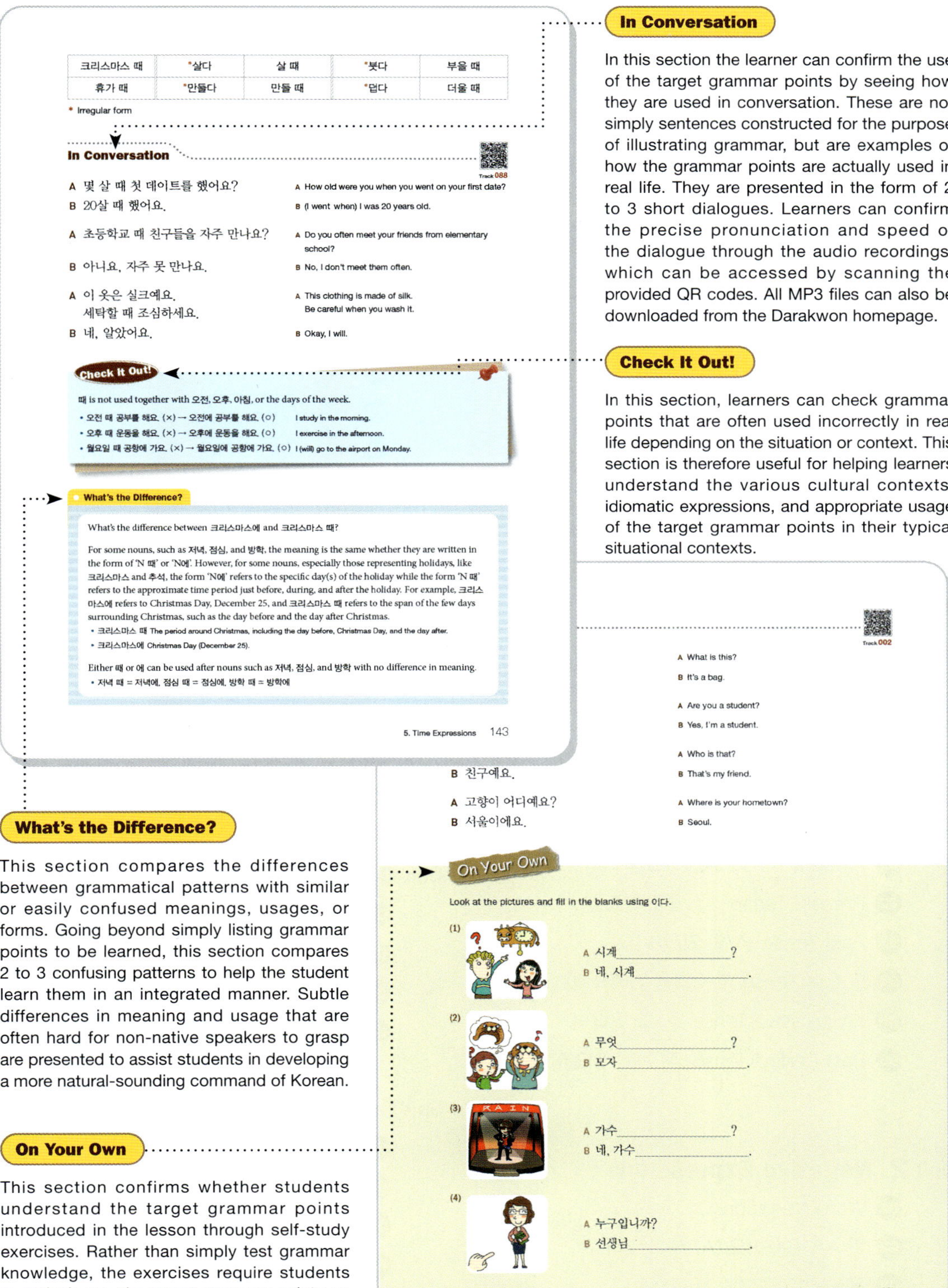

크리스마스 때	*살다	살 때	*붓다	부을 때
휴가 때	*만들다	만들 때	*덥다	더울 때

* Irregular form

In Conversation

Track 088

A 몇 살 때 첫 데이트를 했어요?
B 20살 때 했어요.

A How old were you when you went on your first date?
B (I went when) I was 20 years old.

A 초등학교 때 친구들을 자주 만나요?
B 아니요, 자주 못 만나요.

A Do you often meet your friends from elementary school?
B No, I don't meet them often.

A 이 옷은 실크예요. 세탁할 때 조심하세요.
B 네, 알았어요.

A This clothing is made of silk. Be careful when you wash it.
B Okay, I will.

Check It Out!

때 is not used together with 오전, 오후, 아침, or the days of the week.

- 오전 때 공부를 해요. (×) → 오전에 공부를 해요. (○) I study in the morning.
- 오후 때 운동을 해요. (×) → 오후에 운동을 해요. (○) I exercise in the afternoon.
- 월요일 때 공항에 가요. (×) → 월요일에 공항에 가요. (○) I (will) go to the airport on Monday.

What's the Difference?

What's the difference between 크리스마스에 and 크리스마스 때?

For some nouns, such as 저녁, 점심, and 방학, the meaning is the same whether they are written in the form of 'N 때' or 'N에'. However, for some nouns, especially those representing holidays, like 크리스마스 and 추석, the form 'N에' refers to the specific day(s) of the holiday while the form 'N 때' refers to the approximate time period just before, during, and after the holiday. For example, 크리스마스에 refers to Christmas Day, December 25, and 크리스마스 때 refers to the span of the few days surrounding Christmas, such as the day before and the day after Christmas.

- 크리스마스 때 The period around Christmas, including the day before, Christmas Day, and the day after.
- 크리스마스에 Christmas Day (December 25).

Either 때 or 에 can be used after nouns such as 저녁, 점심, and 방학 with no difference in meaning.

- 저녁 때 = 저녁에, 점심 때 = 점심에, 방학 때 = 방학에

5. Time Expressions 143

Track 002

A What is this?
B It's a bag.

A Are you a student?
B Yes, I'm a student.

A Who is that?
B 친구예요.
B That's my friend.

A 고향이 어디예요?
B 서울이에요.

A Where is your hometown?
B Seoul.

On Your Own

Look at the pictures and fill in the blanks using 이다.

(1) A 시계________?
B 네, 시계________.

(2) A 무엇________?
B 모자________.

(3) A 가수________?
B 네, 가수________.

(4) A 누구입니까?
B 선생님________.

Getting Ready 27

In Conversation

In this section the learner can confirm the use of the target grammar points by seeing how they are used in conversation. These are not simply sentences constructed for the purpose of illustrating grammar, but are examples of how the grammar points are actually used in real life. They are presented in the form of 2 to 3 short dialogues. Learners can confirm the precise pronunciation and speed of the dialogue through the audio recordings, which can be accessed by scanning the provided QR codes. All MP3 files can also be downloaded from the Darakwon homepage.

Check It Out!

In this section, learners can check grammar points that are often used incorrectly in real life depending on the situation or context. This section is therefore useful for helping learners understand the various cultural contexts, idiomatic expressions, and appropriate usage of the target grammar points in their typical situational contexts.

What's the Difference?

This section compares the differences between grammatical patterns with similar or easily confused meanings, usages, or forms. Going beyond simply listing grammar points to be learned, this section compares 2 to 3 confusing patterns to help the student learn them in an integrated manner. Subtle differences in meaning and usage that are often hard for non-native speakers to grasp are presented to assist students in developing a more natural-sounding command of Korean.

On Your Own

This section confirms whether students understand the target grammar points introduced in the lesson through self-study exercises. Rather than simply test grammar knowledge, the exercises require students to actively use the target grammar points on their own.

Contents

Introduction to the Korean Language

1. Korean Sentence Structure
2. Conjugation of Verbs and Adjectives
3. Connecting Sentences
4. Sentence Types
5. Honorific Expressions

1. Korean Sentence Structure

Korean sentences consist of either "a subject + predicate (verb)" or "a subject + object + predicate (verb)."

Eric eats an apple.

Eric reads a book in the library.

Particles are attached to words in Korean sentences. They express the role that their respective words play in the sentence. After the subject of a sentence, the particle **이** or **가** is used. After an object, the particle **을** or **를** is used. And after an adverbial, particles such as **에** and **에서** are used. (See also Unit 3. Particles)

While the predicate of a Korean sentence always comes at the very end of the sentence, the order of subjects, objects, and adverbials changes depending on the intention of the speaker. Regardless of their order in the sentence, however, the role of each of these parts can still be identified because of the particle attached to it.

사과를		에릭이		먹어요.
object	+	subject	+	verb
an apple		Eric		eats

책을		도서관에서		에릭이		읽어요.
object	+	adverb	+	subject	+	verb
a book		in the library		Eric		reads

In addition, when the subject can be clearly understood from the context, it can be omitted.

A 에릭이 뭐 해요? What is Eric doing?
B (에릭이) 사과를 먹어요. (He is) eating an apple.

A 어디에 가요? Where do (you) go?
B 학교에 가요. (I) go to school.

2. Conjugation of Verbs and Adjectives

One of the characteristics of Korean verbs and adjectives is that they both are conjugated according to tense, politeness level, passive and causative forms, and speech styles. Verbs and adjectives consist of a word stem and word ending, with their base forms comprised of the word stem plus **다**. This form is also called the 'dictionary form'. Accordingly, a dictionary search for such words will reveal their base forms, such as **가다** (to go), **오다** (to come), **먹다** (to eat), and **입다** (to wear). When conjugated, the word stems of verbs and adjectives do not change; rather, **다** is replaced with the appropriate form depending on the speaker's intention.

Verbs

Base Form	
가 다 ↑ word stem ↑ word ending (to go)	갑니다 (go/goes) 가(다) + –ㅂ니다 (present formal ending)
	가십니다 (go/goes) (referring to a superior/elder) 가(다) + –시– (honorific) + –ㅂ니다 (present formal ending)
	갔습니다 (went) 가(다) + –았– (past tense) + –습니다 (present formal ending)

Adjectives

Base Form	
좋 다 ↑ word stem ↑ word ending (to be good)	좋습니다 (is good) 좋(다) + −습니다 (present formal ending)
	좋았습니다 (was good) 좋(다) + −았− (past tense) + −습니다 (present formal ending)
	좋겠습니다 (seems be good) 좋(다) + −겠− (guess) + −습니다 (formal ending)

3. Connecting Sentences

There are two ways to connect sentences in Korean. One is by using conjunctive adverbs (e.g., **그리고** (and), **그렇지만** (but), **그래서** (so/therefore)), and the other is by using conjunctive endings.

(1) And

Conjunctive Adverb Connection	바람이 불어요. 그리고 추워요. It's windy. And It's cold.
Conjunctive Ending Connection	바람이 불고 추워요. It's windy and cold.

(2) But

Conjunctive Adverb Connection	김치는 맵습니다. 그렇지만 맛있습니다. Kimchi is spicy. But it tastes good.
Conjunctive Ending Connection	김치는 맵지만 맛있습니다. Kimchi is spicy but tastes good.

(3) So/Therefore

Conjunctive Adverb Connection	눈이 와요. 그래서 길이 많이 막혀요. It's snowing. Therefore the traffic is bad.
Conjunctive Ending Connection	눈이 와서 길이 많이 막혀요. It's snowing, so the traffic is bad.

When connecting two sentences with a conjunctive adverb, it is sufficient simply to place the conjunctive adverb between the two sentences. However, when using a conjunctive ending, the ending must be attached to the word stem of the predicate of the preceding sentence to connect the two sentences.

(1) 바람이 **불다** + **-고** + 추워요 → 바람이 불고 추워요.
(2) 김치가 **맵다** + **-지만** + 맛있어요 → 김치가 맵지만 맛있어요.
(3) 눈이 **오다** + **-아서** + 길이 많이 막혀요 → 눈이 와서 길이 많이 막혀요.

(See also Good Things to Know 4. Connective Adverbs)

4. Sentence Types

Korean has four main sentence types: declarative, interrogative, imperative, and propositive. Moreover, the sentence type is influenced by the location that the speech is occurring and the target, which can be divided into two main types: formal polite and informal polite (including informal plain). The formal polite style –(스)ㅂ니다 is used most in formal or public situations, including the military, news reporting, presentations, meetings, and lectures. The informal polite style –아/어요 is the honorific form used most in daily life. Compared to the formal polite style, the informal polite style is softer and less formal, and therefore it is used mainly among family members, friends, and other close acquaintances. Furthermore, although the formal polite style has different forms for each of the four sentence types (declarative, interrogative, imperative, and propositive), the informal polite style uses the same form for all four types. Thus, sentence types in this style are determined by the situation and sentence intonation. For this reason, the informal polite style is less complicated than the formal polite style. As for the informal plain style –아/어, it is mainly used among intimate friends, by superiors toward persons of lower-rank, and among family members. It is considered rude to use the informal plain style with somebody you do not know personally or with whom you are not very close. Here we examine the formal polite and informal polite styles only.

(1) Declarative Sentence

Declarative sentences are used when explaining something or responding to a question.
(See also Unit 1. Tenses 01 Present Tense)

① Formal Polite Style

Declarative formal polite sentences are made by adding –(스)ㅂ니다 to the word stem.

- 저는 학교에 갑니다. I go to school.
- 저는 빵을 먹습니다. I eat bread.

② **Informal Polite Style**

Declarative informal polite sentences are made by adding **–아/어요** to the word stem.

- 저는 학교에 가요. I go to school.
- 저는 빵을 먹어요. I eat bread.

(2) Interrogative Sentences

Interrogative sentences are used when asking a question. (See also Unit 1. Tenses 01 Present Tense)

① **Formal Polite Style**

Interrogative formal polite sentences are made by adding **–(스)ㅂ니까?** to the word stem.

- 학교에 갑니까? Do you go to school?
- 빵을 먹습니까? Do you eat bread?

② **Informal Polite Style**

Interrogative informal polite sentences are made by adding **–아/어요?** to the word stem. Because they have the same form as declarative sentences, they are made interrogative by being spoken with a rising intonation at the end of the sentence (and also by adding a question mark to the written form).

- 학교에 가요? Do you go to school?
- 빵을 먹어요? Do you eat bread?

(3) Imperative Sentences

Imperative sentences are used when making a demand or giving advice.
(See also Unit 7. Demands and Obligations, Permission and Prohibition 01 V–(으)세요)

① **Formal Polite Style**

Imperative formal polite sentences are made by adding **–(으)십시오** to the word stem.

- 공책에 쓰십시오. Please write in your notebook.
- 책을 읽으십시오. Please read the book.

② Informal Polite Style

Imperative informal polite sentences can be made by adding **-아/어요** to the word stem, just like in the other sentence types described above. However, using **-(으)세요** in place of **-아/어요** is considered a more polite expression, and therefore **-(으)세요** should be used.

- 공책에 쓰세요. Please write in your notebook.
- 책을 읽으세요. Please read the book.

(4) Propositive Sentences

Propositive sentences are used when making a suggestion or agreeing with someone else's suggestion. (See also Unit 12. Asking Opinions and Making Suggestions 03 V-(으)ㅂ시다)

① Formal Polite Style

Propositive formal polite sentences are made by adding **-(으)ㅂ시다** to the word stem. **-(으)ㅂ시다** can be used when the person being spoken to is younger or the same age as the speaker. It cannot be used when speaking to a superior. It is considered improper etiquette to use this expression toward a superior or elder.

- 11시에 만납시다. Let's meet at 11 o'clock.
- 여기에서 점심을 먹읍시다. Let's eat lunch here.

② Informal Polite Style

Propositive informal polite sentences are made by adding **-아/어요**, just like in the other sentence types described above.

- 11시에 만나요. Let's meet at 11 o'clock.
- 여기에서 점심을 먹어요. Let's eat lunch here.

The preceeding sentence types are summarized below using the verb **가다** (to go). The subject is omitted and understood by the situation or context.

	Formal Polite Style	Informal Polite Style
Declarative	갑니다.	가요. ↘ (I) go. (I) am going.
Interrogative	갑니까?	가요? ↗ Shall (we) go?
Imperative	가십시오.	가세요. ↓ Go!
Propositive	갑시다.	가요. → Let's go.

(※ Red arrows indicate the degree of rising, falling, or unchanging intonation at the end of the sentence.)

5. Honorific Expressions

Due to the influence of Confucian thought on Korean society, it is common for Korean speakers to use both honorific and humble forms of speech in conversation according to age, family relationships, social status, and social distance (degree of intimacy).

(1) Honoring the Subject of the Sentence

Honorifics are used when the subject of a sentence is a person older than the speaker, a senior member of one's family, or a person of higher social rank. To honor the subject, **–(으)시–** is added to the stems of adjectives and verbs. For verb stems ending in a vowel, **–시–** is added, and for those ending in a consonant, **–으시–** is added.

가다 (to go)

가 + **–시–** + –ㅂ니다 → 가십니다
가 + **–시–** + –어요 → 가세요
가 + **–시–** + –었어요 → 가셨어요
가 + **–시–** + –(으)ㄹ 거예요 → 가실 거예요

읽다 (to read)

읽 + **–으시–** + –ㅂ니다 → 읽으십니다
읽 + **–으시–** + –어요 → 읽으세요
읽 + **–으시–** + –었어요 → 읽으셨어요
읽 + **–으시–** + –(으)ㄹ 거예요 → 읽으실 거예요

- 선생님께서 한국말을 가르치십니다. The teacher teaches Korean.
- 아버지께서는 작년에 부산에 가셨어요. My father went to Busan last year.

(2) Honoring the Listener

Honorifics are used when the listener is older or of higher social status than the speaker and also when the speaker and listener are not acquainted with each other, regardless of age. Final endings are used to express the degree of respect, and they can be formed from each of the formal polite, informal polite.

(See also Introduction to the Korean Language 4. Sentence Types)

도와주셔서 감사합니다. (formal polite style)
도와주셔서 감사해요. (informal polite style)
※ 도와줘서 고마워. is an informal plain style

(3) Other Honorifics

① The honorific forms of some verbs are not expressed by adding –(으)시– to the verb stem but rather by using a different verb form altogether.

Base Form	Honorific Form	Base Form	Honorific Form
자다 (to sleep)	주무시다	죽다 (to die)	돌아가시다
말하다 (to speak)	말씀하시다	데려가다 (to take)	모셔가다
먹다 (to eat)	잡수시다/드시다	있다 (to exist)	계시다
마시다 (to drink)	드시다	있다 (to have)	있으시다

- 어머니께서 집에 안 **계세요.** Mother is not home right now.
- 내일 시간 **있으세요**? Do you have time tomorrow?

② Some nouns have honorific counterparts.

Base Form	Honorific Form	Base Form	Honorific Form
나이 (age)	연세	생일 (birthday)	생신
말 (words)	말씀	집 (house)	댁
밥 (meal/food)	진지	이름 (name)	성함
사람 (person)	분	아내 (wife)	부인

- 할아버지, **진지** 잡수세요. Grandpa, please have some dinner.
- **부인**께서도 안녕하십니까? How is your wife?

③ Honorific particles can be used after nouns indicating people.

이/가 → 께서　　은/는 → 께서는　　에게(한테) → 께

- 동생**이** 친구에게 선물을 줍니다. My younger sibling gives a present to a friend.
- 할아버지**께서** 동생에게 선물을 주십니다. Grandpa gives a present to a brother.
- 저**는** 딸기를 좋아해요. I like strawberries.
- 할머니**께서는** 딸기를 좋아하세요. Grandma likes strawberries.

④ Nouns designating persons can be made honorific by adding the suffix –님.

Base Form	Honorific Form	Base Form	Honorific Form
선생 (teacher)	선생님	교수 (professor)	교수님
사장 (president)	사장님	박사 (doctor)	박사님
목사 (pastor)	목사님	원장 (director)	원장님

- 저희 사장**님**은 마음이 넓으십니다.
  Our company president is a generous person.
- 목사**님**, 기도해 주셔서 감사합니다.
  Pastor, thank you for your prayer.

⑤ Respect can be expressed toward the listener or target of an action by using the following words.

Base Form	Honorific Form	Base Form	Honorific Form
말하다 (to speak)	말씀드리다	묻다 (to ask)	여쭙다
주다 (to give)	드리다	보다/만나다 (to meet)	뵙다

- 아버지께 **말씀드릴까요**? Shall we speak with Dad?
- 할아버지께 이 책을 **드리세요**. Please give this book to Grandpa.

⑥ The speaker can also show respect toward the listener by lowering his or her own status.

나 → 저 I　　**우리 → 저희** Our　　**말 → 말씀** Words

- **저**도 그 소식을 들었어요. I also heard that news.
- **저희** 집에 한번 놀러 오세요. Please stop by our house sometime.
- 부장님, 드릴 **말씀**이 있습니다. Chief, I have something to tell you.

(4) Things to Remember when Using Honorifics

① In Korean it is common to address others by repeatedly using their name or title rather than pronouns such as **당신** (you), **너** (you), **그** (he/him), **그녀** (she/her), and **그들** (they/them).

"요코 씨, 어제 회사에서 재준 씨를 만났어요? 재준 씨가 (그가(×)) 요코 씨를 (당신을(×)) 찾았어요. 그러니까 요코 씨가 (당신이(×)) 재준 씨한테 (그한테(×)) 전화해 보세요."

"Yoko, did you see Jaejun at work yesterday? Jaejun (He) was looking for Yoko (you), so Yoko (you) need to give Jaejun (him) a call."

당신 is a mutual title of address used mainly between husband and wife, and therefore it is not used to address anyone other than one's spouse. Similarly, **너** is a mutual title used only among close friends.

- 여보, 아까 **당신**이 나한테 전화했어요? Dear, did you call me?
- **너**는 오늘 뭐 하니? What are you going to do today?

② Special expressions such as **성함이 어떻게 되세요?** (What is your name?) and **연세가 어떻게 되세요?** (How old are you?) are used when asking the name or age of someone you don't know or when the person you are asking is older or has a higher social status than you.

- 할아버지, **성함이 어떻게 되세요?** (◯) Sir (elderly), may I ask your name?
  할아버지, 이름이 뭐예요? (×)
- 사장님 **연세가 어떻게 되세요?** (◯) Mr. President (of a company), may I ask your age?
  사장님 나이가 몇 살이에요? (×)

③ In most cases, the word **살** is not used to refer to the age of someone older than the speaker.

A 캐럴 씨, 할아버지 **연세**가 어떻게 되세요? Carol, how old is your grandfather?
B 올해 일흔다섯이세요. (◯) He will be 75 this year.
올해 일흔다섯 살이세요. (×)

④ The two honorific forms of **주다** are **드리다** and **주시다**.
When the giver is younger than the receiver, then **드리다** is used, but when the actor is older than the recipient of the action, **주시다** is used.

- 나는 선물을 어머니께 **드렸어요**. I gave a present to Mom.
- 어머니께서 나에게 선물을 **주셨어요**. Mom gave a present to me.
- 나는 동생에게 선물을 **주었어요**. I gave a present to my little brother/sister.

Getting Ready

01 이다 (to be)

Track 001

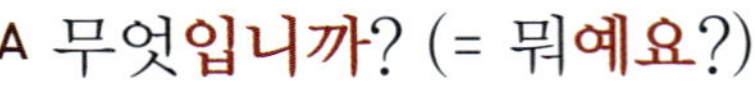

A 무엇**입니까**? (= 뭐**예요**?)

What's this?

B 의자**입니다**. (= 의자**예요**.)

It's a chair.

A 한국 사람**입니까**? (= 한국 사람**이에요**?)

Is she Korean?

B 네, 한국 사람**입니다**. (= 한국 사람**이에요**.)

Yes, she's Korean.

A 어디**입니까**? (= 어디**예요**?)

Where is it?

B 한국**입니다**. (= 한국**이에요**.)

It's Korea.

Grammar Focus

이다 attaches to the end of a noun to make it the predicate of the sentence. **이다** is used to express that the subject and predicate are the same thing. **이다** can also be used to specify something. The formal descriptive form is **입니다**, and its interrogative form is **입니까?** The corresponding informal forms, **예요/이에요**, are the same for both the descriptive and interrogative forms, with the interrogative form rising in intonation as it is pronounced: **예요?/이에요?** When the preceding noun ends in a vowel, **예요** is used, and when the noun ends in a consonant, **이에요** is used. The negative form of **이다** is **아니다**. (See also Unit 2. Negative Expressions 01 Word Negation)

Informal Polite Style		Formal Polite Style
Noun With Final Vowel	Noun With Final Consonant	
예요	**이에요**	**입니다**
사과**예요**. 나비**예요**. 어머니**예요**.	책상**이에요**. 연필**이에요**. 학생**이에요**.	사과**입니다**. : 책상**입니다**. 나비**입니다**. : 연필**입니다**. 어머니**입니다**. : 학생**입니다**.

In Conversation

Track 002

A 무엇입니까? A What is this?
B 가방입니다. B It's a bag.

A 학생입니까? A Are you a student?
B 네, 학생입니다. B Yes, I'm a student.

A 누구예요? A Who is that?
B 친구예요. B That's my friend.

A 고향이 어디예요? A Where is your hometown?
B 서울이에요. B Seoul.

Look at the pictures and fill in the blanks using 이다.

(1)

A 시계______________?
B 네, 시계______________.

(2)

A 무엇______________?
B 모자______________.

(3)

A 가수______________?
B 네, 가수______________.

(4)

A 누구입니까?
B 선생님______________.

있다 (to exist/be, to have)

Track 003

개가 의자 위에 **있어요**.
(= 개가 의자 위에 **있습니다**.)
There's a dog on the chair.

우리 집이 신촌에 **있어요**.
(= 우리 집이 신촌에 **있습니다**.)
Our house is in Sinchon.

남자 친구가 **있어요**.
(= 남자 친구가 **있습니다**.)
I have a boyfriend.

Grammar Focus

1 있다 expresses the existence or location of something and means 'to be located in/on' in English. Although 있다 is typically used in the form of 'N이/가 N(place)에 있다', the order of the subject and place in the sentence can be changed with no change in meaning: 'N(place)에 N이/가 있다'. The opposite of 있다 is 없다. When 'N에 있다' expresses a place, the following location nouns can be used.

앞, 뒤, 위, 아래 (= 밑), 옆 (오른쪽, 왼쪽), 가운데, 사이, 안, 밖

① 책상 위 on the desk	② 책상 아래 (= 책상 밑) under the desk	③ 책상 앞 in front of the desk	④ 책상 뒤 behind the desk

⑤ 책상 옆
beside the desk

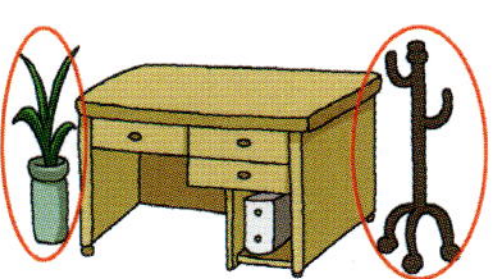

⑥ 책상 왼쪽
left of the desk

⑦ 책상 오른쪽
right of the desk

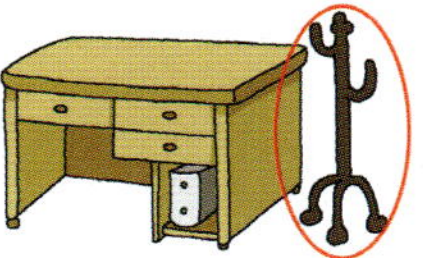

⑧ 사이
in between

⑨ 책상 가운데
in the middle of the desk

⑩ 집 안
inside the house

⑪ 집 밖
outside the house

① 책상 위에 컴퓨터가 있어요.	The computer is on the desk.
② 책상 아래 (= 책상 밑에) 구두가 있어요.	The shoes are under the desk.
③ 책상 앞에 의자가 있어요.	The chair is in front of the desk.
④ 책상 뒤에 책장이 있어요.	The bookshelf is behind the desk.
⑤ 책상 옆에 화분하고 옷걸이가 있어요.	The plant and coat hanger are beside the desk.
⑥ 책상 왼쪽에 화분이 있어요.	The plant is to the left of the desk.
⑦ 책상 오른쪽에 옷걸이가 있어요.	The coat hanger is to the right of the desk.
⑧ 화분과 옷걸이 사이에 책상이 있어요.	The desk is between the plant and the coat hanger.
⑨ 책상 가운데에 인형이 있어요.	The teddy bear is in the middle of the desk.
⑩ 집 안에 강아지가 있어요.	The dog is inside the house.
⑪ 집 밖에 고양이가 있어요.	The cat is outside the house.

2 **있다** is also used in the form 'N**이/가 있다**' to express possession, meaning 'to have' in English. The opposite of **있다** is **없다**.

(See also Unit 2. Negative Expressions 01 Word Negation)

- 나는 언니가 있어요. 동생이 없어요.
  I have an older sister. I don't have a younger sibling.
- 자전거가 있어요. 차가 없어요.
  I have a bicycle. I don't have a car.

In Conversation

Track 004

A 책이 어디에 있어요?
B 가방 안에 있어요.

A Where is the book?
B It's in my bag.

A 은행이 어디에 있어요?
B 학교 옆에 있어요.

A Where is the bank?
B It's next to the school.

A 한국 친구가 있어요?
B 네, 한국 친구가 있어요.

A Do you have any Korean friends?
B Yes, I have Korean friends.

A 컴퓨터가 있어요?
B 네, 있어요.

A Do you have a computer?
B Yes, I have one.

On Your Own

Describe this room. Look at the picture and write the appropriate word in each blank as shown in the example.

보기 전화가 텔레비전 옆 에 있어요.

(1) 텔레비전 _____ 에 꽃병이 있어요.

(2) 이민우 씨 _____ 에 캐럴 씨가 있어요.

(3) _____ 씨 왼쪽에 가방이 있어요.

(4) 가방 _____ 에 책이 있어요.

(5) 신문이 가방 _____ 에 있어요.

(6) 이민우 씨가 _____ 오른쪽에 있어요.

03 Numbers

Track 005

Sino-Korean Numbers

0	1	2	3	4	5	6	7	8	9	10
영/공	일	이	삼	사	오	육	칠	팔	구	십
	11	20	30	40	50	60	70	80	90	100
	십일	이십	삼십	사십	오십	육십	칠십	팔십	구십	백
	1,000	10,000	100,000	1,000,000						
	천	만	십만	백만						

Grammar Focus

There are two ways to express numbers in Korean. One is by using Sino-Korean numbers, and the other is by using native Korean numbers. Sino-Korean numbers are used to express such things as telephone numbers, bus route numbers, height, weight, address numbers, years, months, minutes, seconds, and prices.

(010-4783-3275)

공일공 사칠팔삼의[에] 삼이칠오

백육십삼 번
(number 163)

백오십 센티미터
사십팔 킬로그램

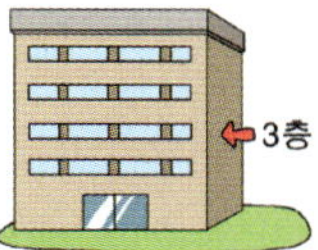

삼 층
(3rd floor)

오백일 호

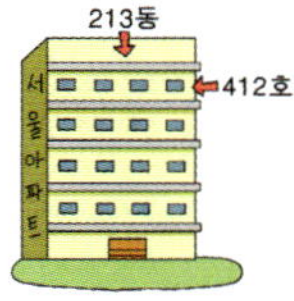

이백십삼 동
사백십이 호
(Building 213, Room 412)

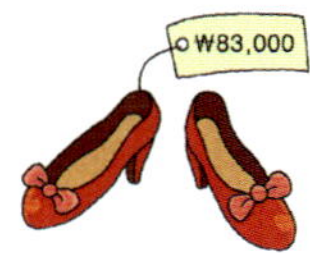

팔만 삼천 원

이백삼십칠만 원

Check It Out!

❶ In Korean, large numbers are read based on units of ten thousand (만) instead of thousands (천). Thus, 354,970 is interpreted as 35,4970 and read as 35만 4970 (→ 삼십오만 사천구백칠십). Similarly, 6,354,790 is interpreted as 635,4790 and read as 635만 4790 (→ 육백삼십오만 사천칠백구십).

- 26354790 → 2635/4790
  이천육백삼십오만 사천칠백구십

❷ When a number larger than 1 begins with 1, the initial 1 (일) is not pronounced.

- 10: 십 〔일십(×)〕 110: 백십 〔일백십(×)〕
- 1,110: 천백십 〔일천백십(×)〕 11,110: 만 천백십 〔일만 천백십(×)〕

❸ 16, 26, 36 ··· 96 are pronounced [심뉵], [이심뉵], [삼심뉵] ··· [구심뉵].

❹ '0' is pronounced as either 공 or 영. When appearing in telephone numbers, 공 is used.

- 6508-8254 → 육오공팔의[에] 팔이오사
- 010-4783-0274 → 공일공 사칠팔삼의[에] 공이칠사

❺ There are two ways to read telephone numbers.

- 7804-3577 → 칠팔공사의[에] 삼오칠칠
  → 칠천팔백사 국의[에] 삼천오백칠십칠 번

* In this case 의 is pronounced [에], not [의].

In Conversation

Track 006

A 사무실이 몇 층이에요?	A What floor is the office on?
B 9층이에요. (구 층)	B The 9th floor.
A 전화번호가 뭐예요?	A What's your phone number?
B 019-8729-9509예요. (공일구 팔칠이구의[에] 구오공구)	B It's 019-8729-9509.
A 몇 번 버스를 타요?	A What bus do you take?
B 705번 버스를 타요. (칠백오 번)	B I take bus number 705.
A 책이 얼마예요?	A How much is the book?
B 25,000원이에요. (이만 오천 원)	B It's 25,000 won.

On Your Own

Write the following numbers in Korean as shown in the example.

보기
A 전화번호가 뭐예요?
B 2734-3698이에요.
(이칠삼사의 삼육구팔)이에요.

(1) A 휴대 전화가 있어요?
B 네, 있어요. 010-738-3509예요.
( )예요.

(2) A 몸무게가 몇 킬로그램(kg)이에요?
B 34킬로그램(kg)이에요.
( )킬로그램(kg)이에요.

(3) A 키가 몇 센티미터(cm)예요?
B 175센티미터(cm)예요.
( )센티미터(cm)예요.

(4) A 치마가 얼마예요?
B 62,000원이에요.
( )원이에요.

Native Korean Numbers

Track 007

1	2	3	4	5	6	7	8	9	10
하나 (= 한)	둘 (= 두)	셋 (= 세)	넷 (= 네)	다섯	여섯	일곱	여덟	아홉	열
11	20	30	40	50	60	70	80	90	100
열하나	스물 (= 스무)	서른	마흔	쉰	예순	일흔	여든	아흔	백

한 분 / 두 마리 / 세 명 / 네 권 / 다섯 개 / 여섯 병

여덟 장 / 세 잔 / 두 대 / 한 살 / 열 송이 / 한 켤레

Grammar Focus

Native Korean numbers are used to express time and units. They are generally used along with unit nouns that express the appropriate unit when counting things or people. Examples of unit nouns include **명**, **마리**, **개**, **살**, **병**, and **잔**. In these cases, the Korean numbers that precede these nouns are written in slighty different forms: **하나** becomes **한** (**학생 한 명**), **둘** becomes **두** (**개 두 마리**), **셋** becomes **세** (**커피 세 잔**), **넷** becomes **네** (**콜라 네 병**), and **스물** becomes **스무** (**사과 스무 개**), etc.

하나 + 개		**한** 개	아홉 + 개		아홉 개
둘 +개		**두** 개	열 + 개		열 개
셋 + 개		**세** 개	열하나 + 개		**열한** 개
넷 + 개	→	**네** 개	열둘 + 개	→	**열두** 개
다섯 + 개		다섯 개	......		......
여섯 +개		여섯 개	스물 + 개		**스무** 개
일곱 + 개		일곱 개	스물한 +개		**스물한** 개
여덟 + 개		여덟 개	스물둘 + 개		**스물두** 개

Unit Nouns

1	한 명	한 분	한 마리	한 권	한 개	한 병
2	두 명	두 분	두 마리	두 권	두 개	두 병
3	세 명	세 분	세 마리	세 권	세 개	세 병
4	네 명	네 분	네 마리	네 권	네 개	네 병
5	다섯 명	다섯 분	다섯 마리	다섯 권	다섯 개	다섯 병
6	여섯 명	여섯 분	여섯 마리	여섯 권	여섯 개	여섯 병
7	일곱 명	일곱 분	일곱 마리	일곱 권	일곱 개	일곱 병
8	여덟 명	여덟 분	여덟 마리	여덟 권	여덟 개	여덟 병
9	아홉 명	아홉 분	아홉 마리	아홉 권	아홉 개	아홉 병
10	열 명	열 분	열 마리	열 권	열 개	열 병
11	열한 명	열한 분	열한 마리	열한 권	열한 개	열한 병
……	……	……	……	……	……	……
20	스무 명	스무 분	스무 마리	스무 권	스무 개	스무 병
?	몇 명	몇 분	몇 마리	몇 권	몇 개	몇 병

In Conversation

Track 008

A 가족이 몇 명이에요?
B 우리 가족은 네 명이에요.

A How many family members do you have?
B We are a family of four.

A 동생이 몇 살이에요?
B 남동생은 스물세 살이에요.
여동생은 스무 살이에요.

A How old are your younger siblings?
B My younger brother is 23, and my younger sister is 20.

A 여기 사과 세 개, 콜라 한 병 주세요.
B 네, 모두 오천육백 원입니다.

A Please give me (I'll take/buy) three apples and one coke.
B Okay, your total is 5,600 won.

Look at the picture and write the appropriate number in Korean in each blank.

보기 남자가 두 명, 여자가 세 명 있어요.

(1) 개가 ____________ 있어요.

(2) 텔레비전이 ____________, 컴퓨터가 __________ 있어요.

(3) 의자가 ______ 개, 사과가 __________ 있어요.

(4) 콜라가 __________, 주스가 __________ 있어요.

(5) 책이 __________ 있어요. 꽃이 ______ 송이 있어요.

04 Dates and Days of the Week

Track 009

2022년 6월 9일 목요일

몇 년? (What Year?)

2022년: 이천이십이 년, 1998년: 천구백구십팔 년, 1864년: 천팔백육십사 년

몇 월? (What Month?)

1월	2월	3월	4월	5월	6월	7월	8월	9월	10월	11월	12월
일월	이월	삼월	사월	오월	**유월**	칠월	팔월	구월	**시월**	십일월	십이월

며칠? (What Date?)

1일	2일	3일	4일	5일	6일	7일	8일	9일	10일
일일	이일	삼일	사일	오일	육일	칠일	팔일	구일	십일

11일	12일	13일	14일	15일	16일	17일	18일	19일	20일
십일일	십이일	십삼일	십사일	십오일	십육일 [심뉴길]	십칠일	십팔일	십구일	이십일

21일	22일	23일	24일	25일	26일	27일	28일	29일	30일	31일
이십일일	이십이일	이십삼일	이십사일	이십오일	이십육일 [이심뉴길]	이십칠일	이십팔일	이십구일	삼십일	삼십일일

무슨 요일? (What Day of the Week?)

일	월	화	수	목	금	**토**
일요일	월요일	화요일	수요일	목요일	금요일	**토요일**

In Conversation

A 오늘이 며칠이에요?
B 5월 5일(오월 오일)이에요.

A 오늘이 무슨 요일이에요?
B 화요일이에요.

A 언제 결혼했어요?
B 2001년(이천일 년)에 결혼했어요.

A What's today's date?
B It's May 5.

A What day of the week is today?
B It's Tuesday.

A When did you get married?
B We got married in 2001.

Check It Out!

❶ The Korean words for June and October are read and written as 유월 and 시월, respectively, not 육월 and 십월.

❷ When asking 'what year', 몇 년 is used, and when asking 'what month', 몇 월 is used. However, when asking 'what day', 며칠 is used in place of 몇 일.

- 오늘이 몇일이에요? (×) → 오늘이 며칠이에요? (○) What is today's date?

On Your Own

Look at each picture and write the appropriate dates in Korean.

보기

1994.3.25.(금) : 천구백구십사 년 삼월 이십오 일 금요일

(1) 

2020.6.6.(토) : ______________________ ______요일

(2) 

2015.11.15.(일) : ______________________ ______요일

(3) 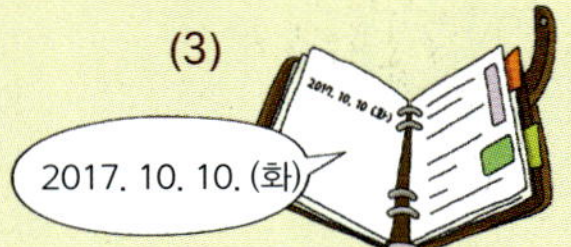

2017.10.10.(화) : ______________________ ______요일

05 Time

Track 011

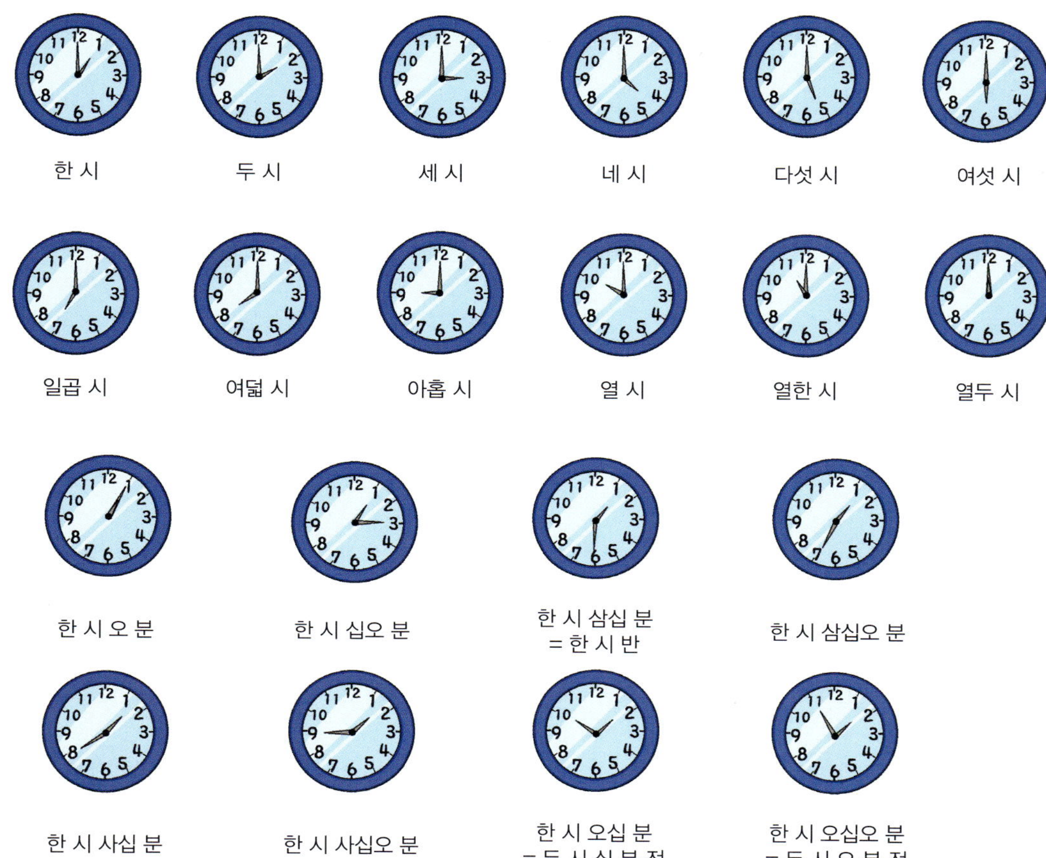

Grammar Focus

In Korean, hours are read using native Korean numbers, while minutes are read using Sino-Korean numbers. When referring to a time when an action takes place, the particle **에** is attached to the end of the time noun.

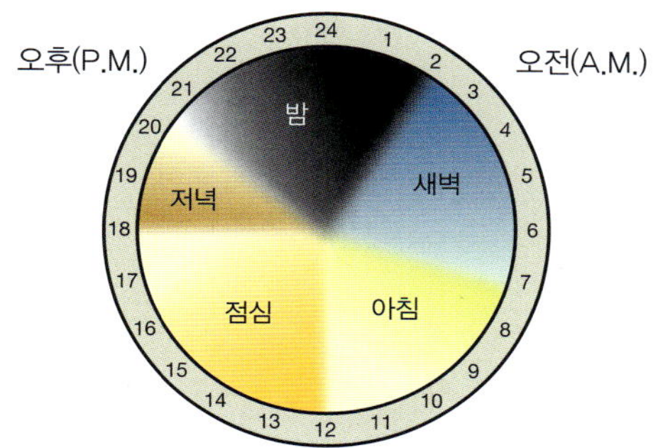

Although the literal meanings of **오전** and **오후** are 'before noon' and 'after noon', respectively, in Korean **오전** is typically used to mean the morning hours while **오후** is used to mean the afternoon hours. Time can also be subdivided into smaller units, including **새벽** (daybreak), **아침** (morning), **점심** (noon, lunchtime), **저녁** (evening), and **밤** (night).

In Conversation

Track 012

A 지금 몇 시예요?
B 오전 아홉 시 십 분이에요. (9:10 A.M.)

A What time is it now?
B It's 9:10 in the morning.

A 지금 몇 시예요?
B 두 시 십 분 전이에요.
(= 한 시 오십 분이에요.) (1:50)

A What time is it now?
B It's ten minutes to two. (= It's 1:50.)

A 몇 시에 일어나요?
B 아침 일곱 시에 일어나요. (7:00)

A What time do you wake up?
B I wake up at 7:00 in the morning.

On Your Own

Look at the pictures and write the appropriate time in the blanks.

보기

오전 일곱 시

(1)

____

(2)

____

(3)

____

(4)

____

(5)

____

(6)

저녁 __________

(7)

밤 __________

(8)

밤 __________

Unit 1.

Tenses

01 Present Tense A/V-(스)ㅂ니다
02 Present Tense A/V-아/어요
03 Past Tense A/V-았/었어요
04 Future Tense V-(으)ㄹ 거예요 ①
05 Progressive Tense V-고 있다 ①
06 Past Perfect Tense A/V-았/었었어요

01 Present Tense A/V-(스)ㅂ니다

Track 013

안녕하십니까?

Good evening.

9시 뉴스**입니다.**

This is the 9 o'clock news.

질문 **있습니까?**

Do you have any questions?

A 이것을 어떻게 **생각합니까?**

What's your opinion of this?

B **좋습니다.**

I think it's good.

Grammar Focus

The present tense of the formal polite style in Korean is made by adding -(스)ㅂ니다. It is used mainly in formal or public situations such as in the military, news broadcasts, presentations, meetings, and lectures.

	Word Stem Ends in Vowel	Word Stem Ends in Consonant
Declarative	-ㅂ니다	-습니다
Interrogative	-ㅂ니까?	-습니까?

Word Stem Ends in Vowel	가다 (to go)	가 +	-ㅂ니다 → 갑니다 (Declarative) -ㅂ니까? → 갑니까? (Interrogative)
	오다 (to come)	오 +	-ㅂ니다 → 옵니다 (Declarative) -ㅂ니까? → 옵니까? (Interrogative)

<table>
<tr><td rowspan="2">Word Stem Ends in Consonant</td><td>먹다
(to eat)</td><td>먹 + -습니다 → 먹습니다 (Declarative)
-습니까? → 먹습니까? (Interrogative)</td></tr>
<tr><td>앉다
(to sit)</td><td>앉 + -습니다 → 앉습니다 (Declarative)
-습니까? → 앉습니까? (Interrogative)</td></tr>
</table>

	Base Form	Declarative	Interrogative
Ends in Vowel + -ㅂ니다 -ㅂ니까?	자다	잡니다	잡니까?
	예쁘다	예쁩니다	예쁩니까?
	이다	입니다	입니까?
	아니다	아닙니다	아닙니까?
	*만들다	만듭니다	만듭니까?
Ends in Consonant + -습니다 -습니까?	읽다	읽습니다	읽습니까?
	작다	작습니다	작습니까?
	있다	있습니다	있습니까?
	없다	없습니다	없습니까?

* Irregular form

In Conversation

Track 014

A 학교에 갑니까?
B 네, 학교에 갑니다.

A Are you going to school?
B Yes, I'm going to school.

A 아침을 먹습니까?
B 네, 먹습니다.

A Do you eat breakfast?
B Yes, I eat breakfast.

A 운동을 합니까?
B 네, 운동을 합니다.

A Do you exercise?
B Yes, I exercise.

Look at the pictures and fill in the blanks as shown in the example.

보기 
(가다)

A 갑니까?
B 네, 갑니다.

보기 
(운동하다)

A 뭐 합니까?
B 운동합니다.

(1) 
(먹다)

A 햄버거를 ___________?
B ________________.

(2) 
(기다리다)

A 뭐 합니까?
B 친구를 ___________.

(3) 
(읽다)

A 신문을 ___________?
B ________________.

(4) 
(만나다)

A 뭐 합니까?
B 친구를 ___________.

(5) 
(쓰다)

A 뭐 합니까?
B 일기를 ___________.

(6) 
(사다)

A 책을 ___________?
B ________________.

02 Present Tense A/V–아/어요

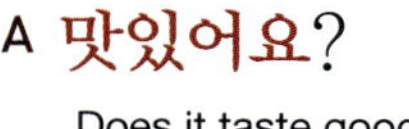

A 맛있어요?

Does it taste good?

Track 015

B 네, 맛있어요.

Yes, it tastes good.

A 어디에 가요?

Where are you going?

B 학교에 가요.

I'm going to school.

사랑해요, 캐럴 씨.

I love you, Carol.

Grammar Focus

The informal polite style is the honorific form used most in daily life. Compared to the formal polite style, this style is softer and less formal and is therefore used mainly among family members, friends, and other close acquaintances. The declarative and interrogative forms of the informal polite style are the same. The declarative form is therefore made by ending the sentence in a falling tone, while the interrogative form is made by ending the sentence in a rising tone.

1. –아요

아요 is used when the word stem ends in ㅏ or ㅗ.

① –아요 is added when the word stem ends in a consonant.

앉다 + **아요** → 앉아요　　받다 → 받아요, 살다 → 살아요

② If the word stem ends in the vowel ㅏ, one ㅏ is deleted.

가다 + **아요** → 가요　　자다 → 자요, 만나다 → 만나요, 끝나다 → 끝나요

③ If the word stem ends in a vowel, the following contraction can also occur.

오다 + **아요** → 와요 (오 + ㅏ요 → 와요)　　보다 → 봐요

<table>
<tr><td>2. −어요</td><td>어요 is used when the word stem ends in a vowel other than ㅏ or ㅗ.
① −어요 is added when the word stem ends in a consonant.
읽다 + 어요 → 읽어요 　먹다 → 먹어요, 입다 → 입어요
② If the word stem ends in the vowel ㅐ, ㅓ, or ㅕ, then the 어 of −어요 is deleted.
보내다 + 어요 → 보내요 　지내다 → 지내요, 서다 → 서요, 켜다 → 켜요
③ If the word stem ends in the vowel ㅜ, then ㅜ and the 어 of 어요 combine to form ㅝ.
배우다 + 어요→ 배워요 (배우 + ㅓ요 → 배워요) 　주다 → 줘요, 바꾸다 → 바꿔요
④ When the word stem ends in the vowel ㅣ, ㅣ and the 어 of 어요 combine to form ㅕ.
마시다 + 어요→ 마셔요 (마시 + ㅓ요 → 마셔요)
기다리다 → 기다려요, 헤어지다 → 헤어져요</td></tr>
<tr><td>3. −하다 → 해요</td><td>When the predicate ends in 하다, it is changed to 해요. (Originally, 여요 was added to 하 to form 하여요, but 하여요 is now shortened to 해요.)
말하다 → 말해요
공부하다 → 공부해요, 전화하다 → 전화해요, 여행하다 → 여행해요, 일하다 → 일해요</td></tr>
<tr><td>4. 예요/이에요</td><td>이다 changes to 예요/이에요, with 예요 used when the preceding word ends in a vowel and 이에요 used when the word ends in a consonant.
① When the noun ends in a vowel: 의사예요 (의사 + 예요)
사과이다 → 사과예요, 어머니이다 → 어머니예요
② When the noun ends in a consonant: 회사원이에요 (회사원 + 이에요)
책상이다 → 책상이에요, 선생님이다 → 선생님이에요</td></tr>
</table>

Base Form	−아요	Base Form	−어요	Base Form	해요
앉다	앉아요	읽다	읽어요	말하다	말해요
살다	살아요	꺼내다	꺼내요	전화하다	전화해요
가다	가요	서다	서요	운동하다	운동해요
만나다	만나요	배우다	배워요	일하다	일해요
오다	와요	마시다	마셔요	숙제하다	숙제해요

이다					
이다	Vowel Ending	예요	간호사예요	의자예요	우유예요
	Consonant Ending	이에요	학생이에요	책상이에요	빵이에요

In Conversation

Track 016

A 지금 뭐 해요?
B 숙제해요.

A What are you doing now?
B I'm doing homework.

A 몇 시에 점심을 먹어요?
B 보통 1시에 점심을 먹어요.

A What time do you eat lunch?
B I normally eat lunch at one o'clock.

A 민우 씨는 직업이 뭐예요?
B 선생님이에요.

A What is Minu's job?
B He's a teacher.

Check It Out!

<Characteristics of Present Tense Forms>

❶ In Korean, the present tense forms include not only the present tense but also the present progressive tense and a future tense in which it is clear that a future event will occur.

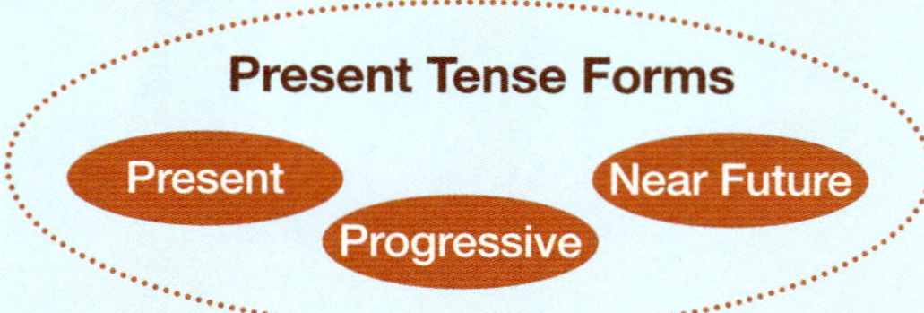

- Present – 저는 대학교에 다닙니다/다녀요. I go to college.
- Progressive – 저는 지금 공부를 합니다/해요. I am studying now.
- Near Future – 저는 내일 학교에 갑니다/가요. I will go to school tomorrow.

❷ The present tense is also used to express general truths and to describe things that occur regularly.

- 지구는 태양 주위를 돌아요. The Earth rotates around the sun.
- 저는 아침마다 달리기를 해요. I run every morning.

On Your Own

1 Look at the pictures and fill in the blanks as shown in the example.

보기
(의자)
A 의자예요?
B 네, 의자예요.

(1) (학생)
A ____________?
B ____________.

(2) (의사)
A ____________?
B ____________.

(3) (책상)
A ____________?
B ____________.

(4) (사과)
A ____________?
B ____________.

2 Look at the pictures and fill in the blanks as shown in the example.

보기
(자다)
A 자요?
B 네, 자요.

보기
(만나다)
A 뭐 해요?
B 친구를 만나요.

(1) (보다)
A 텔레비전을 ______?
B 네, 텔레비전을 ______.

(2) (전화하다)
A 뭐 해요?
B ____________.

(3) (읽다)
A 책을 ______?
B 네, 책을 ______.

(4) (먹다)
A 냉면을 ______?
B 네, 냉면을 ______.

(5) (공부하다)
A 뭐 해요?
B ____________.

(6) (마시다)
A 물을 ______?
B 네, 물을 ______.

03 Past Tense A/V-았/었어요

Track 017

2021년 3월 5일에 **태어났어요**.

(The baby) was born on March 5, 2021.

2018. 2. 25

2018년 2월에 대학교를 **졸업했어요**.

I graduated from college in February 2018.

작년에 **결혼했어요**.

We got married last year.

Grammar Focus

The past tense form of adjectives and verbs is formed by adding **-았/었-** to their word stems. When the word stem ends in the vowel ㅏ or ㅗ, **-았어요** is added, and when it ends in any other vowel, **-었어요** is added. For verbs and adjectives ending in **하다**, **-였어요** is added to form **하+였어요**, which is then shortened to **했어요**. In the case of the formal polite style, **-았/었습니다** and **했습니다** are used.

Word Stem Ends in ㅏ or ㅗ	Word Stem Ends in Vowel Other than ㅏ or ㅗ	Word Ends in 하다
앉다 + **-았어요** → 앉았어요	먹다 + **-었어요** → 먹었어요	공부하다 → 공부했어요

Base Form	-았어요	Base Form	-었어요	Base Form	했어요
보다	봤어요	씻다	씻었어요	청소하다	청소했어요
만나다	만났어요	*쓰다	썼어요	입학하다	입학했어요
닫다	닫았어요	있다	있었어요	운동하다	운동했어요

팔다	팔았어요	열다	열었어요	요리하다	요리했어요
잡다	잡았어요	*줍다	주웠어요	숙제하다	숙제했어요
*모르다	몰랐어요	*부르다	불렀어요	게임하다	게임했어요

이다	Vowel Ending	였어요	간호사였어요
	Consonant Ending	이었어요	학생이었어요
아니다	Vowel Ending	가 아니었어요	간호사가 아니었어요
	Consonant Ending	이 아니었어요	학생이 아니었어요

* Irregular form

In Conversation

Track 018

A 어제 뭐 했어요?
B 공부했어요.

A What did you do yesterday?
B I studied.

A 토요일에 영화를 봤어요?
B 네, 봤어요. 재미있었어요.

A Did you see a movie on Saturday?
B Yes, I saw a movie. It was interesting.

A 주말에 뭐 했어요?
B 음악을 들었어요.

A What did you do over the weekend?
B I listened to music.

Check It Out!

While the past tense of 주다 can be written either as 주었어요 or 줬어요, and the past tense of 보다 can be written either as 보았어요 or 봤어요, the past tense of 오다 is written only as 왔어요, not 오았어요.

- 주다 + -었어요 → 주었어요 (○) 줬어요 (○)
- 보다 + -았어요 → 보았어요 (○) 봤어요 (○)
- 오다 + -았어요 → 왔어요 (○) 오았어요 (×)

On Your Own

What did Carol do this week? Refer to the calendar and choose the appropriate word from below to fill in each blank using –았/었어요.

가다	만나다	맛있다	먹다	보다	부르다
사다	싸다	아프다	재미있다	청소하다	

- 12월 7일: (1) 친구를 ______________.
  (2) 피자를 ______________.
  (3) 피자가 ______________.
- 12월 8일: (4) 백화점에 ______________.
  (5) 구두를 ______________.
  (6) 구두가 ______________.
- 12월 9일: (7) 머리가 ______________. 병원에 갔어요.
- 12월 10일: (8) 노래를 ______________.
- 12월 11일: (9) ______________.
- 12월 12일: (10) 영화를 ______________.
  (11) 영화가 ______________.

04 Future Tense V–(으)ㄹ 거예요 ①

Track 019

2년 후에 차를 **살 거예요**.

I'll buy a car two years from now.

주말에 낚시를 **할 거예요**.

I'll go fishing this weekend.

방학에 중국에 **갈 거예요**.

I'll visit China during my vacation.

Grammar Focus

This pattern is used to express a future plan or intention and means the same as 'will' or 'is going to' in English. It is formed by adding **–(으)ㄹ 거예요** to the stems of verbs. **–ㄹ 거예요** is used when the verb stem ends in ㄹ or a vowel, and **–을 거예요** is used when the verb stem ends in a consonant.

Verb Stem Ends in Vowel or ㄹ	Verb Stem Ends in Consonant
가다 + **–ㄹ 거예요** → 갈 거예요	먹다 + **–을 거예요** → 먹을 거예요

Base Form	–ㄹ 거예요	Base Form	–을 거예요
보다	볼 거예요	입다	입을 거예요
주다	줄 거예요	받다	받을 거예요
만나다	만날 거예요	씻다	씻을 거예요
공부하다	공부할 거예요	*듣다	들을 거예요
*살다	살 거예요	*붓다	부을 거예요
*만들다	만들 거예요	*돕다	도울 거예요

* Irregular form

In Conversation

Track 020

A 언제 고향에 돌아갈 거예요?
B 내년에 돌아갈 거예요.

A When will you return to your hometown?
B I'll return next year.

A 주말에 뭐 할 거예요?
B 자전거를 탈 거예요.

A What will you do over the weekend?
B I'll ride my bike.

On Your Own

The following calendar is from Wang Jing's daily planner. What will Wang Jing do this week? Choose the appropriate word from below to fill in each blank using –(으)ㄹ 거예요.

가다 공부하다 놀다 먹다 부르다 쉬다 타다

오늘은 5월 4일이에요. 내일은 5월 5일 '어린이날'이에요. 그래서 내일 학교에 안 가요. 내일 나는 롯데월드에 (1)________________. 롯데월드에서 친구들하고 같이 (2)________________. 스케이트를 (3)________________. 목요일에 한국어 시험이 있어요. 그래서 수요일에 학교 도서관에서 (4)________________. 금요일은 캐럴 씨의 생일이에요. 우리는 불고기를 (5)________________ 그리고 노래방에서 노래를 (6)________________. 토요일은 집에서 (7)________________.

05 Progressive Tense V-고 있다 ①

Track 021

댄 씨가 지금 음악을 **듣고 있어요**.

Dane is listening to music now.

민우 씨가 지금 집에 **가고 있어요**.

Minu is going home now.

어제 친구가 웨슬리 씨한테 전화했어요.
그때 웨슬리 씨는 **자고 있었어요**.

Yesterday, a friend called Wesley on the phone. Wesley was sleeping at that time.

Grammar Focus

This pattern expresses the progression or continuation of an action and is the equivalent of '-ing' in English. It is formed by adding **-고 있다** to the stems of verbs. To express the continuation of an action that occurred sometime in the past, **-고 있었다** is used.

가다 + **-고 있다** → 가고 있다　　　먹다 + **-고 있었다** → 먹고 있었다

Base Form	-고 있어요	Base Form	-고 있어요
사다	사고 있어요	찾다	찾고 있어요
보다	보고 있어요	만들다	만들고 있어요
만나다	만나고 있어요	일하다	일하고 있어요
오다	오고 있어요	공부하다	공부하고 있어요

In Conversation

Track 022

A 왕징 씨, 지금 시장에 같이 가요.
B 미안해요, 지금 숙제를 하고 있어요.

A Wang Jing, let's go to the market together.
B I'm sorry, but I'm doing my homework right now.

A 왜 아까 전화를 안 받았어요?
B 샤워하고 있었어요.

A Why didn't you answer the phone a while ago?
B I was taking a shower.

A 지금 어디에서 살고 있어요?
B 서울에서 살고 있어요.

A Where are you living now?
B I'm living in Seoul.

Check It Out!

To express that an action simply occurred in the past, the simple past form –았/었어요 is used.

A 어제 뭐 했어요? — What did you do yesterday?
B 집에서 쉬고 있었어요. (×) → 집에서 쉬었어요. (○) — I relaxed at home.

On Your Own

Look at the pictures and fill in the blanks as shown in the example.

보기

A 지금 뭐 해요?
B 피아노를 치고 있어요.
(피아노를 치다)

(1)

A 지금 뭐 해요?
B ______________.
(세수하다)

(2)

A 요즘 뭐 해요?
B ______________.
(한국어를 배우다)

(3)

A 운룡 씨가 지금 공부를 해요?
B 아니요, ______________.
(밥을 먹다)

(4)

A 무엇을 찾고 있었어요?
B ______________.
(반지를 찾다)

06 Past Perfect Tense A/V-았/었었어요

미국에 **갔었어요**.

I have been to the U.S.
(I went to, and have already returned from, the U.S.)

중국에서 **살았었어요**.

I (have) lived in China.
(I don't live in China now.)

아버지가 **뚱뚱했었어요**.

My father was overweight.
(He's not overweight now.)

Grammar Focus

This pattern is used to express something or a situation that occurred in the past but did not continue, or something separate from the present because it occurred much earlier than when the speaker is describing it. It approximates to 'did/had (in the past)' in English. It is formed by adding **-았었어요** to the stems of verbs and adjectives with stems ending in the vowel ㅏ or ㅗ. Otherwise, **-었었어요** is added. For verbs ending in **하다**, **했었어요** is added.

Verb Stem Ends in Vowel ㅏ or ㅗ	Verb Stem Ends in Vowel Other than ㅏ or ㅗ	Verb Ends in 하다
살다 + **-았었어요** → 살았었어요	먹다 + **-었었어요** → 먹었었어요	공부하다 → 공부했었어요

Base Form	-았/었었어요	Base Form	-았/었었어요
가다	갔었어요	많다	많았었어요
사다	샀었어요	싸다	쌌었어요
배우다	배웠었어요	길다	길었었어요

읽다	읽었었어요	친절하다	친절했었어요
일하다	일했었어요	한가하다	한가했었어요
*듣다	들었었어요	*어렵다	어려웠었어요

* Irregular form

In Conversation

Track 024

A 담배를 안 피워요?

B 작년에는 담배를 피웠었어요.
그렇지만 지금은 안 피워요.

A You don't smoke?

B I smoked last year. But I don't smoke now.

A 요즘 바다에 사람이 없어요.

B 여름에는 사람이 많았었어요.

A There's nobody at the seaside these days.

B There were many people (there) in the summer.

A 주말에 뭐 했어요?

B 롯데월드에 갔었어요.
아주 재미있었어요.

A What did you do over the weekend?

B I went to Lotte World. It was really interesting.

What's the Difference?

-았/었어요

Expresses that something simply occurred in the past or that an action or situation that ended in the past has remained that way.

- 댄 씨는 작년에 한국에 왔어요.
(Dane may still be in Korea. We don't know what happened after he came to Korea. He may be in some place other than Korea.)
- 댄 씨는 서울에서 1년 동안 살았어요.
(Dane has been living in Seoul for one year.
He previously lived in Seoul for one year, but we don't know where he lives now.)

-았/었었어요

Expresses a past occurrence that does not continue to the present.

- 댄 씨는 작년에 한국에 왔었어요.
(Dane came to Korea and later left; he is not in Korea now.)
- 댄 씨는 서울에서 1년 동안 살았었어요.
(Dane previously lived in Seoul for one year, but now he does not live in Seoul.)

What was Hayeong like 10 years ago? Look at the pictures and fill in the blanks as shown in the example.

보기

(10년 전 / 현재)

하영 씨는 안경을 안 썼었어요.
(안경을 안 쓰다)

(1)

(10년 전 / 현재)

하영 씨는 ______________________.
(키가 작다)

(2)

(10년 전 / 현재)

하영 씨는 ______________________.
(머리가 길다)

(3)

(10년 전 / 현재)

하영 씨는 ______________________.
(고기를 안 먹다)

(4)

(10년 전 / 현재)

하영 씨는 ______________________.
(치마를 안 입다)

Unit 2.

Negative Expressions

01 Word Negation
02 안 A/V-아/어요 (A/V-지 않아요)
03 못 V-아/어요 (V-지 못해요)

01 Word Negation

Track 025

한국 사람이에요.

She is Korean.

한국 사람이 **아니에요**.

She is not Korean.

돈이 있어요.

I have money.

돈이 **없어요**.

I don't have any money.

한국말을 알아요.

I know Korean.

한국말을 **몰라요**.

I don't know Korean.

Grammar Focus

Negative sentences can be made either by negating the entire sentence or by negating a word. When making a negative sentence by negating a word, **이다** is changed to **아니다**, **있다** is changed to **없다**, and **알다** is changed to **모르다**. Of these, **아니다** is written in the form **이/가 아니다**, but when used in the spoken form, **이/가** is often omitted.

	Formal Polite Style	Informal Polite Style
아니다 ↔ 이다	**아닙니다**	**아니에요**
없다 ↔ 있다	**없습니다**	**없어요**
모르다 ↔ 알다	**모릅니다**	**몰라요**

In Conversation

Track 026

A 민우 씨가 학생이에요?
B 아니요, 학생이 아니에요. 선생님이에요.
(= 아니요, 학생이 아니라 선생님이에요.)

A Is Minu a student?
B No, he's not a student. He's a teacher.

A 오늘 시간 있어요?
B 아니요, 오늘 시간 없어요. 바빠요.

A Do you have some time today?
B No, I don't have any time today. I'm busy.

A 일본어를 알아요?
B 아니요, 몰라요.

A Do you know Japanese?
B No, I don't know Japanese.

On Your Own

Look at the pictures and fill in the blanks as shown in the example.

보기

A 미국 사람이에요?
B 아니요, 미국 사람이 아니에요. 영국 사람이에요.

(1) 

A 남자 친구예요?
B 아니요, 남자 친구________________. 동생이에요.

(2) 

A 집에 개가 있어요?
B 아니요, 개________________.

(3) 

A 교실에 댄 씨가 있어요?
B 아니요, 댄 씨________________.

(4) 

A 선생님의 전화번호를 알아요?
B 아니요, 저는 선생님의 전화번호를 ________________.
요코 씨가 알아요.

02 안 A/V-아/어요 (A/V-지 않아요)

저는 오징어를 **안 먹어요**.
(= 저는 오징어를 **먹지 않아요**.)
I don't eat squid.

그 구두는 **안 예뻐요**.
(= 그 구두는 **예쁘지 않아요**.)
Those shoes aren't pretty.

방이 **안 넓어요**.
(= 방이 **넓지 않아요**.)
The room is not spacious.

Grammar Focus

This pattern is added to verbs and adjectives to negate an action or state. It approximates to 'not' in English. It is formed by adding 안 to the front of verbs and adjectives or -지 않아요 to the end of verb and adjective stems.

안 + 가다 → 안 가요	가다 + **-지 않아요** → 가지 않아요
안 + 크다 → 안 커요	크다 + **-지 않아요** → 크지 않아요

Because verbs that end in 하다 are comprised of 'Noun + 하다', they are negated by adding 안 to the front of the verb, forming 'Noun 안 하다'. Adjectives, on the other hand, are negated by adding 안 to the front, as in '안 + Adjective'. Note, however, that for the verbs 좋아하다 (to like) and 싫어하다 (to dislike), because they are not verbs in the form of 'Noun + 하다', but rather indivisible, single verbs, they are written as 안 좋아하다/좋아하지 않다 and 안 싫어하다/싫어하지 않다.

안 + 일하다 → 일 안 해요 | 일하다 + -지 않아요 → 일하지 않아요
안 + 친절하다 → 안 친절해요 | 친절하다 + -지 않아요 → 친절하지 않아요
안 + 좋아하다 → 안 좋아해요/좋아하지 않아요 (○) 좋아 안 해요 (×)

Base Form	안 -아/어요	-지 않아요
타다	안 타요	타지 않아요
멀다	안 멀어요	멀지 않아요
불편하다	안 불편해요	불편하지 않아요
공부하다	공부 안 해요	공부하지 않아요
*덥다	안 더워요	덥지 않아요
*걷다	안 걸어요	걷지 않아요

* Irregular form

Although **안** and **-지 않다** can be used in declarative and interrogative sentences, they cannot be used in imperative or propositive sentences.

- 안 가십시오 (×), 가지 않으십시오 (×)
  → 가지 마십시오 (○) Please don't go.
- 안 먹읍시다 (×), 먹지 않읍시다 (×)
  → 먹지 맙시다 (○) Let's not eat.

In Conversation

Track 028

A 불고기를 좋아해요?
B 아니요, 저는 고기를 안 먹어요.

A Do you like Korean bulgogi?
B No, I don't eat meat.

A 토요일에 회사에 가요?
B 아니요, 토요일에는 가지 않아요.

A Do you go to the office on Saturdays?
B No, on Saturdays I don't go to work.

A 집이 멀어요?
B 아니요, 안 멀어요. 가까워요.

A Is your house far away?
B No, it's not far away. It's close.

Look at the pictures and fill in the blanks as shown in the example.

보기

A 교회에 다녀요?

B 아니요, <u>안 다녀요. / 다니지 않아요.</u>

(1)

A 오늘 영화를 봐요?

B 아니요, ______________________.

(2)

A 매일 운동해요?

B 아니요, ______________________.

(3)

A 물이 깊어요?

B 아니요, ______________________.

(4)

A 식당 아저씨가 친절해요?

B 아니요, ______________________.

03 못 V-아/어요 (V-지 못해요)

Track 029

저는 수영을 **못해요**.
(= 저는 **수영하지 못해요**.)
I can't swim.

오늘은 술을 **못 마셔요**.
(= 오늘은 술을 **마시지 못해요**.)
I can't drink today.

저는 노래를 **못 불러요**.
(= 저는 노래를 **부르지 못해요**.)
I can't sing.

Grammar Focus

This pattern expresses the subject's lack of ability to do something or the fact that something does not go according to one's wish or hope due to some external factor. It corresponds to the English 'cannot' and is formed by adding **못** in front of a verb or **–지 못해요** to the end of a verb stem.

(See also Unit 6. Ability and Possibility 01 V–(으)ㄹ 수 있다/없다)

못 + 가다 → 못 가요　　가다 + **–지 못해요** → 가지 못해요
못 + 요리하다 → 요리 못해요 (O)　못 요리해요 (×)

Base Form	못 –아/어요	–지 못해요
타다	못 타요	타지 못해요
읽다	못 읽어요	읽지 못해요
숙제하다	숙제 못해요	숙제하지 못해요
*쓰다	못 써요	쓰지 못해요
*듣다	못 들어요	듣지 못해요

* Irregular form

In Conversation

Track 030

A 운전해요?

B 아니요, 운전 못해요.
운전을 안 배웠어요.

A Do you drive?

B No, I can't drive. I never learned how.

A 왜 밥을 안 먹어요?

B 이가 아파요. 그래서 먹지 못해요.

A Why aren't you eating?

B My teeth hurt, so I can't eat.

What's the Difference?

안 (-지 않다)	못 (-지 못하다)
❶ Combines with both verbs and adjectives. • 학교에 안 가요. (○) (I) don't go to school. • 치마가 안 예뻐요. (○) The skirt isn't pretty.	❶ Combines with verbs, but not normally with adjectives. • 학교에 못 가요. (○) (I) can't go to school. • 치마가 못 예뻐요. (×)
❷ Expresses not doing something regardless of ability or external conditions. • 저는 운전을 안 해요. I don't drive. (I know how but don't want to.) • 오늘은 쇼핑을 하지 않아요. I won't go shopping today. (I simply don't feel like going shopping.)	❷ Used when one is unable, or it is impossible, to do something. • 저는 운전을 못해요. I can't drive. (I would like to be able to drive but can't due to some external circumstance, such as a leg injury.) • 오늘은 쇼핑을 하지 못해요. I can't go shopping today. (I want to go shopping but can't due to some external circumstance, such as a lack of money or time.)

On Your Own

Look at the pictures and fill in the blanks using 못 as shown in the example.

보기

A 요코 씨, 술을 마셔요?

B 아니요, 못 마셔요. / 마시지 못해요.

(1)

A 숙제 다 했어요?

B 아니요, ________________.
어려워요.

(2)

A 티루엔 씨의 생일 파티에 가요?

B 아니요, ________________.
바빠요.

(3)

A 어제 영화 봤어요?

B 아니요, ________________.
표가 없었어요.

Unit 3.

Particles

01 N이/가
02 N은/는
03 N을/를
04 N와/과, N(이)랑, N하고
05 N의
06 N에 ①
07 N에 ②
08 N에서
09 N에서 N까지, N부터 N까지
10 N에게/한테
11 N도
12 N만
13 N밖에
14 N(으)로
15 N(이)나 ①
16 N(이)나 ②
17 N쯤
18 N처럼, N같이
19 N보다
20 N마다

01 N이/가

Track 031

날씨가 좋아요.

The weather is nice.

옛날에 공주가 있었어요.

A long time ago, there was a princess.

저기 재준 씨가 와요.

There's Jaejun coming (this way).

Grammar Focus

1 이/가 is added to the end of a subject to designate it as the subject of the sentence. For words ending a vowel, 가 is added, and for words ending in a consonant, 이 is added.

- 조엘 씨가 빵을 먹어요. Joel eats bread.
- 과일이 너무 비싸요. The fruit is too expensive.

2 이/가 also functions to particularly emphasize the preceding subject.

A 누가 음식을 준비할 거예요? Who's going to prepare the food?
B 준호 씨가 음식을 준비할 거예요. Junho will prepare the food.
(Meaning that Junho, not anybody else, will do it.)

A 누가 안 왔어요? Who hasn't arrived?
B 요코 씨가 안 왔어요. Yoko hasn't arrived.

3 이/가 is used to express new information in a sentence, that is, the introduction of a new topic.

- 옛날에 한 남자가 살았어요. 그 남자는 아이들이 두 명 있었어요.
  Once upon a time, there lived a man. He had two sons.
- 저기 민우 씨가 와요.
  Minu is coming this way.

Noun Ending in Vowel + 가	Noun Ending in Consonant + 이
친구**가** 바빠요. 학교**가** 가까워요. 준호**가** 학교에서 공부해요.	선생님**이** 키가 커요. 방**이** 작아요. 동생**이** 지금 자요.

In Conversation

Track 032

A 누가 제이슨 씨예요?
B 저 사람이 제이슨 씨예요.

A Which one is Jason?
B That person (over there) is Jason.

A 어디가 아파요?
B 배가 아파요.

A Where does it hurt?
B My stomach hurts.

A 넥타이가 멋있어요.
B 고맙습니다.

A Your tie looks nice.
B Thank you.

Check It Out!

When 가 is added to 나, 저, and 누구, they combine as follows:

나 + **가** → 내가	저 + **가** → 제가	누구 + **가** → 누가

- 내가 리처드예요. I'm Richard.
  나가 리처드예요. (×)
- 제가 할게요. I'll do it.
  저가 할게요. (×)
- 누가 청소하겠어요? Who will clean up?
  누구가 청소하겠어요? (×)

On Your Own

1 Some friends have gathered to have a party. What will each of the following people be doing? Look at the pictures and fill in the blanks using 이/가.

(1) A 누가 사진을 찍을 거예요?
B ________________ 사진을 찍을 거예요.

(2) A 누가 케이크를 만들 거예요?
B ________________ 케이크를 만들 거예요.

(3) A 그럼, 누가 음료수를 살 거예요?
B 아, ________________ 음료수를 살 거예요.

(4) A 그리고 누가 음악을 준비할 거예요?
B ________________ 음악을 준비할 거예요.

2 Look at the pictures and fill in the blanks using 이/가.

(1) 날씨______ 더워요.

(2) 비빔밥_____ 맛있어요.

(3)  드라마_______ 재미없어요.

(4)  꽃_____ 예뻐요.

02 N은/는

Track 033

안녕하세요? 저는 댄이에요.

Hello. I'm Dane.

형은 키가 커요. 동생은 키가 작아요.

My older brother is tall. My younger brother is short.

부디 씨는 운동을 잘해요. 그렇지만 공부는 못해요.

Budi is good at sports. However, he is not good at studying.

Grammar Focus

1 은/는 is added to the end of what the speaker wants to talk about or explain in the sentence to designate it as the main idea, topic, or issue of discussion. Thus it means the same as 'as for' or 'regarding'. For words ending in a vowel, 는 is added, and for words ending in a consonant, 은 is added.

- 저는 한국 사람입니다. I'm Korean.
- 리처드 씨는 29살입니다. Richard is 29 years old.
- 제 직업은 변호사입니다. I'm a lawyer.

2 은/는 is also used when referring to something mentioned earlier in a conversation or when talking about something already known by both sides in the conversation. In other words, 은/는 is used when expressing 'old' information.

- 저는 내일 요코 씨를 만나요. 요코 씨는 일본에서 왔어요.
  I'll meet Yoko tomorrow. Yoko (She) came from Japan.
- 저는 작년에 뉴욕에 갔었어요. 뉴욕은 정말 아름다웠어요.
  I went to New York last year. New York (It) was really beautiful.
- 어렸을 때 옆집에 한 아이가 있었어요. 그 아이는 착하고 친절했어요.
  When I was young, there was a child who lived next door. That child was good and kind.

3 은/는 is used when comparing or contrasting two things, and in such cases it can be attached not only to subjects but also the objects or other parts of the sentence.

- 에릭은 미국 사람이에요. 그렇지만 준호는 한국 사람이에요.
  Eric is American. Junho, however, is Korean. (subject comparison)
- 저는 축구는 좋아해요. 그렇지만 야구는 좋아하지 않아요.
  I like soccer. However, I don't care for baseball. (object contrast)
- 서울에는 눈이 왔어요. 그렇지만 부산에는 눈이 오지 않았어요.
  Snow fell in Seoul. In Busan, however, snow did not fall. (location contrast)

A 사과 있어요? — Do you have apples?

B 아니요, 배는 있어요. — No, (but) we have pears. (alludes to the fact that while there are no apples, there are, however, pears)

Noun Ending in Vowel + 는	Noun Ending in Consonant + 은
소냐는 겨울을 좋아해요. 제주도는 섬이에요.	제이슨은 의사예요. 서울은 한국에 있어요.

In Conversation

Track 034

A 부모님 직업이 뭐예요?
B 아버지는 회사원이에요.
그리고 어머니는 선생님이에요.

A What do your parents do?
B My father works for a company.
And my mother is a teacher.

A 도쿄가 어때요?
B 도쿄는 많이 복잡해요.

A How's Tokyo?
B Tokyo is really crowded.

A 안녕하세요? 저는 댄입니다.
B 안녕하세요? 저는 캐럴이에요.
미국 사람이에요.

A Hello. I'm Dane.
B Hello. I'm Carol. I'm American.

On Your Own

1 The following is Tiruen's self-introduction. Read it and fill in the blanks appropriately with 은/는.

안녕하세요? (1) 제 이름_____ 티루엔이에요. (2) 저_____ 베트남 사람이에요. (3) 제 고향_____ 하노이예요. (4) 하노이____ 아주 복잡해요. 저는 가족이 3명 있어요. (5) 아버지_____ 회사원이에요. (6) 그리고 어머니_______ 선생님이에요. (7) 동생_____ 학생이에요. (8) 동생_____ 음악을 좋아해요. (9) 저_____ 운동을 좋아해요. 그래서 운동을 많이 해요. (10) 그렇지만 수영_____ 못해요.

2 Look at the pictures and fill in the blanks using 은/는.

(1) 이 사람_____ 왕징 씨예요.

(2) 왕징 씨_____ 중국 베이징에서 왔어요.

(3) 한국_____ 겨울이에요.

(4) 시드니_____ 여름이에요.

(5) 작년에 파리에 갔었어요. 파리_____ 아름다웠어요.

03 N을/를

Track 035

부디 씨가 영화를 봐요.

Budi watches a movie.

아버지가 신문을 읽어요.

Dad reads the newspaper.

요코 씨가 음악을 들어요.

Yoko listens to music.

Grammar Focus

The object particle 을/를 is added to a noun to express that the noun is the object of the sentence. For nouns ending in a vowel, 를 is added, and for nouns ending in a consonant, 을 is added. Common verbs that require this object particle include **먹다** (to eat), **마시다** (to drink), **좋아하다** (to like), **읽다** (to read), **보다** (to see), **만나다** (to meet), **사다** (to buy), **가르치다** (to teach), **배우다** (to learn), and **쓰다** (to write). In colloquial speech, 을/를 is sometimes omitted.

Noun Ending in Vowel + 를	Noun Ending in Consonant + 을
커피를 마셔요. 영화를 봐요. 친구를 만나요. 구두를 사요. 노래를 들어요.	물을 마셔요. 신문을 봐요. 선생님을 만나요. 옷을 사요. 음악을 들어요.

In Conversation

Track 036

A 무슨 운동을 좋아해요?
B 축구를 좋아해요.

A What kind of exercise do you like?
B I like soccer.

A 무엇을 배워요?
B 한국어를 배워요.

A What do you study?
B I study Korean.

A 오늘 누구를 만나요?
B 여자 친구를 만나요.

A Who will you meet today?
B I'll meet my girlfriend.

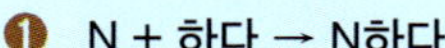

Check It Out!

❶ N + 하다 → N하다

When 을/를 is omitted from verbs like 공부를 하다, 수영을 하다, 운동을 하다, and 산책을 하다, the form becomes shortened to a single one-word form: 공부하다, 수영하다, 운동하다, and 산책하다. However, for the verbs 좋아하다 and 싫어하다, because 좋아– and 싫어– are not nouns, the forms 좋아하다 and 싫어하다 are the one-word verb forms.

❷ 뭐 해요?

The question noun 무엇 can be shortened to 무어, which can be further shortened to 뭐. Thus, the question 뭐를 해요? can be shortened to 뭘 해요?, which can be further shortened to 뭐 해요? This form is often used in conversation.

- 무엇 → 무어 → 뭐
- 무엇을 해요? → 뭐를 해요? → 뭘 해요? → 뭐 해요?

On Your Own

Look at the pictures and fill in the blanks using 을/를.

(1)

A 민우 씨가 무엇을 해요?
B 노래______ 불러요.

(2)

A 웨슬리 씨가 뭐를 해요?
B 한국어______ 배워요.

(3)

A 요코 씨가 뭐 해요?
B ____________________.

(4)

A 티루엔 씨가 뭐 해요?
B ____________________.

04 N와/과, N(이)랑, N하고

Track 037

저는 수박과 딸기를 좋아해요.
I like watermelons and strawberries.

(= 저는 딸기와 수박을 좋아해요.)
I like strawberries and watermelons.

어제 가방이랑 모자를 샀어요.
Yesterday, I bought a bag and a hat.

(= 어제 모자랑 가방을 샀어요.)
Yesterday, I bought a hat and a bag.

햄버거하고 콜라 주세요.
I'll have a hamburger and coke, please.

Grammar Focus

1 These particles express the listing of various things or people and correspond to 'and' in English. **와/과** is used mainly in writing, presentations, and speeches while **(이)랑** and **하고** are used in everyday conversation. For nouns ending in a vowel, **와** or **랑** is used, and for nouns ending in a consonant, **과** or **이랑** is used. **하고** is used regardless of whether a final consonant is present.

Noun Ending in Vowel + 와/랑/하고	Noun Ending in Consonant + 과/이랑/하고
의자**와** 책상이 있습니다. 엄마**랑** 아빠는 회사에 가요. 불고기**하고** 비빔밥을 먹어요.	신문**과** 잡지를 봅니다. 동생**이랑** 저는 아이스크림을 좋아해요. 옷**하고** 운동화를 살 거예요.

2 These particles can also indicate the person with which the subject performs an action and correspond to '(together) with' in English. When indicating such a relationship, **같이** and **함께** normally follow the particle.

- 내일 친구**하고 같이** 영화를 볼 거예요. I plan to see a movie (together) with my friend tomorrow.

• 가족**과 함께** 여행을 가고 싶어요. — I want to go on a trip (together) with my family.

• 우리 선생님**하고 같이** 식사할까요? — Shall we have lunch (together) with the teacher?

In Conversation

Track 038

A 교실에 누가 있습니까? — A Who's in the classroom?

B 선생님과 학생들이 있습니다. — B The teacher and students (are in the classroom).

A 무슨 음식을 좋아해요? — A What kind of food do you like?

B 냉면이랑 김밥을 좋아해요. — B I like naengmyeon and gimbap.

Check It Out!

❶ When functioning as particles to list things, (이)랑 and 하고 can be added to the final noun in the list, but 와/과 cannot.

- 바지랑 가방을 샀어요. (○) I bought pants and a bag.
- 바지하고 가방을 샀어요. (○)
- 바지와 가방을 샀어요. (○)
- 옷이랑 가방이랑 사요. (○) I buy clothes and a bag.
- 옷하고 가방하고 사요. (○)
- 옷과 가방과 사요. (×)

❷ Although 와/과, (이)랑, and 하고 can all be used similarly to list things, they cannot be mixed within the same sentence.

- 저는 딸기와 바나나하고 귤이랑 감을 좋아해요. (×)
- 저는 딸기와 바나나와 귤과 감을 좋아해요. (○) I like strawberries, bananas, tangerines, and persimmons.
- 저는 딸기하고 바나나하고 귤하고 감을 좋아해요. (○)
- 저는 딸기랑 바나나랑 귤이랑 감을 좋아해요. (○)

On Your Own

Look at the pictures and fill in the blanks using 와/과 or (이)랑 or 하고.

(1) 

A 무엇을 좋아해요?

B 비빔밥________ 불고기를 좋아해요.

(2)  

A 어제 집에서 뭘 했어요?

B 청소________ 빨래를 했어요.

(3) 

A 누구하고 여행을 할 거예요?

B __________ 여행을 할 거예요.

(4) 

A 누구랑 살아요?

B __________ 같이 살아요.

05 N의

Track 039

이것은 웨슬리의 책이에요.
(= 이것은 웨슬리 책이에요.)
This is Wesley's book.

이분은 부디 씨의 선생님입니다.
(= 이분은 부디 씨 선생님입니다.)
This is Budi's teacher.

제 이름은 요코입니다.
(= 저의 이름은 요코입니다.)
My name is Yoko.

Grammar Focus

의 expresses the possessive relationship of the first noun being the possessor of the second noun. It corresponds to the possessive 'of' or '(Noun)'s', in English. When 의 is used in this possessive sense, it can be pronounced as either [의] or [에] although [에] is used most often. Furthermore, the particle 의 is often omitted in colloquial speech. In the case of pronouns representing people, such as 나, 저, and 너, rather than being omitted, 의 combines with each to form 나의 → 내, 저의 → 제, and 너의 → 네. In a sentence, 의 is placed between the possessor and the possession.

Noun + 의
리처드의 어머니 (= 리처드 어머니)
우리의 선생님 (= 우리 선생님)
나의 친구/내 친구
저의 이름/제 이름
너의 책/네 책

In Conversation

Track 040

A 이것은 누구의 우산입니까?
B 재준 씨의 우산입니다.

A Whose umbrella is this?
B It's Jaejun's umbrella.

A 이분은 누구예요?
B 제이슨 씨의 어머니예요.

A Who is this person?
B (She's) Jason's mother.

A 이름이 뭐예요?
B 제 이름은 이민우예요.

A What's your name?
B My name is Lee Minu.

Check It Out!

When referring to a group with which one is associated (home, family, company, country, or school), it is common to use the pronouns 우리/저희 in place of 나. Also, 우리 is used in place of 제 and 내 when referring to one's family members. However, in the case of 동생, 내 동생 and 제 동생 are used more often than 우리 동생 (our younger brother/sister).

- 내 집 (my house) → 우리 집 (my/our house)
- 내 가족 (my family) → 우리 가족 (my/our family)
- 제 회사 (my company) → 우리 회사 (my/our company)
- 제 나라 (my country) → 우리나라 (my/our country)
- 제 학교 (my school) → 우리 학교 (my/our school)

- 내 어머니 (my mother) → 우리 어머니 (my/our mother)
- 제 아버지 (my father) → 우리 아버지 (my/our father)
- 제 언니 (my older sister) → 우리 언니 (my/our older sister)
- 제 남편/아내 (my husband/wife) → 우리 남편/아내 (my husband/wife)
- 제 딸/아들 (my daughter/son) → 우리 딸/아들 (my/our daughter/son)

* 제 동생/내 동생 (my younger brother/sister)

When showing respect to the listener, 저희, the humble from of 우리, is used. Examples include 저희 어머니 and 저희 아버지. However, when referring to one's country, only 우리나라 is used, not 저희 나라.

On Your Own

Look at the pictures and fill in the blanks using 의.

(1)

A 이것은 누구의 가방이에요?

B ____________ 가방이에요.
(저)

(2)

A 그것은 누구의 지갑이에요?

B ____________ 지갑이에요.
(부디 씨)

(3)

A 저 남자분은 누구세요?

B ______________________.
(김 선생님, 남편)

(4)

A 이분은 누구세요?

B 이분은 ______________________.
(우리, 어머니)

06 N에 ①

Track 041

친구가 한국**에** 와요.

My friend is coming to Korea.

동생이 대학교**에** 다녀요.

My little brother goes to school.

다음 달에 고향**에** 돌아가요.

I go back to my hometown next month.

Grammar Focus

1 에 is used mainly with the verbs **가다** (to go), **오다** (to come), **다니다** (to attend/commute), **돌아가다** (to return), **도착하다** (to arrive), **올라가다** (to go up), and **내려가다** (to go down). It expresses the direction in which a particular behavior proceeds. It corresponds to 'to' in English.

Noun + 에 가다/오다
매일 회사**에** 가요. 우리 집**에** 오세요. 교회**에** 다녀요.

2 에 is also used with **있다** and **없다** to express the location of a person or thing. It corresponds to 'in' or 'on' in English. (See also Getting Ready 02 있다 (to be))

- 소파 위에 강아지가 있어요.
  The dog is on the sofa.
- 지금 집에 어머니와 동생이 있어요.
  Right now my mother and little brother/sister are in the house.

In Conversation

Track 042

A 어디에 가요?
B 백화점에 가요.

A Where are you going?
B I'm going to the department store.

A 요코 씨가 생일 파티에 와요?
B 아니요, 안 와요.

A Is Yoko coming to the birthday party?
B No, she isn't coming.

A 오늘 오후에 뭐 해요?
B 서점에 가요.

A What will you do this afternoon?
B I'm going to the bookstore.

On Your Own

Look at the pictures and fill in the blanks using 에.

(1)

A 캐럴 씨가 어디에 가요?
B ______________________________.

(2)

A 운룽 씨가 학교를 졸업했어요?
B 네, 졸업했어요. 요즘 ______________________________.

(3)

A 지금 동생이 어디에 있어요?
B ______________________________.

(4)

A 핸드폰이 어디에 있어요?
B ______________________________.

07 N에 ②

Track 043

저는 아침 8시**에** 일어나요.

I wake up at 8:00 in the morning.

3월 2일**에** 한국에 왔어요.

I came to Korea on March 2.

토요일**에** 만나요.

See you on Saturday.

Grammar Focus

에 is also added to nouns that indicate time and expresses the time when some action, event, or situation occurs. It corresponds to 'at' or 'on' in English. **에** can also combine with the particles **는** and **도** to form **에는** and **에도**.

Noun Indicating Time + 에	
년/해 (Year)	2009년**에**, 작년**에**, 올해**에**, 내년**에**
월/달 (Month)	4월**에**, 지난달**에**, 이번 달**에**, 다음 달**에**
날 (Day)	4월 18일**에**, 생일**에**, 어린이날**에**, 크리스마스**에**
요일 (Day of Week)	월요일**에**, 토요일**에**, 주말**에**
시간 (Time)	한 시**에**, 오전**에**, 오후**에**, 아침**에**, 저녁**에**
계절 (Season)	봄**에**, 여름**에**, 가을**에**, 겨울**에**

Of the nouns that indicate time, **에** cannot be added to **그제 (= 그저께)** (the day before yesterday), **어제 (= 어저께)** (yesterday), **오늘** (today), **내일** (tomorrow), **모레** (the day after tomorrow), or **언제** (when).

- 어제에 친구를 만났어요. (×) → 어제 친구를 만났어요. (○)
  I met my friend yesterday.
- 내일에 영화를 볼 거예요. (×) → 내일 영화를 볼 거예요. (○)
  I plan to see a movie tomorrow.
- 언제에 일본에 가요? (×) → 언제 일본에 가요? (○)
  When will you go to Japan?

In Conversation

Track 044

A 보통 몇 시에 자요?
B 보통 밤 11시에 자요.

A What time do you normally go to sleep?
B I usually go to sleep at 11:00 P.M.

A 언제 고향에 돌아갈 거예요?
B 내년 6월에 돌아갈 거예요.

A When will you go back to your hometown?
B I plan to go back in June of next year.

A 주말에 시간이 있어요?
B 네, 주말에 시간이 있어요.

A Do you have time on the weekend?
B Yes, I have time on the weekend.

Check It Out!

When more than one noun representing time is used in a sentence, then 에 is added to the final noun only.

- 다음 주에 토요일에 오전에 10시 30분에 만나요. (×)
  → 다음 주 토요일 오전 10시 30분에 만나요. (○)
  Let's meet next Saturday at 10:30 A.M.

On Your Own

Look at the pictures and fill in the blanks using 에.

(1)

A 일요일 몇 시에 만나요?

B ______________________________.

(2)

A 한국에 언제 왔어요?

B ______________________________.

(3)

A 댄 씨의 생일 파티를 언제 해요?

B ______________________________.

(4)

A 부디 씨는 언제 결혼해요?

B ______________________________.

08 N에서

Track 045

학교에 가요. 학교**에서** 공부를 해요.

I'm going to school. I study at school.

영화관에 갔어요. 영화관**에서** 영화를 봤어요.

I went to the theater. I saw a movie at the theater.

식당에 갈 거예요. 식당**에서** 밥을 먹을 거예요.

I'm going to the cafeteria. I'll eat at the cafeteria.

Grammar Focus

에서 is added to the end of nouns to express the place at which some action or behavior occurs. It corresponds to 'at' or 'in' in English.

Location Noun + 에서
백화점**에서** 쇼핑해요.
도서관**에서** 공부해요.
우체국**에서** 편지를 보내요.
커피숍**에서** 커피를 마셔요.
헬스클럽**에서** 운동해요.

In Conversation

Track 046

A 어디에서 살아요?
B 서울에서 살아요.

A Where do you live?
B I live in Seoul.

A 어제 뭐 했어요?
B 명동에서 친구를 만났어요.

A What did you do yesterday?
B I met my friend at Myeongdong.

A 내일 뭐 할 거예요?
B 도서관에서 공부할 거예요.

A What will you do tomorrow?
B I'll study at the library.

Check It Out!

When used before the verb 살다, the particles 에 and 에서 can both be used. There is very little difference in meaning.

- 저는 서울에 살아요. (○) (Describes the state of living or existing in Seoul.)
- 저는 서울에서 살아요. (○) (Emphasizes the act or behavior of living in Seoul.)

What's the Difference?

에	에서
Indicates the place where a person or thing is located or moves and is mainly used with verbs denoting movement, location, or existence. • 시청은 서울에 있어요. (○) City Hall is in Seoul. • 집에 에어컨이 없어요. (○) The house does not have an air conditioner. • 식당에 밥을 먹어요. (×) • 학교에 한국어를 배웠어요. (×)	Indicates the place where an action occurs and is used with a variety of verbs. • 시청은 서울에서 있어요. (×) • 집에서 에어컨이 없어요. (×) • 식당에서 밥을 먹어요. (○) I eat in the dining room. • 학교에서 한국어를 배웠어요. (○) (I) learned Korean at school.

On Your Own

Look at the pictures and fill in the blanks using 에서.

(1) 

A 어디에서 일해요?

B ______________________________.

(2) 

A 어디에서 기차를 타요?

B ______________________________.

(3) 

A 토요일에 뭐 할 거예요?

B ______________________________.

(4) 

A 어제 저녁에 뭐 했어요?

B ______________________________.

09 N에서 N까지, N부터 N까지

Track 047

학교**에서** 집**까지** 걸어왔어요.

I walked home from school.

서울**에서** 부산**까지** 시간이 얼마나 걸려요?

How long does it take to get from Seoul to Busan?

오전 9시**부터** 오후 5시**까지** 일해요.

I work from 9:00 A.M. until 5:00 P.M.

Grammar Focus

These particles express the physical or temporal range over which an action or event occurs and correspond to 'from... to...' and 'from... until...' in English. When expressing physical locations, normally 'Noun**에서** Noun**까지**' is used, and when expressing a range of time, 'Noun**부터** Noun**까지**' is used. Sometimes, however, both expressions can be used with no distinction.

Place에서 Place까지 (Range of Locations)	Time부터 Time까지 (Range of Times)
집**에서** 학교**까지** 버스로 20분쯤 걸려요. 한국**에서** 일본**까지** 배로 갈 수 있어요. 여기**에서** 저기**까지** 몇 미터(m)예요? (= 여기부터 저기까지 몇 미터(m)예요?)	점심시간은 오후 1시**부터** 2시**까지**입니다. 월요일**부터** 금요일**까지** 학교에 가요. 7월**부터** 8월**까지** 방학이에요. (= 7월에서 8월까지 방학이에요.)

In Conversation

Track 048

A 여기에서 학교까지 멀어요?
B 네, 버스로 한 시간쯤 걸려요.

A Is it far from here to school?
B Yes, it takes about one hour by bus.

A 이 도서관은 토요일에 문을 엽니까?
B 네, 토요일은 오전 10시부터 오후 4시까지 엽니다.

A Is this library open on Saturdays?
B Yes, on Saturdays it's open from 10 A.M. until 4 P.M.

A 명동에서 동대문까지 어떻게 가요?
B 지하철 4호선을 타고 가세요.

A How do you get from Myeongdong to Dongdaemun?
B Please take subway line 4.

On Your Own

Look at the pictures and fill in the blanks using either 에서 ~까지 or 부터 ~까지.

(1)

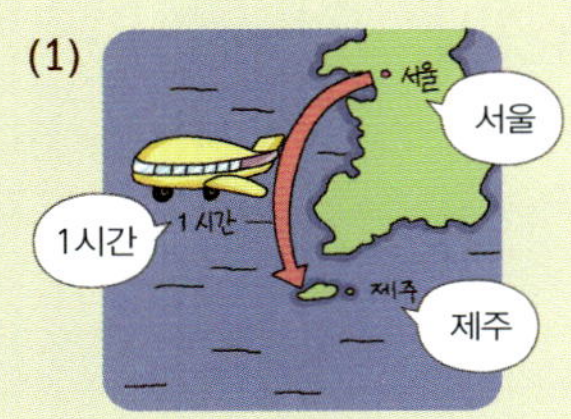

A 서울________ 제주도________ 얼마나 걸립니까?
B 비행기로 1시간 걸립니다.

(2)

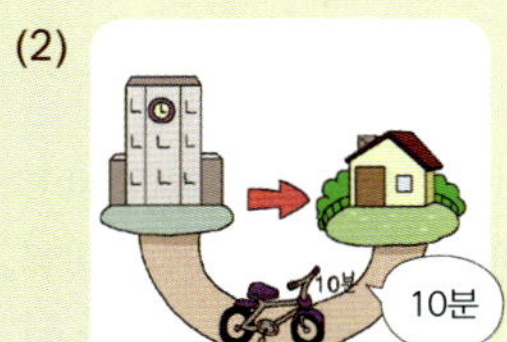

A ____________________ 얼마나 걸려요?
B 자전거로 10분 걸려요.

(3)

A 몇 시부터 몇 시까지 점심시간이에요?
B 오후 1시________ 2시________ 점심시간입니다.

(4)

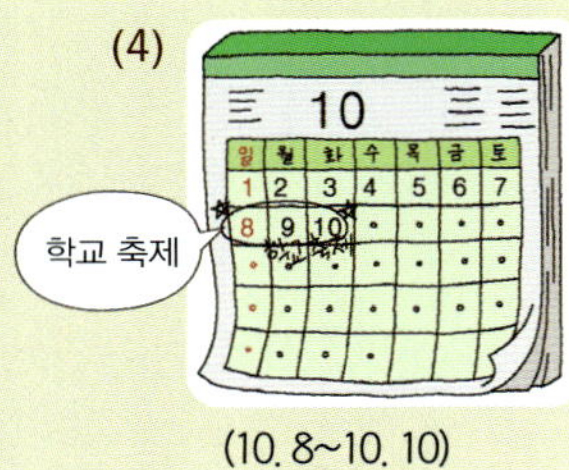

(10. 8~10. 10)

A 언제부터 언제까지 학교 축제예요?
B ____________________ 학교 축제예요.

10 N에게/한테

Track 049

재준 씨가 캐럴 씨**에게** 선물을 줍니다.

Jaejun gives a present to Carol.

선생님이 학생들**에게** 한국어를 가르칩니다.

The teacher teaches Korean to the students.

동생이 개**한테** 밥을 줘요.

My little sister feeds the dog.

Grammar Focus

에게/한테 are added to nouns representing people or other living creatures and indicate that the noun is the recipient or target of an action. **한테** is more colloquial than **에게**. **에게/한테** are only used when the preceding noun is a person or other living creature. Otherwise, (for plants, things, places, etc.) **에** is used.

에게/한테 cannot be used with all verbs. The limited number of verbs they can be used with include **주다** (to give), **선물하다** (to give a present), **던지다** (to throw), **보내다** (to send), **부치다** (to ship/send), **쓰다** (to write), **전화하다** (to phone), **묻다** (to ask), **가르치다** (to teach), **말하다** (to speak), **팔다** (to sell), **가다** (to go), and **오다** (to come).

Person · Animal + 에게/한테	Thing · Plant · Place + 에
개**에게** 줘요	나무**에** 물을 줘요
친구**에게** 소포를 보내요	중국**에** 소포를 보내요
선생님**한테** 물어봐요	회사**에** 물어봐요
친구**한테** 전화해요	사무실**에** 전화해요
아기가 엄마**한테** 와요	친구가 우리 집**에** 와요

In Conversation

Track 050

A 누구한테 편지를 써요?
B 고향 친구한테 편지를 써요.

A Who are you writing a letter to?
B I'm writing a letter to my friend back home.

A 왜 꽃을 샀어요?
B 여자 친구한테 선물할 거예요.

A Why did you buy flowers?
B I'm going to give them to my girlfriend as a present.

A 선생님, 남산도서관 전화번호가 몇 번이에요?
B 미안해요. 잘 몰라요. 114에 전화해 보세요.

A Teacher, what is the phone number for Namsan Library?
B I'm sorry, but I don't know. Please call 114 (directory assistance).

Check It Out!

1. When giving or doing something for someone equal or lower in social status than the speaker, 에게 주다 is used. However, when the target of the action is someone of higher social status to whom the speaker must show respect, the honorific 께 is used in place of 에게/한테, and 드리다 is used in place of 주다. (See also Introduction to the Korean Language 5. Honorific Expressions)

   - 나는 할아버지**에게** 선물을 **주었습니다**. → 나는 할아버지**께** 선물을 **드렸습니다**.
     I gave a present to my Grandpa.
   - 사장님**에게 전화를 했습니다**. → 사장님**께 전화를 드렸습니다**.
     I made a call to the boss.
   - 아버지**에게 말했습니다**. → 아버지**께** 말씀**드렸습니다**.
     I told my father.

2. When receiving or learning something from another person, 에게서 받다/배우다 or 한테서 받다/배우다 is used. 서 can also be omitted, in which case the expression becomes 에게 받다/배우다 or 한테 받다/배우다. When the thing being received or learned comes from a person of higher social status, the honorific 께 is used in place of 에게서 and 한테서.

   - 내 생일에 친구**에게서** 선물을 받았습니다. = 내 생일에 친구**에게** 선물을 받았습니다.
     I got a present from my friend on my birthday.
   - 이정아 선생님**한테서** 한국말을 배웠습니다. = 이정아 선생님**한테** 한국말을 배웠습니다.
     I learned Korean from my teacher, Lee Jeonga.
   - 어렸을 때 할아버지**께** 한자를 배웠습니다.
     I learned Chinese characters from my grandfather when I was little.

On Your Own

Look at the pictures and fill in the blanks using 에(게)/한테.

(1) 

캐럴 씨가 남자 친구________ 전화해요.

(2) 

아이가 칠판________ 그림을 그립니다.

(3) 

댄 씨가 __________________ 공을 던집니다.

(4) 

요코 씨가 꽃_________ 물을 줍니다.

11 N도

무쿨 씨는 인도 사람이에요.
그리고 친구**도** 인도 사람이에요.

Mukul is Indian. And his friend is also Indian.

아버지는 키가 커요. 그리고 저**도** 키가 커요.

My father is tall. And I am tall, too.

왕징 씨는 사과를 좋아해요. 그리고 딸기**도** 좋아해요.

Wang Jing likes apples. And she likes strawberries, too.

Grammar Focus

도 is used after subject and object nouns to express the listing of subjects and objects or the addition of a subject or object to one mentioned previously. This meaning corresponds to 'also' or 'too' in English.

Noun + 도
나는 한국 사람입니다. 그리고 친구**도** 한국 사람입니다.
아버지는 돈이 많습니다. 그리고 시간**도** 많습니다.
나는 사과를 좋아합니다. 그리고 수박**도** 좋아합니다.
나는 공부를 잘합니다. 그리고 운동**도** 잘합니다.

When added to a subject particle, the subject particle is omitted, leaving only 도.

- 나는 한국 사람이에요. 그리고 친구**는도** 한국 사람이에요. (×)
  → 나는 한국 사람이에요. 그리고 친구**도** 한국 사람이에요. (○)
  I'm Korean. And my friend is also Korean.

Similarly, when added to the object particle, 을/를 is omitted, leaving only 도.

- 나는 사과를 좋아해요. 그리고 딸기를도 좋아해요. (×)
  → 나는 사과를 좋아해요. 그리고 딸기도 좋아해요. (○)
  I like apples. And (I like) strawberries, too.

When 도 is added to particles other than subject or object particles, however, the other particle is not omitted.

- 일본에 친구가 있어요. 그리고 미국에도 친구가 있어요. (○)
  I have a friend in Japan. And (I have a friend) in the USA, too.
  일본에 친구가 있어요. 그리고 미국도 친구가 있어요. (×)
- 집에서 공부해요. 그리고 도서관에서도 공부해요. (○)
  I study at home. And (I study) in the library, too.
  집에서 공부해요. 그리고 도서관도 공부해요. (×)
- 친구에게 선물을 주었어요. 그리고 동생에게도 선물을 주었어요. (○)
  I gave a present to my friend. And (I gave a present) to my younger sister, too.
  친구에게 선물을 주었어요. 그리고 동생도 선물을 주었어요. (×)

In Conversation

Track 052

A 무엇을 먹을 거예요?
B 비빔밥을 먹을 거예요.
그리고 된장찌개도 먹을 거예요.

A What will you have to eat?
B I'll have bibimbap. And I'll have doenjang stew, too.

A 요즘 무엇을 배워요?
B 한국어를 배워요.
그리고 태권도도 배워요.

A What do you study these days?
B I study Korean. And I also learn taekwondo.

A 어제 생일 파티에 누가 왔어요?
B 마틴 씨가 왔어요.
그리고 요코 씨도 왔어요.

A Who came to the birthday party yesterday?
B Martin came. And Yoko also came.

On Your Own

Look at the pictures and fill in the blanks using 도.

(1)

A 무슨 음식을 좋아해요?

B 불고기를 좋아해요. 그리고 비빔밥________ 좋아해요.

(2)

A 누가 예뻐요?

B 하영 씨가 예뻐요.

그리고 ______________________.

(3)

A 어제 누구를 만났어요?

B 친구를________________.

그리고 여자 친구________________.

(4)

A 어제 시장에서 무엇을 샀어요?

B 바지를 ________________.

그리고 ______________________.

12 N만

Track 053

오늘 학교에 캐럴 씨**만** 왔어요.

Today, only Carol came to school.

댄 씨는 야채는 안 먹어요. 고기**만** 먹어요.

Dane doesn't eat vegetables. (He) only eats meat.

5분**만** 기다려 주세요.

Please wait for just five minutes.

Grammar Focus

만 expresses the choosing of one thing to the exclusion of other things. It corresponds to 'only' or 'just' in English. When used after a number, it can also mean 'minimum'. It is used by adding **만** to the end of the word being chosen or stated to the exclusion of other things.

Noun + 만
캐럴 씨는 바지**만** 입어요. 그 식당은 월요일**만** 쉬어요. 영원히 제니퍼 씨**만** 사랑할 거예요. 우리 아이는 하루 종일 게임**만** 해요.

The particle **만** can be used either in place of the particles **이/가**, **은/는**, and **을/를**, or it can be used together with them. When used together, **만** is added first, followed by **이**, **은**, or **을**, to form **만이**, **만은**, and **만을**.

- 준호만 대학에 입학했어요. (○) = 준호만이 대학에 입학했어요. (○)
  Only Junho was accepted to the university.
- 민우는 다른 책은 안 읽고 만화책만 읽어요. (○)
  = 민우는 다른 책은 안 읽고 만화책만을 읽어요. (○)
  Minu reads comic books only, and no other books.

However, when used with particles other than **이/가**, **은/는**, and **을/를**, **만** comes after the particle, to form **에서만**, **에게만**, and **까지만**, for example.

- 우리 딸은 학교에서만 공부하고 집에서는 공부하지 않아요. (◯)
  Our daughter studies only at school, and doesn't study at home.
  우리 딸은 학교만에서 공부하고 집에서는 공부하지 않아요. (×)
- 준호 씨에게만 선물을 줬어요. (◯) I gave a present just to Junho.
  준호 씨만에게 선물을 줬어요. (×)
- 제이슨 씨는 12시까지만 공부하고 자요. (◯) Jason studies only until 12 o'clock, and then sleeps.
  제이슨 씨는 12시만까지만 공부하고 자요. (×)

In Conversation

Track 054

A 학생들이 다 왔어요?
B 부디 씨만 안 왔어요.
다른 학생들은 다 왔어요.

A Have all the students arrived?
B Only Budi hasn't arrived.
The others have all arrived.

A 커피에 설탕과 크림 다 넣으세요?
B 설탕만 넣어 주세요.

A Do you take both sugar and cream in your coffee?
B Just sugar, please.

Look at the pictures and fill in the blanks using 만.

(1)

A 캐럴 씨와 댄 씨 모두 미국 사람이에요?
B 아니요, ______________________________.
(캐럴 씨)

(2)

A 동생에게도 편지를 썼어요?
B 아니요, ______________________________.
(부모님)

(3)

A 남편이 집에서도 회사 일을 해요?
B 아니요, ______________________________.
(회사)

13 N밖에

Track 055

사과가 한 개**밖에** 안 남았어요.

There's only one apple left.

냉장고에 우유**밖에** 없어요.

There's nothing but milk in the refrigerator.

선물을 한 개**밖에** 못 받았어요.

I only received one present.

Grammar Focus

밖에 expresses the only thing or option available, with no possibility of anything else. It corresponds to 'only' or 'nothing but' in English. The word that comes before **밖에** has a connotation of being very small or few in number, and a negative form must follow it.

	Negative form	Example
Noun + 밖에	안 (= -지 않다)	학생들이 두 명**밖에** 안 왔어요.
	못 (= -지 못하다)	그 돈으로는 사과를 한 개**밖에** 못 사요.
	없어요	음식이 조금**밖에** 없어요.
	몰라요	한국어는 '안녕하세요'**밖에** 몰라요.

Although **밖에** is always followed by a negative form, it cannot be followed by **아니다**, nor can it be followed by imperative or propositive forms.

- 민우는 학생밖에 아니에요. (×)
- 토마토를 조금밖에 사지 마세요. (×) → 토마토를 조금만 사세요. (○)
  Please buy only a few tomatoes.

• 10분밖에 기다리지 맙시다. (×) → 10분만 기다립시다. (○)
Let's wait just 10 minutes.

(Compare with Unit 3. Particles 12 N만,16 N(이)나 ①)

In Conversation

Track 056

A 그 책을 많이 읽었어요?
B 어려워서 다섯 쪽밖에 못 읽었어요.

A Did you read much of that book?
B It's difficult, so I could only read five pages.

A 파티에 사람들이 많이 왔어요?
B 30명을 초대했어요. 그런데 20명밖에 안 왔어요.

A Did a lot of people come to the party?
B I invited 30 people, but only 20 came.

A 시간이 얼마나 남았어요?
B 10분밖에 안 남았어요.

A How much time is left?
B There are only 10 minutes remaining.

What's the Difference?

The particles 밖에 and 만 have similar meanings, but while 만 can be used in both positive and negative sentences, 밖에 is used in negative sentences only.

밖에

• 교실에 재준 씨밖에 있어요. (×)
교실에 재준 씨밖에 없어요. (○)
Only Jaejun is in the classroom.

• 가게에서 과일밖에 샀어요. (×)
가게에서 과일밖에 안 샀어요. (○)
I only bought fruit at the store.

만

• 교실에는 재준 씨만 있어요. (○)
Only Jaejun is in the classroom.
교실에는 재준 씨만 없어요. (○)
Everyone but Jaejun is in the classroom.
(All the other students are present.)

• 가게에서 과일만 샀어요. (○)
I only bought fruit at the store.
가게에서 과일만 안 샀어요. (○)
I bought things other than fruit at the store.
(I bought all the other ingredients.)

On Your Own

Look at the pictures and fill in the blanks using 밖에.

(1)

A 집에서 회사까지 시간이 많이 걸려요?

B 아니요, 집에서 회사까지 10분__________ 안 걸려요.

(2)

A 어제 많이 잤어요?

B 아니요, 세 시간__________ 못 잤어요.

(3)

A 반에 여학생이 많아요?

B ____________________________________.

(4)

A 집에 에어컨이 있어요?

B 아니요, ______________________________.

14 N(으)로

Track 057

여기에서 오른쪽으로 가세요.

Please go to the right from here.

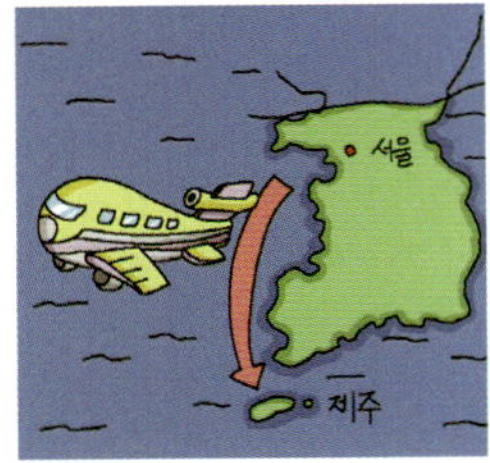

서울에서 제주도까지 비행기로 가요.

(I) go from Seoul to Jeju Island by airplane.

가위로 종이를 잘라요.

(I) cut the paper with scissors.

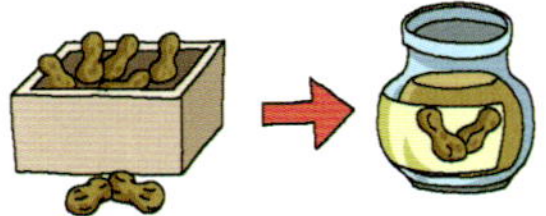

땅콩으로 잼을 만들었어요.

(I) made jam from peanuts.

Grammar Focus

1 (으)로 expresses a direction (toward a place). It means 'to' or 'toward' in English. When the preceding noun ends in a vowel or ㄹ, 로 is used, and when the noun ends in a consonant, 으로 is used.

- 오른쪽으로 가세요. 은행이 나와요. Please go to the right. You'll see a bank.
- 앞으로 쭉 가세요. 우체국이 있어요. Please go straight forward. There's a post office.

2 (으)로 is also used when expressing means of transport, other means, tools, and materials used to make something. This meaning corresponds to 'by' or 'with/using' and 'from' in English.

- 부산에 기차로 갈 거예요. I'll go to Busan by train.
- 가위로 종이를 잘라요. I cut the paper with scissors.
- 밀가루로 빵을 만들어요. I make bread from flour.

Noun Ending in Vowel or ㄹ + 로	Noun Ending in Consonant + 으로
버스로 가요.	왼쪽으로 가세요.
비행기로 왔어요.	오른쪽으로 가세요.
지하철로 갈 거예요.	트럭으로 가요.
한국어로 말하세요.	콩으로 만들어요.
칼로 잘라요.	젓가락으로 먹어요.

In Conversation

Track 058

A 실례합니다. 은행이 어디에 있어요? A Pardon me. Where is the bank?
B 저 약국 앞에서 오른쪽으로 가세요. B Please go to the right from that pharmacy (over there).

A 서울에서 부산에 어떻게 가요? A How do you get to Busan from Seoul?
B 기차로 가세요. 기차가 빨라요. B (Please) go by train. The train is fast.

A 이 과자가 맛있어요. 뭐로 만들었어요? A This candy is good. What's it made of?
B 이 과자는 쌀로 만들었어요. B This candy is made of rice.

A 한국 사람은 숟가락으로 밥을 먹어요. A Koreans eat rice with a spoon.
B 일본 사람은 젓가락으로 밥을 먹어요. B The Japanese eat rice with chopsticks.

Check It Out!

When a means of transport is represented by a verb instead of a noun, -아/어서 is added to the verb, such as in 걸어서, 뛰어서, 달려서, 운전해서, and 수영해서.

- 학교에서 집까지 걸어서 가요. I go home from school by foot.
- 서울에서 부산까지 운전해서 갔어요. I went from Seoul to Busan by driving a car.
- 부산에서 제주도까지 수영해서 갈 거예요. I plan to swim (go by swimming) from Busan to Jeju Island.

What's the Difference?

❶ What is the difference between 차로 왔어요 and 운전해서 왔어요?

차로 왔어요 refers to getting in a car and traveling, with the subject either driving the car or riding as a passenger. However, 운전해서 왔어요 can only be used when the subject actually drove the car.

민우 씨가 차로 왔어요.	민우 씨가 운전해서 왔어요.
* Can be used when expressing that Minu traveled by car. * Can be used when Minu drove the car. * Can be used even when Minu was not the one who drove.	* Can be used when expressing that Minu traveled by driving a car. * Can be used when Minu drove the car. * Cannot be used when Minu was not the one who drove.

❷ What is the difference between (으)로 가다 and 에 가다?

(으)로 가다 expresses going toward a particular direction, with the focus being on the direction. 에 가다, on the other hand, focuses on the destination, and thus only the destination is expressed because no sense of direction is conveyed.

(으)로 가다	에 가다
* Focus on direction: 에릭 씨가 집으로 가요. (○) Eric goes to his home. 오른쪽으로 가세요. (○) Go to the right.	* Focus on destination: 에릭 씨가 집에 가요. (○) Eric goes to his home. 오른쪽에 가세요. (×)

Look at the pictures and fill in the blanks using (으)로.

(1)

A 집에서 회사까지 어떻게 가요?

B ______________ 가요.

C ______________ 가요.

D ______________ 가요.

(2)

A 집에서 한강공원까지 어떻게 가요?

B ______________ 가요.

(3)

숙제를 __________ 하지 마세요. __________ 쓰세요.

(4)

계란하고 밀가루 ________ 빵을 만들어요.

15 N(이)나 ①

Track 059

아침에 빵**이나** 밥을 먹어요.

In the mornings, I eat bread or rice.

목이 말라요. 물**이나** 주스 주세요.

I'm thirsty. Please give me some water or juice.

방학에 제주도**나** 설악산에 가고 싶어요.

I want to go to Jeju Island or Mt. Seorak during the school vacation.

Grammar Focus

(이)나 means that one of the two or more listed nouns will be chosen. When the preceding noun ends in a vowel, **나** is used, and when the noun ends in a consonant, **이나** is used. In the case of adjectives and verbs, **-거나** is added to the verb stem. (See also Unit 4. Listing and Contrast 02 V-거나)

Noun Ending in Vowel + 나	Noun Ending in Consonant + 이나
잡지**나** 신문을 봐요.	신문**이나** 잡지를 봐요.
딸기**나** 수박을 사요.	수박**이나** 딸기를 사요.
우유**나** 물을 마셔요.	물**이나** 우유를 마셔요.
바다**나** 산에 가요.	산**이나** 바다에 가요.
축구**나** 수영을 해요.	수영**이나** 축구를 해요.

When **(이)나** is added to a subject or object, the subject or object particle is omitted, leaving only **(이)나** in place of **이/가** or **을/를**, respectively.

- 어머니**가나** 아버지가 요리해요. (×) → 어머니**나** 아버지가 요리해요. (◯)
  My mother or father cooks.
- 빵**을이나** 밥을 먹어요. (×) → 빵**이나** 밥을 먹어요. (◯) (I) eat bread or rice.

When **(이)나** is used together with the particle **에**, **에서**, or **에게**, it can be either be used 1) by itself with the first word(s) in the list, while **에**, **에서**, or **에게** is used only with the final word in the list, or 2) together with **에**, **에서**, or **에게** to form **에나**, **에서나**, or **에게나**. However, the use of **(이)나** by itself is more natural.

- 토요일**에나** 일요일에 운동해요. (◯) = 토요일**이나** 일요일에 운동해요. (◯)
  (I) exercise on Saturday or Sunday.
- 산**에나** 바다에 가요. (◯) = 산**이나** 바다에 가요. (◯)
  (I) go to the mountain or sea. / Let's go to the mountain or sea.
- 공원**에서나** 커피숍에서 데이트해요. (◯) = 공원**이나** 커피숍에서 데이트해요. (◯)
  (We) go on dates to the park or a coffee shop.
- 선생님**에게나** 한국 친구에게 질문해요. (◯) = 선생님**이나** 한국 친구에게 질문해요. (◯)
  (I) ask questions to my teacher or Korean friend.

In Conversation

Track 060

A 무엇을 살 거예요?
B 구두나 가방을 살 거예요.

A What will you buy?
B I plan to buy some shoes or a bag.

A 이 문법 문제를 잘 모르겠어요.
B 이 선생님이나 김 선생님에게 물어보세요.

A I don't understand this grammar question.
B Please ask instructor Lee or instructor Kim.

On Your Own

Look at the pictures and fill in the blanks using (이)나

(1)

A 명동에 어떻게 가요?
B 지하철 ____________ 버스를 타세요.

(2)

A 어디에서 책을 읽을 거예요?
B 도서관 ____________ 공원에서 읽을 거예요.

(3)

A 방학에 어디에 갈 거예요?
B ________________________ 갈 거예요.

16 N(이)나 ②

Track 061

친구를 두 시간**이나** 기다렸어요.

I waited for my friend for no less than two hours.

아이가 여덟 명**이나** 있어요.

(We) have (as many as) eight children.

사과가 맛있어요. 그래서 열 개**나** 먹었어요.

The apples are tasty. So I ate (as many as) ten of them.

Grammar Focus

(이)나 indicates that the number or amount of something is much higher or more than expected, or that it is at a level higher than what is generally considered normal. It corresponds to 'as many as' or 'no less than' in English. When added to words ending in a vowel, 나 is added, and when added to words ending in a consonant, 이나 is added.

Noun Ending in Vowel + 나	Noun Ending in Consonant + 이나
바나나를 일곱 개**나** 먹었어요. 한 시간 동안 30페이지**나** 읽었어요.	친구에게 다섯 번**이나** 전화했어요. 어제 열두 시간**이나** 잤어요.

(Compare with Unit 3. Particles 13 N밖에)

In Conversation

Track 062

A 어제 술을 많이 마셨어요?
B 네, 맥주를 열 병이나 마셨어요.

A 기차 시간이 얼마나 남았어요?
B 30분이나 남았어요.

A 마틴 씨는 자동차가 많아요?
B 네, 5대나 있어요.

A Did you drink a lot of alcohol yesterday?
B Yes, I drank (no less than) 10 bottles.

A How much time is left before the train arrives?
B There's (still as much as) thirty minutes remaining.

A Does Martin have a lot of cars?
B Yes, he's got (as many as) five.

What's the Difference?

While the particle 밖에 indicates that a number or amount is less than expected or doesn't meet a general standard, (이)나 indicates that a number or amount is more than expected or exceeds a general standard. Depending on the perspective, a certain quantity can be viewed as either smaller or larger than expected, and thus 밖에 and (이)나 can be used to express such views.

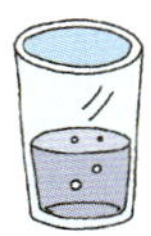

- 물이 반**밖에** 없어요.
  (The amount is less than expected.)
- 물이 반**이나** 있어요.
  (The amount is more than expected.)

A 우리는 아이가 네 명**밖에** 없어요.
(The number is not viewed as very many.)
B 네 명**이나** 있어요? 저는 한 명인데요.
(The number is viewed as more than usual.)

댄 이번 시험에서 80점**이나** 받았어요.
(Dane normally scores around 70, so, to him, 80 is a better than expected score.)
왕징 이번 시험에서 80점**밖에** 못 받았어요.
(Wang Jing normally scores around 90, so, to her, 80 is a worse than expected score.)

On Your Own

Look at the pictures and fill in the blanks using (이)나.

(1) 

A 오늘 길이 너무 막혔어요.
B 맞아요. 회사까지 ____________ 걸렸어요.
(1시간)

(2) 

A 그 영화가 재미있어요?
B 네, 너무 재미있어요. 그래서 ____________ 봤어요.
(3번)

(3) 

A 책이 그렇게 어려워요?
B 네, ____________ 읽었어요. 그런데 아직도 모르겠어요.
(5번)

(4) 

A 조엘 씨 집에는 개가 정말 많아요.
B 몇 마리 있어요?
A ____________ 있어요.
(10마리)

(5) 

A 티루엔 씨는 커피를 정말 많이 마셔요.
B 맞아요. 하루에 ____________ 마셔요.
(6잔)

17 N쯤

Track 063

파티에 20명쯤 왔어요.

About 20 people came to the party.

공항에 한 시쯤 도착했어요.

I arrived at the airport around 1 o'clock.

요즘 토마토가 3,000원쯤 해요.

These days, tomatoes cost about 3,000 won.

Grammar Focus

쯤 is added to nouns denoting numbers, quantities, and time to indicate approximation. It corresponds to 'about' or 'around' in English.

Noun + 쯤
한 시쯤 만납시다. 10,000원쯤 있어요. 두 달쯤 배웠어요. 5번쯤 만났어요.

In Conversation

Track 064

A 내일 몇 시쯤 만날까요?

B 1시쯤 어때요?
수업이 12시 50분에 끝나요.

A At about what time shall we meet tomorrow?

B How's around 1 o'clock?
My class ends at 12:50.

A 학교에서 집까지 얼마나 걸려요?
B 버스로 30분쯤 걸려요.

A How long does it take you to get to school from home?
B It takes me about 30 minutes by bus.

A 한국에 언제 오셨어요?
B 1년 전쯤 왔어요.

A When did you come to Korea?
B I came about a year ago.

Check It Out!

When referring to approximate prices, 'Noun쯤 하다' is used more often than 'Noun 쯤이다'.

A 사과가 요즘 얼마쯤 해요? — About how much are apples these days?
B 요즘 3개에 2,000원쯤 해요. — Recently they cost about 2,000 won for three.

A 중국까지 비행기 표가 얼마쯤 해요? — About how much is the airfare to China?
B 글쎄요, 300,000원쯤 할 거예요. — Um, it will probably cost around 300,000 won.

On Your Own

Look at the pictures and fill in the blanks using 쯤.

(1)

A 오늘 몇 시에 일어났어요?
B ______________________________.

(2)

A 고향까지 얼마나 걸려요?
B ______________________________.

(3)

A 영국에서 얼마나 여행했어요?
B ______________________________.

(4)

A 남대문시장에서 청바지가 얼마쯤 해요?
B ______________________________.

18 N처럼, N같이

Track 065

가수**처럼** 노래를 잘 불러요.

He sings like a professional singer.

하영 씨는 천사**같이** 착해요.

Hayeong is as kind as an angel.

영화배우**같이** 잘생겼어요.

He's as handsome as a movie actor.

Grammar Focus

처럼/같이 expresses that some action or thing appears the same or very similar to the preceding noun. It corresponds to 'like' or 'as ... as' in English.

Noun + 처럼/같이
인형**처럼** 예뻐요. (= 인형**같이** 예뻐요.)
아기**처럼** 웃어요. (= 아기**같이** 웃어요.)
엄마**처럼** 친절해요. (= 엄마**같이** 친절해요.)
실크**처럼** 부드러워요. (= 실크**같이** 부드러워요.)
하늘**처럼** 높아요. (= 하늘**같이** 높아요.)

In Conversation

Track 066

A 댄 씨가 정말 한국말을 잘하지요?

B 네, 저도 댄 씨처럼 한국말을 잘했으면 좋겠어요.

A Dane is really good at Korean, right?

B Yes, I wish I was as good at Korean as Dane is.

A 그 남자가 어때요?
B 코미디언같이 재미있어요.

A How is that man?
B He's as funny as a comedian.

A 서울이 복잡해요?
B 네, 일본 도쿄처럼 복잡해요.

A Is Seoul crowded?
B Yes, it's crowded like Tokyo, Japan.

Check It Out!

처럼/같이 are often used in Korean to express characteristics metaphorically by comparing them to animals or other things in nature. Thus you will often encounter the following figures of speech used to describe people: someone scary is 호랑이처럼 무섭다, someone cute is 토끼처럼 귀엽다, someone slow to act is 거북이처럼 느리다, and someone generous is 바다처럼 마음이 넓다.

On Your Own

Look at the pictures and write the appropriate answer for each item in the space provided.

(1) 우리 언니는 요리사처럼 요리를 잘해요. (　　　)
(2) 슬퍼서 아이처럼 울었어요. (　　　)
(3) 눈이 별처럼 빛나요. (　　　)
(4) 우리 할아버지는 호랑이처럼 무서워요. (　　　)
(5) 돌고래처럼 수영을 잘해요. (　　　)
(6) 우리는 가족같이 친해요. (　　　)

19 N보다

Track 067

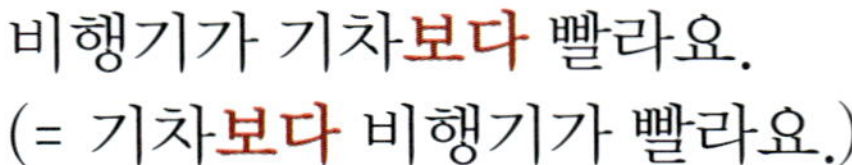

비행기가 기차**보다** 빨라요.
(= 기차**보다** 비행기가 빨라요.)

Airplanes are faster than trains.

동생이 언니**보다** 더 커요.
(= 언니**보다** 동생이 더 커요.)

My little sister is bigger than my elder sister.

백화점이 시장**보다** 더 비싸요.
(= 시장**보다** 백화점이 더 비싸요.)

The department store is more expensive than the market.

Grammar Focus

보다 indicates that the word preceding it is the standard from which a comparison will be made. It corresponds to 'more … than' or '-er than' in English. Though **보다** is added to a noun to form 'N 이/가 N보다 ~하다', the order of the subject and noun with **보다** added can be reversed with no change in meaning. Also, while the adverbs **더** and **덜** are generally used together with **보다**, they can be omitted.

Noun + 보다
사과**보다** 딸기를 (더) 좋아해요. 동생**보다** 수영을 (더) 잘해요. 어제**보다** 오늘이 (덜) 추워요. 작년**보다** 올해 눈이 많이 왔어요.

In Conversation

Track 068

A 봄을 좋아해요, 여름을 좋아해요?
B 여름보다 봄을 더 좋아해요.

A Do you like spring or summer?
B I like spring more than summer.

A 댄 씨, 토요일이 바빠요, 일요일이 바빠요?
B 저는 일요일에 교회에 가요. 그래서 토요일보다 일요일이 더 바빠요.

A Dane, are you busy on Saturday or Sunday?
B I go to church on Sunday. So I'm busier on Sunday than Saturday.

A 제주도하고 서울하고 어디가 더 따뜻해요?
B 제주도가 서울보다 더 따뜻해요.

A Which is warmer, Jeju Island or Seoul?
B Jeju Island is warmer than Seoul.

On Your Own

Look at the pictures and fill in the blanks using 보다.

(1)

(적비, 5kg)

(운룡, 3kg)

A 누구의 가방이 더 무거워요?
B ____________________.

(2)

A 소파가 편해요, 의자가 편해요?
B ____________________.

(3)

(₩50,000)

(₩30,000)

A 어느 것이 더 싸요?
B ____________________.

(4)

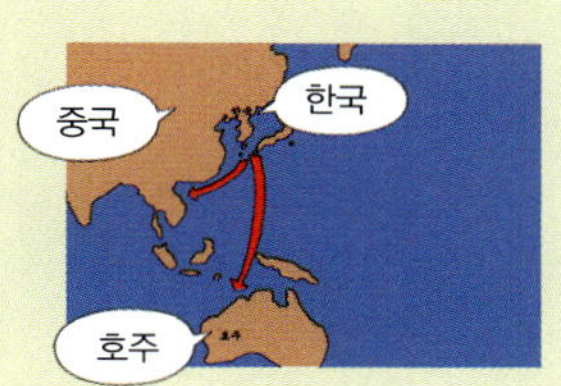

A 한국에서 어느 나라가 더 가까워요?
B ____________________.

20 N마다

Track 069

웨슬리 씨는 일요일**마다** 교회에 가요.

Wesley goes to church every Sunday.

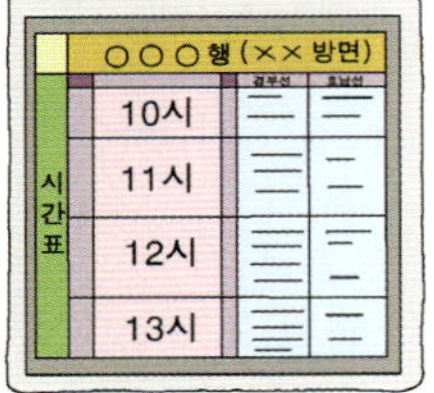

기차는 한 시간**마다** 있어요.

The train comes once every hour.

나라**마다** 국기가 달라요.

Every country has a different flag.

Grammar Focus

1 **마다** is added to time nouns. It expresses the repetition of the same or a similar situation or behavior over a set period of time. It corresponds to 'every' or 'once every' in English.

- 두 달마다 머리를 잘라요. I cut my hair (once) every two months.
- 오 분마다 지하철이 와요. The subway train comes (once) every five minutes.

2 **마다** can also indicate all, or every one, of something, with no exceptions. In this sense, it corresponds to 'every' or 'all' in English. **마다** is added to the noun being described.

- 주말마다 여행을 가요. I take a trip every weekend.
- 점심시간에는 식당마다 자리가 없어요.
  During lunchtime, all the cafeterias become full (have no seats available).

Noun + 마다
1시간**마다** 버스가 출발해요.
날**마다** 청소해요.
해**마다** 외국 여행을 해요.
토요일**마다** 가족하고 전화해요.

In Conversation

Track 070

A 이번 주 금요일 저녁에 시간 있어요?

B 금요일마다 태권도를 배워요. 그래서 시간이 없어요.

A Do you have time this Friday evening?

B I have taekwondo lessons every Friday. So I don't have any time.

A 비행기가 자주 있어요?

B 이틀마다 있어요.

A Are there a lot of flights?

B There's a flight every two days.

A 컴퓨터가 교실마다 있어요?

B 네, 모든 교실에 다 있어요.

A Are there computers in every classroom?

B Yes, all classrooms have them.

Check It Out!

❶ The phrases 날마다, 일주일마다, 달마다, and 해마다 can also be written as 매일, 매주, 매월/매달, and 매년.

- 날마다 회사에 가요. = 매일 회사에 가요.
  I go to work (at the company) daily. = I go to work (at the company) every day.
- 일주일마다 회의가 있어요. = 매주 회의가 있어요.
  We have a meeting weekly. = We have a meeting every week.
- 달마다 잡지가 나와요. = 매월/매달 잡지가 나와요.
  The magazine is published monthly. = The magazine is published every month.
- 해마다 이사해요. = 매년 이사해요.
  I move (change residences) once a year. = I move every year.

❷ In the case of the word 집, 집집마다 is used instead of 집마다.

- 요즘에는 집집마다 인터넷을 사용해요. These days, all households use the Internet.

On Your Own

Look at the pictures and fill in the blanks using 마다.

(1)

A 부디 씨, 고향에 자주 가세요?

B ____________________.
(방학)

(2)

A 한국 사람은 젓가락, 숟가락으로 식사해요.

B 미국 사람은 나이프와 포크, 인도 사람은 손으로 식사해요.
__________ 식사 방법이 달라요.
(나라)

(3)
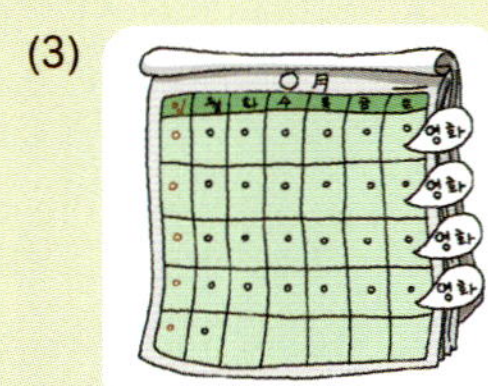

A 영화를 보세요?

B 네, __________ 봐요.
(토요일)

(4)

A 몇 분마다 지하철이 와요?

B 출근 시간에는____________________.
(5분)

Unit 4.

Listing and Contrast

01 A/V-고
02 V-거나
03 A/V-지만
04 A/V-(으)ㄴ/는데 ①

01 A/V-고

Track 071

캐럴 씨는 키가 **크고** 날씬해요.
Carol is tall and slender.

민우 씨는 한국 사람**이고** 댄 씨는 영국 사람입니다.
Minu is Korean, and Dane is British.

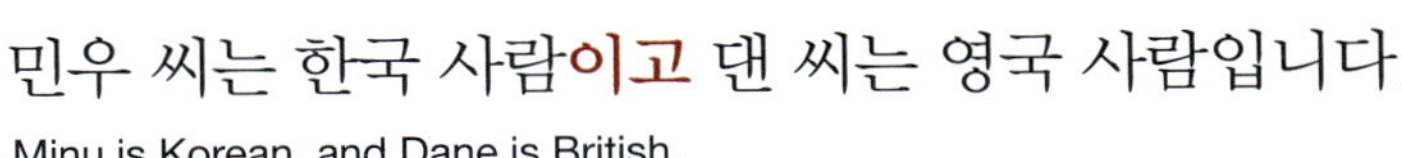

어제 파티에서 티루엔 씨가 노래도 **부르고** 춤도 췄어요.
At yesterday's party, Tiluen sang songs and danced.

Grammar Focus

1 –고 is used to list two or more actions, states, or facts. It corresponds to 'and' in English. –고 is added to the stems of verbs and adjectives.

- 형은 **커요. 그리고** 동생은 작아요. My older brother is big. And my younger brother is small.
  → 형은 **크고** 동생은 작아요. My older brother is big, and my younger brother is small.

2 –고 is also used to express that the action in the first clause was performed before the action in the second clause. It corresponds to 'and (then)' in English. Tense is only expressed in the second clause, not the first.
(See also Unit 5. Time Expressions 03 V-고 나서)

- 어제 밥을 **먹었어요. 그리고** 숙제를 했어요.
  Yesterday, I ate dinner. And I did my homework.
  → 어제 밥을 **먹고** 숙제를 했어요. [어제 밥을 먹었고 숙제를 했어요. (×)]
  Yesterday, I ate dinner, and then did my homework.

가다 + **–고** → 가고	크다 + **–고** → 크고

Base Form	-고	Base Form	-고
오다	오고	예쁘다	예쁘고
보다	보고	바쁘다	바쁘고
읽다	읽고	넓다	넓고
찾다	찾고	작다	작고
공부하다	공부하고	날씬하다	날씬하고

Check It Out!

The form 'N도 Vst고 N도 V' is used when combining two or more facts about the same subject.

- 형은 수영을 잘해요. 그리고 농구도 잘해요.
  My older brother is good at swimming. And (he's) also good at basketball.
  → 형은 수영**도** 잘**하고** 농구**도** 잘해요.
  My older brother is good at swimming and also good at basketball.
- 저는 딸기를 좋아해요. 그리고 바나나도 좋아해요.
  I like strawberries. And (I) like bananas, too.
  → 저는 딸기**도** 좋아**하고** 바나나**도** 좋아해요.
  I like strawberries and also (I) also like bananas.

In Conversation

Track 072

A 내일 뭐 할 거예요?
B 오전에는 친구를 만나고
오후에는 도서관에 갈 거예요.

A What will you do tomorrow?
B In the morning, I'll meet a friend,
and in the afternoon, (I'll) go to the library.

A 어제 뭐 했어요?
B 피자도 먹고 영화도 봤어요.

A What did you do yesterday?
B I ate pizza and saw a movie.

A 여자 친구가 어때요?
B 똑똑하고 예뻐요.

A What do you think of your girlfriend?
B (She's) smart and pretty.

On Your Own

Look at the pictures and fill in the blanks using -고.

(1)

A 날씨가 어때요?

B 바람이 __________ 추워요.
(불다)

(2)

A 디나 씨 남자 친구가 어때요?

B ____________________.
(멋있다, 친절하다)

(3)

A 가족들은 주말에 보통 뭐 해요?

B 오빠는 __________, 언니는 __________.
(운동하다, 데이트하다)

(4)

A 어제 왕징 씨의 집에서 뭐 했어요?

B ________도 ________고 ________도 ________.
(요리를 하다, 텔레비전을 보다)

02 V-거나

Track 073

아침에 빵을 **먹거나** 우유를 마셔요.

In the morning, I (either) eat bread or drink milk.

주말에 음악을 **듣거나** 영화를 볼 거예요.

On the weekend, I plan to listen to music or watch a movie.

바쁘거나 가방이 무거울 때 택시를 타요.

I take a taxi when I'm busy or my bag is too heavy.

Grammar Focus

-거나 is added to the stem of a verb or adjective to express a choice between that verb or adjective and the one following it. It means the same as 'or' in English. Usually, it is used only once to connect two verbs or adjectives, but it can also be used to connect three or more. Also, in the same way **-거나** is added to the stems of verbs and adjectives, **-(이)나** can be added to nouns to express the same meaning.

(See also Unit 3. Particles 15 N(이)나 ①)

보다 + **-거나** → 보거나　　　　먹다 + **-거나** → 먹거나

Base Form	-거나	Base Form	-거나
자다	자거나	듣다	듣거나
만나다	만나거나	돕다	돕거나
만들다	만들거나	공부하다	공부하거나

In Conversation

Track 074

A 이번 주말에 뭐 할 거예요?
B 운동을 할 거예요.
테니스를 치거나 수영을 할 거예요.

A What will you do this weekend?
B I'll go exercise.
I'll (either) play tennis or go swimming.

A 목이 아파요.
B 그럼 생강차를 마시거나 사탕을 드세요.

A I have a sore throat.
B Then (you should) drink some ginger tea or eat some candy.

A 결혼기념일에 뭐 할 거예요?
B 여행을 가거나 외식을 할 거예요.

A What will you do on your wedding anniversary?
B (We'll) take a trip or go out to eat.

On Your Own

Look at the pictures and fill in the blanks using –거나.

(1)

A 너무 피곤해요. 저녁 식사 어떻게 해요?
B ____________ 피자를 주문합시다.
(외식을 하다)

(2)

A 안녕! 잘 있어요. 건강하세요. 2년 후에 올게요.
B 잘 가요. 가끔 편지를 ____________ 이메일을 보내세요!
(쓰다)

(3)

A 이 단어를 잘 몰라요.
B 한국어 선생님에게 ____________ 사전을 찾으세요.
(물어보다)

(4)

A 시간이 있으면 보통 뭐 하세요?
B ____________ 그림을 그려요.
(영화를 보다)

03 A/V-지만

Track 075

한국말은 **어렵지만** 재미있어요.

Korean is difficult but interesting.

형은 **크지만** 동생은 작아요.

My older brother is big, but my younger brother is small.

하영 씨는 많이 **먹지만** 날씬해요.

Hayeong eats a lot, but (she's) slim.

Grammar Focus

-지만 is used when the information in the second clause of the sentence is opposite or contrary to that in the first. It corresponds to 'but' in English. **-지만** is added to the stems of verbs and adjectives, and in the case of the past tense, **-았/었지만** is added.

사다 + **-지만** → 사지만　　　　좋다 + **-지만** → 좋지만

Base Form	-지만	Base Form	-지만
보다	보지만	슬프다	슬프지만
먹다	먹지만	배고프다	배고프지만
배우다	배우지만	작다	작지만
수영하다	수영하지만	편하다	편하지만

(Compare with Unit 4. Listing and Contrast 04 A/V-(으)ㄴ/는데 ①)

In Conversation

Track 076

A 오늘 날씨가 어때요?
B 바람이 불지만 춥지는 않아요.

A How is the weather today?
B It's windy but not cold.

A 요코 씨, 아파트가 어때요?
B 작지만 깨끗해요.

A How is your apartment, Yoko?
B It's small but clean.

A 댄 씨가 한국말을 잘해요?
B 네, 외국 사람이지만 한국말을 잘해요.

A Can Dane speak Korean well?
B Yes, (he's) a foreigner, but (he) can speak Korean well.

Look at the pictures and fill in the blanks using –지만.

(1)

A 한국 음식이 어때요?
B ______________________________.
(맵다, 맛있다)

(2)

A 언니가 학생이에요?
B 저는 ____________________ 언니는 ____________________.
(학생이다) (회사원이다)

(3)

A 주말에도 바빠요?
B 평일에는 ____________________ 주말에는 ____________________.
(바쁘다) (한가하다)

(4)

A 나탈리아 씨, 추워요?
B 네, ______________________________.
(옷을 많이 입다, 춥다)

04 A/V-(으)ㄴ/는데 ①

Track 077

낮에는 차가 **많은데** 밤에는 차가 없어요.

In the afternoon there are a lot of cars, but at night there aren't any.

저는 오빠는 **있는데** 언니는 없어요.

I have an older brother, but not an older sister.

노래는 **못하는데** 춤은 잘 춰요.

I can't sing, but I can dance well.

Grammar Focus

This pattern is used when the information in the second clause of the sentence is opposite of, in contrast to, or an unexpected result of what is presented in the first clause. It corresponds to 'but' in English. When added to an adjective ending in a vowel, **-ㄴ데** is added, while **-은데** is added to an adjective ending in a consonant. As for present tense verbs, past tense verbs, and **있다/없다**, **-는데** is added.

Adjectives, Present Tense 이다		Present Tense Verbs	Past Tense Verbs, Adjectives
No Final Consonant	Final Consonant		
-ㄴ데	**-은데**	**-는데**	**-았/었는데**
예쁜데 학생인데	높은데 적은데	오는데 읽는데 있는데 없는데	왔는데 많았는데 의사였는데 학생이었는데

Base Form	-(으)ㄴ/는데	Base Form	-(으)ㄴ/는데
크다	큰데	가다	가는데

낮다	낮은데	마시다	마시는데
*멀다	먼데	일하다	일하는데
*덥다	더운데	*듣다	듣는데
*빨갛다	빨간데	*살다	사는데
귀여웠다	귀여웠는데	만났다	만났는데

* Irregular form

(Compare with Unit 4. Listing and Contrast 03 A/V-지만)

In Conversation

Track 078

A 왜 그 시장에 안 가요?
B 가격은 싼데 너무 멀어요.

A Why don't you go to that market?
B The prices are cheap, but it's too far away.

A 회사가 어때요?
B 일은 많은데 월급은 적어요.

A How's your job at the company?
B There are many things to do, but the salary is small.

On Your Own

Look at the pictures and fill in the blanks using -(으)ㄴ/는데.

(1) 

A 그 식당 어때요?
B ______________________.
(맛있다, 비싸다)

(2) 

A 티루엔 씨 집이 어때요?
B 방은 ____________ 화장실은 ____________.
(크지 않다) (2개이다)

(3) 

A 캐럴 씨는 결혼했어요?
B 아니요, 아직 ____________ 남자 친구는 있어요.
(결혼 안 하다)

(4)

A 저녁 먹었어요?
B 네, ____________ 배가 고파요.
(먹다)

Unit 5.

Time Expressions

01 N 전에, V-기 전에

Track 079

2년 **전에** 한국에 왔습니다.

I came to Korea two years ago.

식사 **전에** 이 약을 드세요.

Please take this medicine before meals.

수영하기 전에 준비운동을 해요.

I do warm-up exercises before swimming.

Grammar Focus

This pattern means 'before a certain period of time' or 'before some action', and corresponds to 'before' or 'ago' in English. It is used in the forms 'Time **전에**', 'Noun **전에**', and 'Verb **-기 전에**' in a sentence.

'Noun **전에**' is used mainly with nouns to which **하다** can be added to make verbs. For this reason, **-기 전에** can be added to the corresponding verb stem to produce the same meaning **(식사 전에, 식사하기 전에)**. However, for all verbs other than **하다** verbs, only **-기 전에** can be used.

Noun + 전에	Verb Stem + -기 전에
식사 + **전에** → 식사 전에	식사하다 + **-기 전에** → 식사하기 전에

Time + 전에	N + 전에	Base Form	V-기 전에
1시간 전에	식사 전에	식사(하다)	식사하기 전에
한 달 전에	여행 전에	여행(하다)	여행하기 전에
2년 전에	방문 전에	방문(하다)	방문하기 전에

1시 전에	수업 전에	수업(하다)	수업하기 전에
하루 전에	운동 전에	자다	자기 전에
–		마시다	마시기 전에
		죽다	죽기 전에

In Conversation

Track 080

A 같이 점심 식사해요.
B 미안해요. 1시간 전에 식사했어요.

A Let's have lunch together.
B Sorry. I ate an hour ago.

A 다음 달에 결혼하지요?
B 네, 결혼하기 전에 이것저것 준비할 게 많네요.

A You're getting married next month, right?
B Yes, there sure are a lot of things to prepare before getting married.

A 한국에 오기 전에 어디에 살았어요?
B 뉴욕에서 살았어요.

A Where did you live before coming to Korea?
B I lived in New York.

What's the Difference?

What's the difference between the expressions 1시 전에 and 1시간 전에?

- 1시 전에 오세요.
  (In this case the person can come any time before 1:00, such as 12:50, 12:00, or even 11:00.)
- 1시간 전에 오세요.
  (In this case the person should come exactly one hour before some previously stated time. For example, if there is a meeting scheduled for 3:00, then the person should come at 2:00.)

What should be done before performing each action shown under (가)? Find the most appropriate answer under (나), connect both actions with a line, and then complete each of the sentences that follow using either 전에 or –기 전에.

(가)			(나)
(1) 	•	• ⓐ	
(2) 	•	• ⓑ	
(3) 	•	• ⓒ	
(4) 	•	• ⓓ	

(1) ______________ 서류를 복사해요.

(2) ______________ 손을 씻어요.

(3) ______________ 전화해요.

(4) ______________ 기도해요.

02 N 후에, V-(으)ㄴ 후에

Track 081

한 달 **후에** 아기가 태어나요.

My baby will be born in one month.

밥을 **먹은 후에** 이를 닦아요.

I brush my teeth after dinner.

대학교 졸업 **후에** 취직을 했어요.

I got a job after college graduation.

(= 대학교를 **졸업한 후에** 취직을 했어요.)

I got a job after graduating from college.

Grammar Focus

This pattern means 'after a certain period of time' or 'after some action' and corresponds to 'after' or 'later' in English. It is used in the forms 'Time **후에**', 'Noun **후에**', and 'V-(으)ㄴ 후에' in a sentence.

When attaching to verbs, **-ㄴ 후에** is added when the stem ends in a vowel, **-은 후에** is added when the stem ends in a consonant, and when the stem ends in ㄹ, ㄹ is deleted and **-ㄴ 후에** is added to the remaining part of the stem. **-(으)ㄴ 다음에** can also be used in place of **-(으)ㄴ 후에**.

Noun	Verb	
Noun+후에	Stem Ending in Vowel	Stem Ending in Consonant
식사 **후에**	가다 + **-ㄴ 후에** → 간 후에	먹다 + **-은 후에** → 먹은 후에

Time 후에	N 후에	Base Form	V-ㄴ 후에	Base Form	V-은 후에
1시 후에	식사 후에	식사하다	식사한 후에	받다	받은 후에
1시간 후에	입학 후에	입학하다	입학한 후에	벗다	벗은 후에
한 달 후에	방학 후에	오다	온 후에	읽다	읽은 후에

3년 후에	졸업 후에	만나다	만난 후에	*듣다	들은 후에
–		*놀다	논 후에	*짓다	지은 후에
		*만들다	만든 후에	*돕다	도운 후에

* Irregular form

In Conversation

Track 082

A 언제 고향에 돌아가요?
B 1년 후에 가요.

A When will you return to your hometown?
B In one year from now.

A '집들이'가 뭐예요?
B 한국에서 이사한 후에 하는 파티예요.

A What is meant by '집들이'?
B It's a Korean housewarming party for someone who just moved into a new house.

A 수업 후에 시간 있어요?
B 미안해요. 바빠요. 수업이 끝난 다음에 식당에서 아르바이트를 해요.

A Do you have time after class?
B Sorry. I'm busy. After class ends, I have a part-time job at a restaurant.

What's the Difference?

What's the difference between the expressions 1시 후에 and 1시간 후에?

- 1시 후에 오세요.
  (In this case the person can come anytime after 1:00, such as 1:10, 2:00, or even 3:00.)
- 1시간 후에 오세요.
  (In this case the person should come exactly one hour after some previously stated time. For example, if there is a meeting scheduled for 3:00, then the person should come at 4:00.)

On Your Own

What should be done after performing each action shown under (가)? Find the most appropriate answer under (나), connect both actions with a line, and then complete each of the sentences that follow using either 후에 or -(으)ㄴ 후에.

(가)

(1) 

(2) 

(3) 

(4) 

(나)

ⓐ 

ⓑ 

ⓒ 

ⓓ 

(1) ______________ 샤워해요. (운동하다)

(2) ______________ 집들이를 해요. (이사하다)

(3) ______________ 지하철을 타요. (내리다)

(4) ______________ 영수증을 받아요. (우유를 사다)

03 V-고 나서

Track 083

일을 **하고 나서** 쉽니다.

I rest after finishing my work.

텔레비전을 **보고 나서** 잡니다.

I sleep after watching TV.

아침을 **먹고 나서** 신문을 봅니다.

I read the newspaper after eating breakfast.

Grammar Focus

-고 나서 expresses the finishing of one behavior followed by the beginning of a subsequent behavior and thus corresponds to 'do (something) after', 'upon finishing' or 'and then' in English. Although in some cases -나서 can be omitted without changing the meaning of the sentence, such as in 일을 하고 나서 쉬세요 and 일을 하고 쉬세요, the inclusion of -고 나서 instead of simply -고 helps clarify the fact that the first behavior has completely ended.

보다 + **-고 나서** → 보고 나서　　먹다 + **-고 나서** → 먹고 나서

Base Form	-고 나서	Base Form	-고 나서
끝나다	끝나고 나서	듣다	듣고 나서
먹다	먹고 나서	돕다	돕고 나서
읽다	읽고 나서	공부하다	공부하고 나서

Because -고 나서 expresses temporal order, it can only be used with verbs. Further, when the subjects of the first and second clauses are the same in sentences using the motion verbs **가다** (to go), **오다** (to come), **들어가다** (to enter), **들어오다** (to exit), **나가다** (to leave), **나오다** (to emerge [from]), **올라가다** (to go up), and **내려가다** (to go down), and the verbs **일어나다** (to get/stand up), **앉다** (to sit), **눕다** (to lie down), and **만나다** (to meet), **–아/어서** is used in place of **–고** and **–고 나서**.

- 나는 학교에 가고 나서 (나는) 공부해요. (×)
  → 나는 학교에 가서 (나는) 공부해요. (○)
  I go to school and (I) study.

- (나는) 오늘 버스에서 앉고 나서 (나는) 왔어요. (×)
  → (나는) 오늘 버스에서 앉아서 (나는) 왔어요. (○)
  Today, (I) rode on the bus and (I) came (here).

In Conversation

Track **084**

A 김 부장님, 서류를 언제까지 드릴까요?
B 회의가 끝나고 나서 주세요.

A Manager Kim, (by) when shall I give you the documents?
B Please give them to me after the meeting.

A 듣기 시험을 어떻게 봐요?
B 문제를 두 번 읽을 거예요.
문제를 잘 듣고 나서 대답을 찾으세요.

A How do you take the listening test?
B They will read the questions twice.
Listen to the questions carefully, and then find the answer.

A '독후감'이 뭐예요?
B 책을 읽고 나서 쓰는 글이에요.

A What does '독후감' mean?
B It's what you write after you finish reading a book.

Look at the pictures and fill in the blanks using either –서 or –고 나서.

댄 씨는 아침에 (1)________________ 샤워를 합니다. (2)__________________________ 아침 식사를 합니다. 한국 음식이 맛있습니다. 아침을 (3)_____________________ 학원에 갑니다. 학원에 (4)_______ 학생들에게 영어를 가르칩니다. 영어 수업은 12시에 끝납니다. 영어를 (5)______________________ 친구하고 영화를 봅니다. 영화를 (6)___________________ 커피를 마십니다.

저녁 6시부터 9시까지 한국어 수업이 있습니다. 한국어는 쉽지 않습니다. 그렇지만 재미있습니다. 한국어 수업이 (7)__________________ 헬스장에 갑니다. 헬스장에서 운동을 합니다. (8)_______________________ 집에 갑니다. 집에 (9)________________ 텔레비전을 봅니다. 한국 드라마가 재미있습니다. 댄 씨는 12시에 잡니다.

04 V-아/어서 ①

바나나를 **까서** 먹었어요.

(The monkey) peeled a banana and ate it.

네 시간 동안 공원에 **앉아서** 이야기했어요.

(We) sat in a park for four hours and talked.

여자 친구에게 목걸이를 **사(서)** 주었어요.

I bought a necklace for my girlfriend and gave it to her.

Grammar Focus

-아/어서 is a connective ending indicating the temporal relationship between events. Specifically, it expresses the occurrence of the action in the second clause after the action in the first clause has occurred. The two actions are so closely related that the second action cannot occur without the first action occurring first. This expression corresponds to 'and' or '(in order) to' in English. Moreover, **서** can often be omitted from **-아/어서**, leaving just **-아/어**, but this is not possible with certain verbs, including **가다** (to go), **오다** (to come), and **서다** (to stand). It is formed by adding **-아서** to stems ending in the vowel ㅏ or ㅗ. Otherwise, **-어서** is added. For verbs ending in **하다**, **해서** is added.

Stem Ending in ㅏ or ㅗ	Stem Ending in Vowel Other than ㅏ or ㅗ	Verb Ending in 하다
가다 + **-아서** → 가서	씻다 + **-어서** → 씻어서	결혼하다 → 결혼해서

Base Form	-아/어서	Base Form	-아/어서
사다	사서	만들다	만들어서
팔다	팔아서	요리하다	요리해서

앉다	앉아서	입학하다	입학해서
만나다	만나서	숙제하다	숙제해서
*쓰다	써서	*굽다	구워서

* Irregular form

In the case of sentences in the past, present, or future tense, the tense is expressed only in the second verb, not the first.

- 어제 친구를 만나서 영화를 봤어요.
  Yesterday, I met a friend and watched a movie.
- 내일 친구를 만나서 영화를 볼 거예요.
  Tomorrow, I will meet a friend and watch a movie.

The subjects of both verbs are the same.

- 나는 어제 친구를 만나서 (나는) 영화를 봤어요. (○)
  Yesterday I met a friend and (I) watched a movie.
  나는 어제 친구를 만나서 친구는 영화를 봤어요. (×)

In Conversation

Track 086

A 왜 사과를 깎지 않고 먹어요?
B 사과를 깎아서 먹으면 맛이 없어요.

A Why do you eat apples without peeling them?
B Apples aren't tasty if you peel and eat them.

A 오늘 학교에 지하철로 왔어요?
B 네, 그런데 한 시간 동안 서서 와서 다리가 아파요.

A Did you come to school by subway today?
B Yes, but on the way I stood for an hour, and (so) my legs are sore.

A 왜 아르바이트를 해요?
B 돈을 벌어서 카메라를 살 거예요.

A Why are you doing that part-time job?
B (I plan) to make some money to buy a camera.

What's the Difference?

❶ –고 is a connective ending similar to –아/어서 in that it indicates the temporal relationship between events. However, while –아/어서 is used when the first and second actions are very closely related, –고 is used to connect two unrelated actions that happen sequentially.

- 과일을 씻어서 (그 과일을) 먹어요.
  (I/You) wash the fruit and eat (the fruit).
- 과일을 씻고 (다른 음식을) 먹어요.
  (I/You) wash the fruit and then eat (something else).
- 친구를 만나서 (그 친구와 같이) 영화를 봤어요.
  I met a friend and (together we) watched a movie.
- 친구를 만나고 (나 혼자 또는 다른 사람과) 영화를 봤어요.
  I met a friend and then (I by myself or with somebody else) watched a movie.

❷ When used with verbs designating the wearing of clothes and accessories, –고 is used in place of –아/어서.

- 코트를 입어서 공부해요. (×) → 코트를 입고 공부해요. (○) I put on a coat and study.
- 사람들이 우산을 써서 가요. (×) → 사람들이 우산을 쓰고 가요. (○)
  People are putting up their umbrellas and going.
- 아이가 안경을 써서 책을 봐요. (×) → 아이가 안경을 쓰고 책을 봐요. (○)
  The child puts on glasses and reads books.

Look at the pictures and choose the appropriate word from below to fill in the blanks using –아/어서.

가다	들어가다	만나다	만들다	사다

(1) 

A 어제 뭐 했어요?
B 어제 고등학교 친구를 __________ 같이 식사했어요.

(2) 

A 오늘 퇴근 후에 뭐 할 거예요?
B 노래방에 _______ 노래할 거예요.

(3) 

A 보통 빵을 _________ 먹어요?
B 아니요, 우리는 빵을 ___________ 먹어요.

(4) 

A 날씨가 추워요.
B 그러면 커피숍에 _____________ 이야기해요.

05 N 때, A/V-(으)ㄹ 때

Track 087

방학 **때** 아르바이트를 해요.
I work a part-time job during vacation.

4살 **때** 사진이에요.
This is a picture of me when I was four years old.

시험 **볼 때** 옆 사람의 시험지를 보지 마세요.
Don't look at your neighbors' answer sheets when taking the test.

Grammar Focus

때 expresses the time when an action or state occurs or its duration. When following a noun, 때 is used, and when following a verb, -ㄹ 때 is used when the stem ends in a vowel or ㄹ, while -을 때 is used when the stem ends in a consonant.

Noun	Verb	
Noun + 때	Stem Ending in Vowel or ㄹ	Stem Ending in Consonant
방학 + **때** → 방학 때	가다 + **-ㄹ 때** → 갈 때	먹다 + **-을 때** → 먹을 때

N 때	Base Form	V-ㄹ 때	Base Form	V-을 때
10살 때	보다	볼 때	있다	있을 때
시험 때	만나다	만날 때	없다	없을 때
고등학교 때	끝나다	끝날 때	받다	받을 때
점심 때	나쁘다	나쁠 때	좋다	좋을 때
저녁 때	피곤하다	피곤할 때	*듣다	들을 때

크리스마스 때	*살다	살 때	*붓다	부을 때
휴가 때	*만들다	만들 때	*덥다	더울 때

* Irregular form

In Conversation

Track 088

A 몇 살 때 첫 데이트를 했어요?
B 20살 때 했어요.

A How old were you when you went on your first date?
B (I went when) I was 20 years old.

A 초등학교 때 친구들을 자주 만나요?
B 아니요, 자주 못 만나요.

A Do you often meet your friends from elementary school?
B No, I don't meet them often.

A 이 옷은 실크예요. 세탁할 때 조심하세요.
B 네, 알았어요.

A This clothing is made of silk. Be careful when you wash it.
B Okay, I will.

Check It Out!

때 is not used together with 오전, 오후, 아침, or the days of the week.

- 오전 때 공부를 해요. (×) → 오전에 공부를 해요. (○) I study in the morning.
- 오후 때 운동을 해요. (×) → 오후에 운동을 해요. (○) I exercise in the afternoon.
- 월요일 때 공항에 가요. (×) → 월요일에 공항에 가요. (○) I (will) go to the airport on Monday.

What's the Difference?

What's the difference between 크리스마스에 and 크리스마스 때?

For some nouns, such as 저녁, 점심, and 방학, the meaning is the same whether they are written in the form of 'N 때' or 'N에'. However, for some nouns, especially those representing holidays, like 크리스마스 and 추석, the form 'N에' refers to the specific day(s) of the holiday while the form 'N 때' refers to the approximate time period just before, during, and after the holiday. For example, 크리스마스에 refers to Christmas Day, December 25, and 크리스마스 때 refers to the span of the few days surrounding Christmas, such as the day before and the day after Christmas.

- 크리스마스 때 The period around Christmas, including the day before, Christmas Day, and the day after.
- 크리스마스에 Christmas Day (December 25).

Either 때 or 에 can be used after nouns such as 저녁, 점심, and 방학 with no difference in meaning.

- 저녁 때 = 저녁에, 점심 때 = 점심에, 방학 때 = 방학에

On Your Own

Look at the pictures and choose the appropriate word from below to fill in the blanks using either 때 or -(으)ㄹ 때.

덥다	식사	없다	크리스마스

(1) 

A ______________ 뭐 해요?

B 친구들과 파티를 할 거예요.

(2) 

A 한국에서는______________ 수저를 사용합니다.

B 미국에서는 포크와 나이프를 사용해요.

(3) 

A 햄버거 좋아해요?

B 시간이______________ 햄버거를 먹어요.

(4) 

A 이게 뭐예요?

B 부채예요.______________ 사용해요.

06 V-(으)면서

Track 089

밥을 **먹으면서** TV를 봅니다.

I eat while watching TV.

우리 언니는 피아노를 **치면서** 노래를 해요.

My/our older sister sings while she plays the piano.

운전하면서 전화하지 마세요. 위험해요.

Don't use the phone while driving. It's dangerous.

Grammar Focus

-(으)면서 indicates that the actions of the first and second verbs occur simultaneously. It means 'while' in English. When the verb stem ends in a vowel or ㄹ, **-면서** is used, and when it ends in a consonant, **-으면서** is used.

Stem Ending in Vowel or ㄹ	Stem Ending in Consonant
가다 + **-면서** → 가면서	먹다 + **-으면서** → 먹으면서

Base Form	-면서	Base Form	-으면서
보다	보면서	받다	받으면서
부르다	부르면서	읽다	읽으면서
기다리다	기다리면서	*듣다	들으면서
공부하다	공부하면서	*걷다	걸으면서
*울다	울면서	*짓다	지으면서
*만들다	만들면서	*돕다	도우면서

* Irregular form

The subjects of both clauses are the same. That is, they must be the same person.

- 하영 씨는 노래를 하면서 재준 씨는 피아노를 칩니다. (×)
  → (하영 씨는) 노래를 하면서 (하영 씨는) 피아노를 칩니다. (○)
  (Hayeong) plays the piano while she (Hayeong) sings.
  → 하영 씨가 노래를 하는 동안 재준 씨는 피아노를 칩니다. (○)
  While Hayeong sings, Jaejun plays the piano.

When the subjects of the two verbs are different, **–는 동안** is used.

- 동생이 청소를 하는 동안 언니는 빨래를 했습니다.
  While my little brother/sister was cleaning the house, my older sister did the laundry.

(See also Unit 5. Time Expressions 09 N 동안, V–는 동안)

Past and future tense endings are not added to the verb preceding **–(으)면서**. It is always written in present tense.

- 어제 하영 씨는 노래를 했으면서 피아노를 쳤습니다. (×)
  → 어제 하영 씨는 노래를 하면서 피아노를 쳤습니다. (○)
  Yesterday, Hayeong sang while she played the piano.

In Conversation

Track 090

A 음악을 좋아해요?	A Do you like music?
B 네, 그래서 음악을 들으면서 공부를 해요.	B Yes, that's why I listen to music while I study.
A 어제 많이 바빴어요?	A Were you very busy yesterday?
B 네, 그래서 샌드위치를 먹으면서 일했어요.	B Yes, that's why I ate a sandwich while working.
A 요즘 왜 피곤해요?	A Why are you tired these days?
B 학교에 다니면서 아르바이트를 해요. 그래서 피곤해요.	B I have a part-time job while attending school. That's why I'm tired.

Look at the pictures and fill in the blanks using -(으)면서.

(1) ______________________________.
(커피를 마시다, 신문을 보다)

(2) ______________________________.
(노래를 하다, 샤워를 하다)

(3) ______________________________.
(아이스크림을 먹다, 걷다)

(4) ______________________________.
(친구를 기다리다, 책을 읽다)

07 N 중, V-는 중

Track 091

지하철 **공사 중**입니다.

The subway is under construction.

(= 지하철 **공사하는 중**입니다.)

The subway is in the middle of being constructed.

사장님은 **회의 중**입니다.

The president is in a meeting.

(= 사장님은 **회의하는 중**입니다.)

The president is currently having a meeting.

지금 집에 **가는 중**이에요.

(I'm) on the way home.

이사할 거예요. 그래서 집을 **찾는 중**이에요.

I intend to move. So I'm looking for a new place to live.

Grammar Focus

This expression is used with a noun that indicates the content of an action and means that the subject is in the process of performing the action. It corresponds to 'in the process/middle of' or 'currently doing' in English. After a noun, 중 is added, and after a verb, -는 중 is added to the verb stem.

Noun + 중	Verb Stem + -는 중
회의 + **중** → 회의 중	회의하다 + **-는 중** → 회의하는 중

Base Form	N 중	V-는 중
수업(하다)	수업 중	수업하는 중
회의(하다)	회의 중	회의하는 중
공사(하다)	공사 중	공사하는 중
통화(하다)	통화 중	통화하는 중
가다	-	가는 중
먹다		먹는 중
배우다		배우는 중
*만들다		만드는 중

* Irregular form

In Conversation

Track 092

A 왜 이렇게 길이 막혀요?
B 백화점이 세일 중이에요.
그래서 길이 막혀요.

A Why is there so much traffic?
B The department store is having a sale.
That's why there's traffic.

A 여보세요? '한국무역회사'입니까?
김 과장님 좀 부탁합니다.
B 김 과장님은 지금 외출 중이십니다.
오후 5시에 들어오실 겁니다.

A Hello? Is this the Korea Trade Company?
I'd like to speak with Section Chief Kim.
B Section Chief Kim is currently out of
the office. He should be back at 5 P.M.

A 운전면허증 있어요?
B 요즘 운전을 배우는 중이에요.
다음 주에 운전면허 시험을 봐요.

A Do you have a driver's license?
B Recently, I've been learning how to drive.
I'll take a driving test next week.

Check It Out!

-는 중이다 and -고 있다 are used in similar ways. However, while -고 있다 has no restrictions regarding what subjects it can be used with, -는 중이다 cannot be used with subjects representing natural phenomena.

- 비가 오는 중이에요. (×) → 비가 오고 있어요. (○) It's raining.
- 눈이 오는 중이에요. (×) → 눈이 오고 있어요. (○) It's snowing.
- 바람이 부는 중이에요. (×) → 바람이 불고 있어요. (○) The wind is blowing.

On Your Own

Look at the pictures and connect each to its appropriate phrase with a line.

(1) • • ⓐ 수리 중

(2)  • • ⓑ 샤워 중

(3)  • • ⓒ 임신 중

(4)  • • ⓓ 통화 중

(5) • • ⓔ 쓰는 중

(6)  • • ⓕ 생각하는 중

(7)  • • ⓖ 만드는 중

(8)  • • ⓗ 읽는 중

08 V-자마자

너무 피곤해서 집에 **오자마자** 잤어요.

I was so tired I went to sleep as soon as I got home.

불이 **나자마자** 소방차가 왔어요.

The fire truck arrived as soon as the fire started.

수업이 **끝나자마자** 학생들은 교실을 나갔어요.

The students left the classroom right after class was over.

Grammar Focus

-자마자 indicates that something occurs immediately following the end of some event or action. It is added to the verb and means 'as soon as' or 'right after' in English.

가다 + **-자마자** → 가자마자 먹다 + **-자마자** → 먹자마자

Base Form	-자마자	Base Form	-자마자
보다	보자마자	씻다	씻자마자
켜다	켜자마자	앉다	앉자마자
끝나다	끝나자마자	듣다	듣자마자
시작하다	시작하자마자	묻다	묻자마자
만들다	만들자마자	눕다	눕자마자

The subjects of the first and second clauses of the sentence can be either the same or different.

- (내가) 집에 오자마자 (내가) 잤어요.
  As soon as I arrived home, I slept.
- 엄마가 나가자마자 아기가 울어요.
  As soon as the mother leaves, the baby starts crying.

Tense is not expressed in the verb of the first clause, but it is in the second.

- 집에 갔자마자 잤어요. (×) → 집에 가자마자 잤어요. (○)
  As soon as I got home, I slept.
- 집에 갈 거자자마자 잘 거예요. (×) → 집에 가자마자 잘 거예요. (○)
  As soon as I get home, I'm going to sleep.

In Conversation

Track 094

A 정아 씨와 언제 결혼할 거예요?	A When will you marry Jeonga?
B 대학교를 졸업하자마자 결혼할 거예요.	B We'll get married as soon as we graduate from college.
A 오늘 왜 기분이 안 좋아요?	A Why are you in a bad mood today?
B 어제 우산을 샀어요. 그런데 우산을 사자마자 잃어버렸어요.	B I bought an umbrella yesterday. But I lost it as soon as I bought it.
A 배가 너무 불러요. 누워서 좀 자고 싶어요.	A I'm so full. I want to lie down and go to sleep.
B 밥을 먹자마자 누우면 건강에 안 좋아요.	B It's not good for your health if you lie down right after eating.

On Your Own

What did the following people do? Connect each picture on the left with a picture on the right with a line, and choose the appropriate word from below to fill in the blanks using –자마자.

끊다	나가다	시작하다	오다

(1)  • • ⓐ

(2)  • • ⓑ

(3)  • • ⓒ

(4)  • • ⓓ

(1) 집에 ____________________ 컴퓨터를 켜요.

(2) 엄마가 방에서 ____________________ 아기가 울어요.

(3) 영화가 ____________________ 자요.

(4) 전화를 ____________________ 나갔어요.

09 N 동안, V-는 동안

Track 095

어제 4시간 **동안** 공부했어요.

Yesterday, I studied for four hours.

곰은 겨울 **동안에** 겨울잠을 자요.

Bears hibernate during winter.

친구들이 점심을 **먹는 동안** 나는 숙제를 했어요.

I did my homework while my friends were eating lunch.

Grammar Focus

This pattern expresses the length of time starting when a certain action or behavior begins and lasting until it ends. It corresponds to 'during' or 'while' in English. After nouns, **동안** is added, and after verbs **-는 동안** is added.

가다 + **-는 동안** → 가는 동안　　먹다 + **-는 동안** → 먹는 동안

N 동안	Base Form	V-는 동안
10분 동안	자다	자는 동안
일주일 동안	읽다	읽는 동안
한 달 동안	듣다	듣는 동안
방학 동안	여행하다	여행하는 동안
휴가 동안	*살다	*사는 동안

* Irregular form

When used in the form 'V–**는 동안**', the subjects of the first and second clauses can be either the same or different.

- (내가) 한국에서 사는 동안 (나는) 좋은 친구들을 많이 만났어요.
  While I lived in Korea, I made a lot of good friends.
- 내가 친구들과 노는 동안 동생은 학교에서 열심히 공부했어요.
  While I played with my friends, my little brother/sister was studying hard at school.

In Conversation

Track **096**

A 얼마 동안 한국에 있을 거예요?
B 3년 동안 있을 거예요.

A How long will you be in Korea?
B I should be (in korea) for three years.

A 방학 동안에 뭐 할 거예요?
B 친척 집을 방문할 거예요.

A What will you do during the vacation?
B I plan to visit my relatives' home.

A 비행기가 2시간 후에 출발해요.
B 그러면 비행기를 기다리는 동안 면세점에서 쇼핑을 합시다.

A The plane will depart in two hours.
B In that case, let's do some shopping at the duty-free shop while we wait for our flight.

What's the Difference?

How are **–(으)면서** and **–는 동안** different?

–(으)면서 is used when one person performs two or more actions simultaneously. However, -는 동안(에) can be used even when the subjects of the first and second clauses are not the same; that is, it can be used to indicate that while the subject of the first clause is performing some action, the subject of the second clause is also performing an action.

–(으)면서	–는 동안에
The subjects of the first and second clauses must be the same. • 하영 씨는 음악을 들으면서 책을 읽었습니다. Hayeong listened to music while (she) read a book. 10:00~10:30	The subjects of the first and second clauses can be different. • 하영 씨가 음악을 듣는 동안에 재준 씨는 책을 읽었습니다. While Hayeong listened to music, Jaejun read a book. 10:00~10:30

On Your Own

Look at the pictures and fill in the blanks using either 동안 or –는 동안.

(1) 

여러분, ______________ 휴식 시간이에요.

(2) 

______________ 식당에서 아르바이트를 했어요.

(3) 

어머니가 ______________ 아버지가 청소를 해요.

(4) 

아이가 ______________ 산타클로스가 선물을 주고 가요.

10 V–(으)ㄴ 지

Track 097

저는 한국에 **온 지** 2년이 되었습니다.
It's been two years since I came to Korea.

담배 **끊은 지** 한 달 되었어요.
It's been one month since (I) stopped smoking.

컴퓨터게임을 **한 지** 5시간이 넘었어요.
It's been over five hours since (you) started playing computer games.

Grammar Focus

–(으)ㄴ 지 indicates how much time has passed since some situation or action occurred and thus corresponds to 'since' in English. It can be expressed in various ways, including **–(으)ㄴ 지 ~ 되다**, **–(으)ㄴ 지 ~ 넘다**, and **–(으)ㄴ 지 ~ 안 되다**. When the verb stem ends in a vowel or **ㄹ**, **–ㄴ 지** is used, and when it ends in a consonant, **–은 지** is used.

Stem Ending in Vowel or ㄹ	Stem Ending in Consonant
가다 + **–ㄴ 지** → 간 지	먹다 + **–은 지** → 먹은 지

Base Form	–ㄴ 지	Base Form	–은 지
오다	온 지	끊다	끊은 지
사귀다	사귄 지	*듣다	들은 지
공부하다	공부한 지	*걷다	걸은 지
*놀다	논 지	*짓다	지은 지
*만들다	만든 지	*돕다	도운 지

* Irregular form

In Conversation

Track 098

A 언제부터 한국어를 공부했어요?
B 한국어를 공부한 지 6개월이 되었어요.

A When did you start studying Korean?
B It's been six months since I began studying Korean.

A 남자 친구와 얼마나 사귀었어요?
B 사귄 지 3년이 넘었어요.

A How long have you been dating your boyfriend?
B We've been dating for over three years.

On Your Own

Look at the timeline and complete the sentences that follow using -(으)ㄴ 지.

(1) 리처드 씨는 대학교를 ______________ 10년 되었습니다.

(2) 리처드 씨는 ______________ 5년 넘었습니다.

(3) 리처드 씨는 한국에 ______________ 4년 되었습니다.

(4) 리처드 씨는 ______________ 4년 되었습니다.

(5) 리처드 씨는 ______________ 1년이 좀 안 되었습니다.

(6) 리처드 씨는 ______________ 4개월이 되었습니다.

(7) 리처드 씨는 ______________ 4년이 좀 넘었습니다.

unit 6.

Ability and Possibility

01 V-(으)ㄹ 수 있다/없다

Track 099

이 영화를 **볼 수 있어요.**

(We) can see this movie.

저 영화를 **볼 수 없어요.**

(We) can't see that movie.

운전면허증이 있어요. 운전**할 수 있어요.**

(I) I have a driver's license. I can drive.

운전면허증이 없어요. 운전**할 수 없어요.**

(I) I don't have a driver's license. I can't drive.

한자를 배웠어요. 한자를 **읽을 수 있어요.**

(I) learned Chinese characters. (I) can read Chinese characters

한자를 안 배웠어요. 한자를 **읽을 수 없어요.**

(I) did not learn Chinese characters. (I) can't read Chinese characters.

Grammar Focus

This pattern expresses ability or possibility. When someone or something is able to do something, or when something is possible, **-(으)ㄹ 수 있다** is used, and when someone or something is not able to do something, or when something is not possible, **-(으)ㄹ 수 없다** is used. In English it means 'can'. When a verb stem ends in a vowel or ㄹ, **-ㄹ 수 있다/없다** is used, and when a verb stem ends in a consonant, **-을 수 있다/없다** is used.

Stem Ending in Vowel or ㄹ	Stem Ending in Consonant
가다 + **-ㄹ 수 있다/없다** → 갈 수 있다/없다	먹다 + **-을 수 있다/없다** → 먹을 수 있다/없다

Base Form	-ㄹ 수 있어요/없어요	Base Form	-을 수 있어요/없어요
가다	갈 수 있어요/없어요	받다	받을 수 있어요/없어요
만나다	만날 수 있어요/없어요	*듣다	들을 수 있어요/없어요
수영하다	수영할 수 있어요/없어요	*걷다	걸을 수 있어요/없어요
*놀다	놀 수 있어요/없어요	*짓다	지을 수 있어요/없어요
*살다	살 수 있어요/없어요	*돕다	도울 수 있어요/없어요

* Irregular form

In Conversation

Track 100

A 무슨 운동을 할 수 있어요?
B 축구를 할 수 있어요. 그리고 태권도도 할 수 있어요. 그렇지만 수영은 할 수 없어요.

A What sports can you play?
B I can play soccer. And I also know (how to do) taekwondo. But I can't swim.

A 요코 씨, 오늘 저녁에 만날 수 있어요?
B 미안해요. 만날 수 없어요. 약속이 있어요.

A Yoko, can you meet me this evening?
B I'm sorry. I can't meet you. I have other plans.

A 한국 드라마를 이해할 수 있어요?
B 네, 드라마는 조금 이해할 수 있어요. 그렇지만 뉴스는 이해할 수 없어요.

A Can you understand Korean TV dramas?
B Yes, I can understand TV dramas somewhat. But I can't understand the news.

Check It Out!

Adding the particle 가 to -(으)ㄹ 수 있다/없다 to form -(으)ㄹ 수가 있다/없다 makes the phrase more emphatic in meaning than -(으)ㄹ 수 있다/없다 alone.

- 떡볶이가 매워서 먹을 수 없어요. The ddeokbokki is spicy, so I can't eat it.
- 떡볶이가 매워서 먹을 수가 없어요. The ddeokbokki is so spicy that I (really) can't eat it.
- 길이 막혀서 갈 수 없어요. There's a lot of traffic, so I won't be able to make it.
- 길이 막혀서 갈 수가 없어요. There's so much traffic that I (really) can't make it (no matter what).

Look at the pictures and choose the appropriate word from below to fill in the blanks using –(으)ㄹ 수 있다/없다.

걷다 고치다 부르다 열다 추다

(1)

A 컴퓨터가 고장 났어요.
B 내가 ____________________.

(2)

A 한국 노래를 ____________________?
B 네, '아리랑'을 ____________________.
한국 춤도 ____________________.

(3)

A 왜 그래요?
B 발이 아파요. ____________________.

(4)

A 이 병을 ____________________.
B 걱정하지 마세요. 내가 ____________________.

02 V-(으)ㄹ 줄 알다/모르다

Track 101

딸기잼을 **만들 줄 알아요**.

I know how to make strawberry jam.

휴대 전화로 사진을 **보낼 줄 몰라요**.

I don't know how to send pictures by mobile phone.

된장찌개를 맛있게 **끓일 줄 알아요**.

I know how to cook a tasty doenjang stew.

Grammar Focus

This pattern expresses whether one knows how, or has the ability, to do something. When the verb stem ends in a vowel or ㄹ, **-ㄹ 줄 알다/모르다** is used, and when the verb stem ends in a consonant, **-을 줄 알다/모르다** is used. It corresponds to 'know how to/doesn't know how to' in English.

Stem Ending in Vowel or ㄹ	Stem Ending in Consonant
보내다 + **-ㄹ 줄 알다/모르다** → 보낼 줄 알다/모르다	입다 + **-을 줄 알다/모르다** → 입을 줄 알다/모르다

Base Form	-ㄹ 줄 알아요/몰라요	Base Form	-을 줄 알아요/몰라요
쓰다	쓸 줄 알아요/몰라요	읽다	읽을 줄 알아요/몰라요
고치다	고칠 줄 알아요/몰라요	접다	접을 줄 알아요/몰라요
사용하다	사용할 줄 알아요/몰라요	*굽다	구울 줄 알아요/몰라요
*만들다	만들 줄 알아요/몰라요	*짓다	지을 줄 알아요/몰라요

* Irregular form

In Conversation

Track 102

A 캐럴 씨, 컴퓨터게임 '스타크래프트'를 할 줄 알아요?
B 아니요, 할 줄 몰라요. 어떻게 해요?

A Carol, do you know how to play the computer game Starcraft?
B No, I don't. How do you play it?

A 무슨 음식을 만들 줄 알아요?
B 저는 잡채하고 스파게티를 만들 줄 알아요.

A What kinds of foods do you know how to make?
B I know how to make Korean japchae and spaghetti.

What's the Difference?

–(으)ㄹ 줄 알다/모르다	–(으)ㄹ 수 있다/없다
Expresses whether one knows how or has the ability to do something. • 나는 딸기잼을 만들 줄 몰라요. I don't know how to make strawberry jam. Cannot be used to express possibility. • 오늘 저녁에 만날 줄 알아요? (×) → 오늘 저녁에 만날 수 있어요? (○) Can we meet tonight?	Used not only to express the ability to do something, but also whether a situation permits something to be done. • 나는 딸기잼을 만들 수 없어요. (1) I don't know how to make strawberry jam. (2) I know how to make strawberry jam, but for some reason (such as a lack of strawberries), I can't make it right now.

On Your Own

Look at the pictures and choose the appropriate word from below to fill in the blanks using –(으)ㄹ 줄 알다/모르다.

두다 사용하다 타다

(1)
A 자전거를 탈 줄 알아요?
B 네, 외발자전거도 ________________.

(2)
A 바둑 ________________?
B 체스는 ________________.
그렇지만 바둑은 ________________.

(3)
A 이거 어떻게 사용해요?
B 글쎄요. 저도 ________________.

Unit 7.

Demands and Obligations, Permission and Prohibition

01 V-(으)세요

Track 103

여기 **앉으세요.**

Please sit here.

책 15쪽을 **보세요.**

Please see (look at) page 15 in the book.

이 길로 쭉 **가세요.**

Please go straight up this road.

Grammar Focus

-(으)세요 is used when politely asking the listener to do something or when making a request and when giving directions or orders. It corresponds to 'please (do)' in English. In such situations, **-아/어요** can also be used, but **-(으)세요** is more polite than **-아/어요**. When the verb stem ends in a vowel, **-세요** is added, and when it ends in a consonant, **-으세요** is added. Some verbs have special forms though. The formal polite style uses **-(으)십시오**.

Stem Ending in Vowel	Stem Ending in Consonant
가다 + **-세요** → 가세요	앉다 + **-으세요** → 앉으세요

Base Form	-세요	Base Form	-(으)세요	Base Form	Special Form
사다	사세요	입다	입으세요	먹다/마시다	드세요
오다	오세요	찾다	찾으세요	자다	주무세요
주다	주세요	받다	받으세요	말하다	말씀하세요
운동하다	운동하세요	벗다	벗으세요	있다	계세요

*만들다	만드세요	*듣다	들으세요	◈ 주다	주세요
*살다	사세요	*걷다	걸으세요		드리세요

＊ Irregular form

◈ (See also Introduction to the Korean Language 5. Honorific Expressions)

When **–(으)세요** is used in the imperative sense to give an order, it can only be used with verbs and not **이다** or adjectives.

- 의사이세요 (×) → 의사가 되세요. (○) Please become a doctor.
- 기쁘세요 (×) → 기뻐하세요. (○) Be happy.
  (※Adjective changed to its verb form)

(See also Unit 18. Changes in Parts of Speech 04 A–아/어하다)

However, there are a number of adjectives ending in **하다** used idiomatically that can be used with **–으세요**.

- 할아버지, 건강하세요. 오래오래 사세요.
  Grandpa, please be healthy. Live a long, long time.
- 민우 씨, 결혼 축하해요. 행복하세요.
  Minu, congratulations on your marriage. I wish you happiness.

In Conversation

Track 104

A 살을 빼고 싶어요.
B 그럼 야채를 많이 드세요.
그리고 운동을 많이 하세요.

A I want to lose some weight.
B Then you should eat a lot of vegetables.
And get lots of exercise.

A 여기에 이름과 전화번호를 쓰세요.
B 알겠습니다.

A Please write down your name and phone number here.
B Okay.

A 여러분, 조용히 하세요!
자, 사장님, 말씀하세요.
B 고마워요, 김 부장.

A Everyone, please be quiet!
Now, Director, please begin (speaking).
B Thank you, Manager Kim.

On Your Own

How should you respond? Look at the pictures and find the most appropriate response from the choices given.

(1)  • • ⓐ 학교에 일찍 오세요.

(2) 

• • ⓑ 들어오세요.

(3)  • • ⓒ 한국어로 말하세요.

(4)  • • ⓓ 많이 드세요.

02 V-지 마세요

술을 **마시지 마세요.**

Please don't drink alcohol.

전화하지 마세요.

Please don't use the phone.

수업 시간에 **자지 마세요.**

Please don't sleep during class.

Grammar Focus

-지 마세요 is used when requesting, persuading, indicating, or ordering the listener not to do something. This is the negative form of **-(으)세요**, and it corresponds to 'please do not (do)' in English. It is used by adding **-지 마세요** to verb stems. The formal polite form is **-지 마십시오**.

가다 + **-지 마세요** → 가지 마세요　　먹다 + **-지 마세요** → 먹지 마세요

Base Form	-지 마세요	Base Form	-지 마세요
사다	사지 마세요	운동하다	운동하지 마세요
오다	오지 마세요	듣다	듣지 마세요
읽다	읽지 마세요	만들다	만들지 마세요

-지 마세요 can only be used with verbs and not **이다** or adjectives.

- 변호사이지 마세요. (×)
- 슬프지 마세요. (×) → 슬퍼하지 마세요. (○)　Please don't feel sad.
- 기분 나쁘지 마세요. (×) → 기분 나빠하지 마세요. (○)　Please don't feel hurt.
  (※Adjective changed to its verb form)

(See also Unit 18. Changes in Parts of Speech 04 A-아/어하다)

In Conversation

Track 106

A 버스를 탈까요?
B 길이 막히니까 버스를 타지 마세요. 지하철을 타세요.

A Shall I take the bus?
B There's a lot of traffic, so don't take the bus. (Please) take the subway.

A 이 영화 어때요? 재미있어요?
B 이 영화를 보지 마세요. 재미없어요.

A How's this movie? Is it interesting?
B (Please) don't see this movie. It's boring.

A 음악을 너무 크게 듣지 마세요. 귀에 안 좋아요.
B 네, 알겠어요.

A (Please) don't listen to music too loudly. It's bad for your ears.
B Okay.

On Your Own

The following friends each have a problem. Look at the pictures and fill in the blanks using –지 마세요.

(1)

A 너무 뚱뚱해요. 살을 빼고 싶어요.
B 그러면 ______________________. (햄버거를 먹다)

(2)

A 요즘 목이 너무 아파요.
B 그러면 ______________________. (담배를 피우다)

(3)

A 요즘 밤에 잠을 못 자요.
B 그럼 ______________________. (커피를 마시다)

(4)

A 요즘 눈이 많이 아파요.
B 그럼 ______________________. (컴퓨터게임을 하다)

03 A/V-아/어야 되다/하다

Track 107

내일 시험이 있어요. 그래서 **공부해야 돼요.**

I have an exam tomorrow. So I must study.

여자 친구 생일이라서 선물을 **사야 돼요.**

It's my girlfriend's birthday, so I have to buy her a present.

먹기 전에 돈을 **내야 해요.**

You have to pay before you eat.

Grammar Focus

-아/어야 되다 or **-아/어야 하다** expresses an obligation or necessity to do something or the necessity of a certain condition. It corresponds to 'must' or 'have (to)' in English. There is no difference in meaning between **-아/어야 되다** and **-아/어야 하다**. If the stem ends in the vowel ㅏ or ㅗ, then **-아야 되다/하다** is used, and for all other vowel endings, **-어야 되다/하다** is used. As for verbs ending in **하다**, the form changes to **해야 되다/하다**. The past tense form is **-아/어야 됐어요/했어요**.

Stem Ending in Vowel ㅏ or ㅗ	Stem Ending in Vowel Other than ㅏ or ㅗ	Verb Ending in 하다
앉다 + **-아야 되다/하다** → 앉아야 되다/하다	기다리다 + **-어야 되다/하다** → 기다려야 되다/하다	공부하다 → 공부해야 되다/하다

Base Form	-아/어야 돼요/해요	Base Form	-아/어야 돼요/해요
가다	가야 돼요/해요	청소하다	청소해야 돼요/해요
보다	봐야 돼요/해요	*쓰다	써야 돼요/해요
읽다	읽어야 돼요/해요	*자르다	잘라야 돼요/해요
배우다	배워야 돼요/해요	*듣다	들어야 돼요/해요

* Irregular form

In Conversation

Track 108

A 주말에 같이 영화 볼까요?
B 미안해요. 어머니 생신이라서 고향에 가야 돼요.

A Shall we see a movie this weekend?
B Sorry, but it's my mother's birthday, and I have to visit home.

A 여름에 제주도에 가려고 해요.
B 비행기 표를 예약했어요? 사람이 많아서 미리 예약해야 돼요.

A I'm planning to go to Jeju Island in the summer.
B Did you reserve a plane ticket? A lot of people will be going there, so you have to reserve your ticket in advance.

A 어제 왜 파티에 안 오셨어요?
B 일이 많아서 회사에서 일해야 됐어요.

A Why didn't you come to the party yesterday?
B I had a lot of things to do, so I had to stay at the office and work.

Check It Out!

–아/어야 되다/하다 has two negative forms, one meaning it is not necessary to do something, –지 않아도 되다, and the other expressing the prohibition of some behavior, –(으)면 안 되다.

❶ –지 않아도 되다 (don't need to, don't have to)
(See also Unit 7. Demands and Obligations, Permission and Prohibition 06 A/V–지 않아도 되다)

A 내일 회사에 가요? Do you go to the office tomorrow?
B 아니요, 내일은 휴가라서 회사에 가지 않아도 돼요. No, tomorrow is a holiday, so I don't have to go to work.

A 공원까지 버스로 가요? (Do you) take the bus to the park?
B 가까워요. 그래서 버스를 타지 않아도 돼요. 걸어가도 돼요.
(The park) is nearby. So I don't need to take the bus. I can walk.

❷ –(으)면 안 되다 (shouldn't, be not allowed to)
(See also Unit 7. Demands and Obligations, Permission and Prohibition 05 A/V–(으)면 안 되다)

- 박물관에서는 사진을 찍으면 안 돼요. You're not allowed to take photographs inside the museum.
- 실내에서 담배를 피우면 안 돼요. You should not smoke indoors.

On Your Own

Look at the pictures and fill in the blanks using -아/어야 되다/하다.

(1) 

A 오늘 시간 있으면 같이 테니스 칠까요?

B 미안해요. 부모님이 한국에 오셔서 ________________.
(공항에 가다)

(2) 

A 파리에서 일하고 싶어요.

B 그러면 ________________.
(프랑스어를 잘하다)

(3) 

A 같이 술 한잔할까요?

B 미안해요. 오늘 ________________.
(운전하다)
그래서 같이 술을 못 마셔요.

(4) 

A 약속이 있어서 시내에 1시까지 가야 해요.

B 그럼 ________________.
(12시에 출발하다)

(5) 

A 어제 왜 헬스클럽에 안 왔어요?

B 몸이 많이 아파서 ________________.
(병원에 가다)

04 A/V-아/어도 되다

Track 109

사진을 **찍어도 돼요**?
May I take a picture?

여기 **앉아도 돼요**?
May I sit here?

펜을 **써도 돼요**?
May I use that pen?

Grammar Focus

-아/어도 되다 expresses permission or approval for a behavior. It corresponds to 'may' or 'be allowed to' in English. If the stem ends in the vowel ㅏ or ㅗ, then **-아도 되다** is used, and for all other vowel endings, **-어도 되다** is used. As for verbs ending in **하다**, the form changes to **해도 되다**. In place of **-아/어도 되다**, **-아/어도 괜찮다** and **-아/어도 좋다** can also be used.

Stem Ending in Vowel ㅏ or ㅗ	Stem Ending in Vowel Other than ㅏ or ㅗ	Verb Ending in 하다
사다 + **-아도 되다** → 사도 되다	마시다 + **-어도 되다** → 마셔도 되다	구경하다 → 구경해도 되다

Base Form	-아/어도 돼요	Base Form	-아/어도 돼요
가다	가도 돼요	*듣다	들어도 돼요
보다	봐도 돼요	*쓰다	써도 돼요
읽다	읽어도 돼요	*자르다	잘라도 돼요
요리하다	요리해도 돼요	*눕다	누워도 돼요

* Irregular form

In Conversation

Track 110

A 밤에 전화해도 돼요?
B 물론이에요. 전화하세요.

A May I call you at night?
B Sure. Please call anytime.

A 창문을 열어도 돼요?
B 그럼요, 열어도 돼요.

A Do you mind if I open the window?
B Not at all. You may open it.

A 라디오를 켜도 돼요?
B 아이가 자고 있어요. 켜지 마세요.

A May I turn on the radio?
B The baby is asleep. Please don't turn it on.

Look at the pictures and choose the appropriate word from below to fill in the blanks using -아/어도 되다.

들어가다	술을 마시다	쓰다	켜다

(1)

A 선생님, ______________________?
B 아니요, 술을 마시지 마세요.

(2)

A 에어컨을 ______________________?
B 네, 켜세요.

(3)

A 지금 ______________________?
B 공연이 시작했어요. 쉬는 시간에 들어가세요.

(4)

A 전화를 ______________________?
B 네, 쓰십시오.

05 A/V-(으)면 안 되다

Track 111

실내에서 담배를 **피우면 안 돼요**.
Smoking indoors is not allowed.

운전 중에 **전화하면 안 돼요**.
Using the phone while driving is not allowed.

지금 길을 **건너면 안 돼요**.
You may not cross the street now.

Grammar Focus

-(으)면 안 되다 expresses the prohibition or limitation of a particular action of the listener. It also can represent social conventions or common sense dictating that a behavior or state is prohibited or not tolerated. It corresponds to 'may not' or 'not allowed to' in English. When the stem ends in a vowel or ㄹ, **-면 안 되다** is used, and when the stem ends in a consonant, **-으면 안 되다** is used.

Stem Ending in Vowel or ㄹ	Stem Ending in Consonant
가다 + **-면 안 돼요** → 가면 안 돼요	먹다 + **-으면 안 돼요** → 먹으면 안 돼요

Base Form	-면 안 돼요	Base Form	-으면 안 돼요
자다	자면 안 돼요	앉다	앉으면 안 돼요
보다	보면 안 돼요	받다	받으면 안 돼요
운동하다	운동하면 안 돼요	*듣다	들으면 안 돼요
*놀다	놀면 안 돼요	*붓다	부으면 안 돼요

* Irregular form

In Conversation

Track 112

A 수업 시간에 영어로 말해도 돼요?

B 수업 시간에는 영어로 말하면 안 돼요. 한국말을 하세요.

A 한국에서는 밥을 먹을 때 코를 풀면 안 돼요.

B 아, 그래요? 몰랐어요.

A 도서관에서 얘기하면 안 돼요.

B 아, 죄송합니다.

A May I speak in English during class?

B During class, you may not speak in English. Please speak in Korean.

A In Korea, you're not supposed to blow your nose when eating.

B Oh, really? I didn't know that.

A You're not allowed to talk in the library.

B Okay, I'm sorry.

Check It Out!

–(으)면 안 되다 can be used in the double negative form, that is, –지 않으면 안 되다, to emphasize that a particular behavior must be performed.

- 8월은 휴가철이니까 비행기 표를 미리 사지 않으면 안 돼요. (= 표를 미리 사야 돼요.)
  August is vacation season, so (you) must buy plane tickets in advance. (Plane tickets have to be bought in advance.)
- 병이 심각해서 수술하지 않으면 안 돼요. (= 수술해야 돼요.)
  Because the illness is serious, surgery must be performed. (We have to perform surgery.)
- 다음 주에 중요한 시험이 있어서 공부하지 않으면 안 돼요. (= 공부해야 돼요)
  Because (I) have an important test next week, I must study. (I have to study.)

On Your Own

Look at the pictures and choose the appropriate word from below to fill in each blank using –(으)면 안 되다.

들어오다	마시다	버리다	키우다

(1) 

A 기숙사에서 개를 키워도 돼요?

B 아니요, 개를 ____________________.

(2) 

A 선생님, 커피를 마셔도 돼요?

B 커피를 ____________________

(3) 

A 여기에 쓰레기를 ____________________.

B 죄송합니다.

(4) 

A 들어가도 돼요?

B ____________________. 옷을 갈아입고 있어요.

06 A/V-지 않아도 되다 (안 A/V-아/어도 되다)

Track 113

유치원생은 버스 요금을 **내지 않아도 돼요**.

Preschool students don't have to pay the bus fare.

평일이니까 영화 표를 미리 **사지 않아도 돼요**.

Because it's a weekday, we don't have to buy tickets in advance.

금요일에는 정장을 **입지 않아도 돼요**.

On Fridays, we don't have to wear suits.

Grammar Focus

-지 않아도 되다 expresses that a particular state of affairs or behavior is not necessary. It is the negative form of **-아/어야 되다/하다**, which expresses the obligation to perform a particular behavior. It corresponds to 'does not have to' in English. It is made by adding **-지 않아도 되다** or **안 -아/어도 되다** to the verb stem.

(See also '-아/어도' conjugation in Unit 16. Conditions and Suppositions 03 A/V-아/어도)

가다 + **-지 않아도 되다**
→ 가지 않아도 되다 (= 안 가도 되다)

먹다 + **-지 않아도 되다**
→ 먹지 않아도 되다 (= 안 먹어도 되다)

Base Form	-지 않아도 돼요	안 -아/어도 돼요
사다	사지 않아도 돼요	안 사도 돼요
보다	보지 않아도 돼요	안 봐도 돼요
기다리다	기다리지 않아도 돼요	안 기다려도 돼요
전화하다	전화하지 않아도 돼요	전화 안 해도 돼요

*듣다	듣지 않아도 돼요	안 들어도 돼요
*쓰다	쓰지 않아도 돼요	안 써도 돼요
*자르다	자르지 않아도 돼요	안 잘라도 돼요

* Irregular form

In Conversation

Track 114

A 오늘 회식에 꼭 가야 돼요?
B 바쁘면 안 가도 돼요.

A Must I go to the dinner today?
B If you're busy, you don't have to go.

A 저는 다이어트해야 돼요!
B 지금도 날씬해요.
다이어트하지 않아도 돼요.

A I've got to go on a diet!
B You're already slender.
You don't need to diet.

On Your Own

Look at the pictures and fill in the blanks using either -지 않아도 되다 or 안 -아/어도 되다.

(1) 

A 많이 기다려야 해요?
B 사람이 없으니까 많이 ______________________.

(2) 

A 주사를 맞아야 돼요?
B 아니요, 심하지 않아서 주사를 ______________________.

(3) 

A 책을 사야 돼요?
B 도서관에 있으니까 ______________________.

(4) 

A 내일도 일찍 일어나요?
B 내일은 수업이 오후에 있으니까 ______________________.

Unit 8.

Expressions of Hope

01 V-고 싶다

02 A/V-았/었으면 좋겠다

01 V-고 싶다

Track 115

한국말을 잘 못해요. 한국말을 **잘하고 싶어요**.

I can't speak Korean well. I want to speak Korean well.

가족을 2년 동안 못 만났어요. 가족이 **보고 싶어요**.

I haven't seen my family for two years. I want to see my family.

딸기를 **먹고 싶어요**.

I want to eat strawberries.

Grammar Focus

-고 싶다 expresses the wish or hope of the speaker and corresponds to 'want to' in English. **-고 싶다** is added to verb stems. If the subject is in the first or second person, then **-고 싶다** is used, but when the subject is in the third person, then **-고 싶어하다** is used.

(See also Check It Out!)

사다 + **-고 싶다** → 사고 싶다　　　읽다 + **-고 싶다** → 읽고 싶다

Base Form	-고 싶어요	Base Form	-고 싶다
가다	가고 싶어요	받다	받고 싶어요
보다	보고 싶어요	먹다	먹고 싶어요
만나다	만나고 싶어요	결혼하다	결혼하고 싶어요
만들다	만들고 싶어요	듣다	듣고 싶어요
울다	울고 싶어요	눕다	눕고 싶어요

In Conversation

Track 116

A 뭐 마시고 싶어요?
B 졸려요. 커피를 마시고 싶어요.

A What do you want to drink?
B I'm sleepy. I want to drink some coffee.

A 크리스마스에 무슨 선물을 받고 싶어요?
B 예쁜 장갑을 받고 싶어요.

A What do you want for Christmas?
B I'd like some nice looking gloves.

Check It Out!

❶ When the subject is in the third person, -고 싶어 하다 is used.
(See also Unit 18. Changes in Parts of Speech 04 A-아/어하다)

- 에릭 씨는 자동차를 사고 싶어요. (×) → 에릭 씨는 자동차를 사고 싶어 해요. (○) Eric wants to buy a car.

❷ Although -고 싶다 cannot be added directly to adjectives, if -아/어지다 is first added to an adjective, making it a verb, then -고 싶다 can be used.
(See also Unit 19. Expressions of State 03 A-아/어지다)

- 날씬하고 싶어요. (×) → 날씬해지고 싶어요. (○) I want to become slim.

❸ -고 싶다 can be combined with the particles 을/를 and 이/가.

- 가족이 보고 싶어요. (○) I want to see my family.
- 가족을 보고 싶어요. (○) I want to see my family.

On Your Own

The following exercise concerns people who have come to Korea. Look at the picture and fill in the blanks with the appropriate sentences using -고 싶다.

(1) ______________________________.
(제주도, 말을 타다)

(2) ______________________________.
(가수, 사인을 받다)

(3) ______________________________.
(휴대 전화, 사다)

(4) ______________________________.
(좋아하는 가수, 만나다)

(5) ______________________________.
(쇼핑, 하다)

02 A/V-았/었으면 좋겠다

차가 **있었으면 좋겠어요.**

I wish I had a car.

돈이 **많았으면 좋겠어요.**

I wish I had a lot of money.

크리스마스에 눈이 **왔으면 좋겠어요.**

I hope it snows on Christmas.

Grammar Focus

-았/었으면 좋겠다 expresses a person's wish or hope about something that has yet to be realized. It can also be used when expressing a desire for a situation to become the opposite of what it currently is. This expression corresponds to 'hope/want' in English. When the verb stem ends in ㅏ or ㅗ, then **-았으면 좋겠다** is used, while **-었으면 좋겠다** is used for all other verb stem endings. As for verbs ending in **하다**, the form changes to **-했으면 좋겠다**.

In addition to **-았/었으면 좋겠다**, **-았/었으면 하다** can also be used, but **-았/었으면 좋겠다** indicates a stronger degree of hope or desire.

Stem Ending in ㅏ or ㅗ	Stem Ending in Vowel Other than ㅏ or ㅗ	Verb Ending in 하다
가다 + **-았으면 좋겠다** → 갔으면 좋겠다	먹다 + **-었으면 좋겠다** → 먹었으면 좋겠다	여행하다 → 여행했으면 좋겠다

Base Form	-았/었으면 좋겠어요	Base Form	-았/었으면 좋겠어요
오다	왔으면 좋겠어요	밝다	밝았으면 좋겠어요
사다	샀으면 좋겠어요	길다	길었으면 좋겠어요
있다	있었으면 좋겠어요	따뜻하다	따뜻했으면 좋겠어요
학생이다	학생이었으면 좋겠어요	친절하다	친절했으면 좋겠어요
부자이다	부자였으면 좋겠어요	*부르다	불렀으면 좋겠어요
작다	작았으면 좋겠어요	*듣다	들었으면 좋겠어요

* Irregular form

In Conversation

Track 118

A 언제 결혼하고 싶어요?
B 따뜻한 봄에 결혼했으면 좋겠어요.

A When do you want to get married?
B It would be nice to get married in the warm spring.

A 요즘도 바빠요?
B 네, 계속 바빠요.
좀 쉬었으면 좋겠어요.

A Are you still busy these days?
B Yes, I'm still busy.
I wish I could have some time off.

A 이번 방학에 뭐 할 거예요?
B 친구들하고 스키장에 갈 거예요.
방학이 빨리 왔으면 좋겠어요.

A What will you do this vacation?
B I plan to go skiing with my friends.
I wish vacation would come sooner.

Check It Out!

-(으)면 좋겠다 can be used in the same sense as -았/었으면 좋겠다, but because -았/었으면 좋겠다 supposes the realization of an as yet unrealized state, it more strongly emphasizes the verb.

- 돈이 많으면 좋겠어요. (The speaker is simply wishing to have a lot of money.)
- 돈이 많았으면 좋겠어요. (The speaker is supposing a situation in which he has a lot of money, which is in contrast to his current situation of having no money; thus the wish is emphasized.)

On Your Own

1 Look at the pictures and fill in the blanks using -았/었으면 좋겠다.

(1) 

A 올해 소원이 뭐예요?

B ____________________. (애인이 생기다)

(2) 

A 죽기 전에 무엇을 하고 싶어요?

B ____________________. (세계 여행을 하다)

(3) 

A 내년에 무엇을 하고 싶어요?

B ____________________. (아파트로 이사하다)

2 Look at the pictures and fill in the blanks as shown in the example.

보기 노래를 못해요. 노래를 잘했으면 좋겠어요.

(1) 

키가 작아요. ____________________.

(2) 

회사 일이 너무 힘들어요. ____________________.
(주말이다)

(3) 

운동을 못해요. ____________________.

Unit 9.

Reasons and Causes

01 A/V-아/어서 ②

02 A/V-(으)니까 ①

03 N 때문에, A/V-기 때문에

01 A/V-아/어서 ②

Track 119

만나서 반갑습니다.
Nice to meet you.

기분이 좋아서 춤을 췄어요.
I was in such a good mood that I danced.

늦어서 죄송합니다.
I'm sorry for arriving late.

Grammar Focus

-아/어서 is used to express that the information in the first clause is the reason for or the cause of the succeeding clause. It corresponds to 'because (of)', 'on account of', and 'so... that...' in English. If the stem ends in the vowel ㅏ or ㅗ, then **-아서** is used. Otherwise, **-어서** is used. As for verbs ending in **하다**, the form changes to **해서**, and in the case of **이다**, **이어서** is used, except in conversation, when **이라서** is used.

Stem Ending in Vowel ㅏ or ㅗ	Stem Ending in Vowel Other than ㅏ or ㅗ	Words Ending in 하다
오다 + **-아서** → 와서	읽다 + **-어서** → 읽어서	날씬하다 → 날씬해서

Base Form	-아/어서	Base Form	-아/어서
가다	가서	좁다	좁아서
살다	살아서	길다	길어서
있다	있어서	피곤하다	피곤해서

이다	이어서(이라서)	*바쁘다	바빠서
운동하다	운동해서	*춥다	추워서
청소하다	청소해서	*듣다	들어서

* Irregular form

–아/어서 cannot be used in imperative or propositive sentences.

- 이 신발은 커서 다른 신발을 보여 주세요. (×)
  → 이 신발은 크니까 다른 신발을 보여 주세요. (○)
  These shoes are big, so please show me a different pair.
- 오늘 약속이 있어서 내일 만날까요? (×)
  → 오늘 약속이 있으니까 내일 만날까요? (○)
  I have to meet someone else today, so shall we meet tomorrow?
- 이게 좋아서 이걸로 삽시다. (×)
  → 이게 좋으니까 이걸로 삽시다. (○)
  I like this one, so let's buy it.

(See also Unit 9. Reasons and Causes 02 A/V–(으)니까 ①)

Tense markers such as **–았/었–** and **–겠–** cannot come before **–아/어서**.

- 밥을 많이 먹었어서 배가 아파요. (×)
  → 밥을 많이 먹어서 배가 아파요. (○)
  My stomach hurts on account of eating so much food.
- 이 옷이 예쁘겠어서 입고 싶어요. (×)
  → 이 옷이 예뻐서 입고 싶어요. (○)
  I want to wear these clothes because they're pretty.

(Compare with Unit 5. Time Expressions 04 V–아/어서)

In Conversation

Track 120

A 토요일에 시간이 있어요?
B 이번 주는 바빠서 시간이 없어요.

A Do you have time on Saturday?
B This week I'm busy and don't have time.

A 이 옷을 왜 안 입어요?
B 그 옷은 작아서 못 입어요.

A Why don't you wear these clothes?
B Those clothes are so small that I can't wear them.

A 집에 갈 때 버스를 타요?
B 아니요, 퇴근 시간에는 차가 많아서 지하철을 타요.

A Do you take the bus when you go home?
B No, there's a lot of traffic when I get off work, so I take the subway.

Look at the pictures and choose the appropriate word from below to fill in each blank using -아/어서.

많다	마시다	맛있다	오다

(1) 

A 왜 이 식당에 사람이 많아요?
B 음식이 ______________ 사람이 많아요.

(2) 

A 내일 영화를 볼까요?
B 숙제가 ______________ 영화를 못 봐요.

(3) 

A 어디에 가요?
B 친구가 한국에 ______________ 공항에 가요.

(4) 

A 왜 약을 먹어요?
B 어제 술을 많이 ______________ 머리가 아파요.

02 A/V-(으)니까 ①

길이 **막히니까** 지하철을 탑시다.

The roads are full of traffic, so let's take the subway.

추우니까 창문 좀 닫아 주세요.

It's cold, so please close the window.

샤워를 **하니까** 기분이 좋아요.

I took a shower, so now I feel good.

Grammar Focus

–(으)니까 expresses the reason or cause for something and corresponds to 'so' or 'because' in English. When the verb stem ends in a vowel or ㄹ, –니까 is used, and when the verb stem ends in a consonant, –으니까 is used.

Stem Ending in Vowel or ㄹ	Stem Ending in Consonant
사다 + **–니까** → 사니까	먹다 + **–으니까** → 먹으니까

Base Form	–니까	Base Form	–으니까
보다	보니까	있다	있으니까
오다	오니까	읽다	읽으니까
이다	이니까	넓다	넓으니까
아프다	아프니까	*듣다	들으니까
크다	크니까	*덥다	더우니까
피곤하다	피곤하니까	*살다	사니까

* Irregular form

In Conversation

Track 122

A 부장님, 이번 주에 회의가 있습니까?
B 이번 주는 바쁘니까 다음 주에 합시다.

A Chief, is there a meeting this week?
B This week I'm busy, so let's have it next week.

A 여자 친구에게 무슨 선물을 할까요?
B 수연 씨가 꽃을 좋아하니까 꽃을 선물하세요.

A What present should I give my girlfriend?
B Sooyeon likes flowers, so give her some flowers.

What's the Difference?

–아/어서

❶ Cannot be used in imperative or propositive sentences.

- 시간이 없어서 빨리 가세요. (×)
- 다리가 아파서 택시를 탈까요? (×)

❷ Tense markers such as –았/었– and –겠– cannot be used.

- 한국에서 살았어서 한국어를 잘해요. (×)

❸ Used mainly to express a general reason.

A 왜 늦었어요? Why were you late?
B 차가 막혀서 늦었어요.
There was a lot of traffic, so I was late.

❹ Can be used with common words of greeting, such as 반갑다, 고맙다, 감사하다, and 미안하다.

- 만나서 반갑습니다. (○) Nice to meet you.

–(으)니까

❶ Can be used with imperative or propositive sentences, i.e., –(으)세요, –(으)ㄹ까요?, and –(으)ㅂ시다.

- 시간이 없으니까 빨리 가세요. (○)
  There's no time, so go quickly.
- 다리가 아프니까 택시를 탈까요? (○)
  My legs are sore, so shall we take a taxi?

❷ Tense markers such as –았/었– and –겠– can be used.

- 한국에서 살았으니까 한국어를 잘해요. (○)
  I can speak Korean well because I lived in Korea.

❸ Used when stating a subjective reason or providing a basis for a particular reason. Further, it is used mainly when the other party also knows about the topic under discussion.

A 왜 늦었어요? Why were you late?
B 차가 막히니까 늦었어요.
I was late because (as you know) there was a lot of traffic.

❹ Cannot be used with common words of greeting, such as 반갑다, 고맙다, 감사하다, and 미안하다.

- 만나니까 반갑습니다. (×)

On Your Own

1 Choose the appropriate word from below to fill in each blank using -(으)니까.

가다	고장 났다	깨끗하다	모르다	일이 많다

(1) A 몇 번 버스가 시청 앞에 가요?
B 저는 잘 __________ 운룡 씨한테 물어보세요.

(2) A 지금 컴퓨터 좀 사용할 수 있어요?
B 이 컴퓨터는 ________________ 옆 컴퓨터를 쓰세요.

(3) A 오늘 피곤해요?
B 네, ________________ 너무 피곤해요.

(4) A 어느 식당으로 갈까요?
B 학교 앞 식당이 맛있고 ________________ 거기로 갈까요?

(5) A 우리 이번 주 토요일에 같이 영화 봐요.
B 이번 주 토요일은 회사에 ________________ 일요일에 봅시다.

2 Circle the correct answers.

(1) 돈이 (없어서 / 없으니까) 쇼핑하지 맙시다.

(2) (더워서 / 더우니까) 에어컨을 켤까요?

(3) 열이 많이 (나서 / 나니까) 병원에 가세요.

(4) (도와주셔서 / 도와주시니까) 감사합니다.

(5) 1시간 전에 (떠났어서 / 떠났으니까) 곧 도착할 거예요.

03 N 때문에, A/V-기 때문에

Track 123

눈 **때문에** 길이 미끄러워요.

The road is slippery because of the snow.

아이 **때문에** 피곤해요.

I'm tired because of the children.

외국인**이기 때문에** 한국말을 잘 못해요.

I can't speak Korean well because I'm a foreigner.

Grammar Focus

때문에 and **-기 때문에** express the reason for or cause of the situation described in the second clause and correspond to 'because' in English. **-기 때문에** is used when expressing a clear reason and is a more literary expression than **-아/어서** and **-(으)니까**. After nouns, **때문에** is added, and after verbs and adjectives, **-기 때문에** is added to the stem.

Noun + 때문에	Verb/Adjective + -기 때문에
아기 + **때문에** → 아기 때문에	바쁘다 + **-기 때문에** → 바쁘기 때문에

Noun	N 때문에	Base Form	A/V-기 때문에
비	비 때문에	살다	살기 때문에
감기	감기 때문에	배우다	배우기 때문에
친구	친구 때문에	크다	크기 때문에
남편	남편 때문에	귀엽다	귀엽기 때문에
교통	교통 때문에	멀다	멀기 때문에

-기 때문에 cannot be used in imperative or propositive sentences.

- 날씨가 춥기 때문에 따뜻한 옷을 입으세요. (×)
  → 날씨가 추우니까 따뜻한 옷을 입으세요. (○)
  The weather is cold, so please wear warm clothes.

- 친구들이 기다리기 때문에 빨리 갑시다. (×)
  → 친구들이 기다리니까 빨리 갑시다. (○)
  Our friends are waiting, so let's go quickly.

- 날씨가 좋기 때문에 산에 갈까요? (×)
  → 날씨가 좋으니까 산에 갈까요? (○)
  The weather is nice, so shall we go to the mountains?

In Conversation

Track 124

A 왜 늦었어요?
B 비 때문에 차가 많이 막혔어요.

A Why were you late?
B There was a lot of traffic due to the rain.

A 토요일에 만날 수 있어요?
B 토요일은 친구 생일이기 때문에 만날 수 없어요.

A Can you meet me on Saturday?
B Saturday is my friend's birthday, so I won't be able to meet you.

A 방학에 여행 갈 거예요?
B 아니요, 가고 싶지만 아르바이트를 하기 때문에 못 가요.

A Will you take a trip during the vacation?
B No, I want to, but because I have a part-time job, I can't go.

What's the Difference?

N 때문에	N이기 때문에
• 아기 때문에 밥을 못 먹어요. I can't eat because of (something related to) the baby. (for example, not going to sleep)	• 아기이기 때문에 밥을 못 먹어요. The baby can't eat because he/she is (still) a baby.
• 학생 때문에 선생님이 화가 나셨어요. The teacher got angry because of (something) the students did. (for example, telling a lie)	• 학생이기 때문에 공부를 열심히 해야 해요. You have to study hard because you are a student.

On Your Own

Look at the pictures and fill in the blanks using either 때문에 or –기 때문에.

(1)

A 오늘 왜 학교에 안 가요?

B ______________________ 학교에 안 가요.
(휴일이다)

(2)

A 내일 주말이에요. 우리 만나서 놀까요?

B ______________________ 못 놀아요.
(약속이 있다)

(3)

A 여보, 오늘 일찍 와요?

B 미안해요. ______________________ 늦을 거예요.
(회사 일)

(4)

A 민우 씨, 왜 그래요? 머리가 아파요?

B 네, ______________________ 머리가 아파요.
(향수 냄새)

Unit **10.**

Making Requests and Assisting

01 V-아/어 주세요, V-아/어 주시겠어요?

02 V-아/어 줄게요, V-아/어 줄까요?

01 V-아/어 주세요, V-아/어 주시겠어요?

Track 125

문 좀 **닫아 주세요**.

Please close the door.

사진 좀 **찍어 주시겠어요?**

Would you please take our picture?

자리를 **안내해 드리세요**.

Please show her to a seat.

Grammar Focus

This pattern expresses a request to someone to perform an action and corresponds to 'please/would you' in English. -아/어 주시겠어요? is a more polite expression that shows more consideration for the listener than -아/어 주세요. When the recipient of the action is someone higher in status than the speaker or someone to be respected, -아/어 드리세요 is used. When the verb stem ends in ㅏ or ㅗ, -아 주세요/주시겠어요? is used. Otherwise -어 주세요/주시겠어요? is used. For verbs that end in 하다, the form changes to -해 주세요/주시겠어요?.

Verb Stem Ends in ㅏ or ㅗ	Verb Stem Ends in Vowel Other than ㅏ or ㅗ	Verbs Ending in 하다
앉다 + **-아 주세요** → 앉아 주세요	찍다 + **-어 주세요** → 찍어 주세요	청소하다 → 청소해 주세요

Base Form	-아/어 주세요	-아/어 주시겠어요?
사다	사 주세요	사 주시겠어요?
켜다	켜 주세요	켜 주시겠어요?

빌리다	빌려 주세요	빌려 주시겠어요?
들다	들어 주세요	들어 주시겠어요?
소개하다	소개해 주세요	소개해 주시겠어요?
안내하다	안내해 주세요	안내해 주시겠어요?
*쓰다	써 주세요	써 주시겠어요?
*끄다	꺼 주세요	꺼 주시겠어요?

* Irregular form

In Conversation

Track 126

A 저 좀 도와주시겠어요?
B 네, 뭘 도와 드릴까요?

A Excuse me. Could you please help me out?
B Sure. How may I help you?

A 왕단 씨, 이 문법 좀 가르쳐 주세요.
B 미안해요. 저도 잘 몰라요.

A Wang Dan, please teach me this grammar.
B Sorry. I don't understand it either.

A 미국 회사에 이메일을 보내야 해요.
이것 좀 영어로 번역해 주시겠어요?
B 네, 그럴게요.

A I have to send an email to a company in the U.S.
Would you please translate this into English?
B Yes, I sure will.

Check It Out!

-아/어 주다, 드리다 is used when the speaker or the subject of the sentence performs an action that assists the listener or another person. When the assistance has already been completed, -아/어 줬어요 or -아/어 드렸어요 is used.

- 형은 제 숙제를 잘 도와줘요. My big brother helps me a lot with my homework.
- 잠깐만 기다려 주세요. Please wait for just a moment.
- 언니가 과일을 깍아 줬어요. My older sister peeled some fruit for me.
- 아직 친구에게 선물 안 해 줬어요. I haven't given a present to my friend yet.

What are the people in the following pictures requesting? Look at the pictures and choose the appropriate word from below to fill in each blank using either –아/어 주세요 or –아/어 주시겠어요?.

문을 열다	조용히 하다	책을 찾다	천천히 이야기하다

(1)

A ______________________________?

B 네, 열어 드릴게요.

(2)

A 재준 씨, ______________________________.

B 네, 다시 잘 들으세요.

(3)

A ______________________________.

B 네, 알겠습니다.

(4)

A ______________________________?

B 네, 알겠어요.

02 V-아/어 줄게요, V-아/어 줄까요?

Track 127

우산이 두 개 있는데 **빌려줄까요?**

I have two umbrellas, so shall I lend you one?

제가 **도와 드릴게요**.

Let me help you with that.

선생님, 제가 **들어 드릴까요?**

Teacher, shall I help you out?

Grammar Focus

This pattern is used when attempting to help someone and corresponds to 'Shall I', 'Allow me', or 'I will' in English. When the person receiving the help is of higher status than the speaker, -아/어 드릴게요 or -아/어 드릴까요? is used. When the verb stem ends in ㅏ or ㅗ, -아 줄게요/줄까요? is used. Otherwise -어 줄게요/줄까요? is used. For verbs that end in 하다, the form changes to -해 줄게요/줄까요?.

Stem Ending in ㅏ or ㅗ	Stem Ending in Vowel Other than ㅏ or ㅗ	Verb Ending in 하다
사다 + **-아 줄게요** → 사 줄게요	기다리다 + **-어 줄게요** → 기다려 줄게요	운전하다 → 운전해 줄게요

Base Form	-아/어 줄게요	-아/어 줄까요?
보다	봐 줄게요	봐 줄까요?
만들다	만들어 줄게요	만들어 줄까요?
빌리다	빌려줄게요	빌려줄까요?

소개하다	소개해 줄게요	소개해 줄까요?
*돕다	도와줄게요	도와줄까요?

* Irregular form

In Conversation

Track 128

A 여기요, 여기 상 좀 치워 주세요.
B 네, 손님, 금방 치워 드릴게요.

A Excuse me, could you please clear this table?
B Okay, I'll clear it off right away.

A 에어컨을 켜 주시겠어요?
B 네, 켜 드릴게요.

A Would you mind turning on the air conditioner?
B Sure, I'll turn it on.

What's the Difference?

–(으)세요

A simple command or request to the listener to do an action for the listener's sake.

- 이 옷이 민우 씨에게 안 어울려요. 다른 옷으로 바꾸세요.
  These clothes do not look good on you (Minu). Please change them with something else. (For the sake of you, Minu.)
- 다리가 아프세요? 여기 앉으세요.
  Does your foot hurt? Please sit down here. (For the sake of the listener.)

–아/어 주세요

A request to the listener to do an action for the sake of the speaker.

- 이 옷이 저에게 안 어울려요. 다른 옷으로 바꿔 주세요.
  These clothes do not look good on me. Please change them with something else. (For my sake.)
- 영화가 안 보여요. 앉아 주세요.
  (I) can't see the screen. Please sit down. (For my sake.)

On Your Own

Look at the pictures and choose the appropriate word from below to fill in each blank using either –아/어 주세요 or –아/어 줄까요?.

내리다　　빌리다

(1) 

A 망치 좀 빌려줄 수 있어요?
B 네, 있어요. ____________________.

(2) 

A 제가 가방을 ____________________?
B 네, 고맙습니다.

Unit 11.

Trying New Things and Experiences

01 V-아/어 보다

02 V-(으)ㄴ 적이 있다/없다

01 V-아/어 보다

Track 129

갈비를 **먹어 봤어요?**

Have you tried Korean ribs?

한번 **입어 보세요.**

Please try it on.

제주도에 **가 보고** 싶어요.

I want to visit Jeju Island.

Grammar Focus

-아/어 보다 expresses trying out or experiencing an action, and corresponds to 'try' in English. When the verb stem ends in ㅏ or ㅗ, **-아 보다** is used. Otherwise **-어 보다** is used. For verbs that end in **하다**, the form changes to **-해 보다**.

In general, when used with the present tense, it expresses trying something, and when used with the past tense, it expresses having the experience of doing something.

- 김치가 맛있어요. 김치를 먹어 보세요. Kimchi tastes good. Please try some kimchi. (try)
- 김치를 먹어 봤어요. 맛있었어요. I've had kimchi. It tastes good. (experience)

Stem Ending in ㅏ or ㅗ	Stem Ending in Vowel Other than ㅏ or ㅗ	Verb Ending in 하다
가다 + **-아 보다** → 가 보다	먹다 + **-어 보다** → 먹어 보다	여행하다 → 여행해 보다

Base Form	-아/어 보세요	-아/어 봤어요
사다	사 보세요	사 봤어요
살다	살아 보세요	살아 봤어요
입다	입어 보세요	입어 봤어요
먹다	먹어 보세요	먹어 봤어요
공부하다	공부해 보세요	공부해 봤어요
등산하다	등산해 보세요	등산해 봤어요
*듣다	들어 보세요	들어 봤어요

* Irregular form

In Conversation

Track 130

A 이 신발 신어 봐도 돼요?
B 네, 신어 보세요.

A May I try on these shoes?
B Yes, please try them on.

A 한국 친구가 있어요?
B 아니요, 없어요. 한국 친구를 사귀어 보고 싶어요.

A Do you have any Korean friends?
B No, I don't. I would like to (have the chance to) make some Korean friends.

A 막걸리를 마셔 봤어요?
B 아니요, 안 마셔 봤어요. 어떤 맛이에요?

A Have you tried drinking Korean rice wine?
B No, I haven't tried it yet. What does it taste like?

On Your Own

1 Look at the picture and make recommendations to a friend to go to the places in Korea shown on the map.

보기 속초에 가면 ___설악산에 가 보세요___.

(1) 민속촌에 가면 ______________________.

(2) 전주에 가면 ______________________.

(3) 제주도에 가면 ______________________.

2 The following is a dialogue. Choose the appropriate word from below to fill in the blanks using –아/어 보다.

가다　　구경하다　　마시다

웨슬리: 왕징 씨, 인사동에 가 봤어요?

왕징: 아니요, (1)__________________. 웨슬리 씨는 (2)__________________?

웨슬리: 네, 지난 주말에 가 봤어요.

왕징: 인사동에서 뭘 했어요?

웨슬리: 옛날 물건을 구경하고 한국 전통차를 (3)__________________.

왕징: 그래요. 저도 인사동에서 전통차를 마셔 보고 싶어요.

웨슬리: 그럼 이번 주말에 인사동을 (4)__________________.

02 V–(으)ㄴ 적이 있다/없다

Track 131

인도 영화를 **본 적이 있어요.**

I've seen an Indian movie.

회사에 **지각한 적이 없어요.**

I've never been late to work.

이탈리아에 **가 본 적이 있어요?**

Have you ever been to Italy?

Grammar Focus

–(으)ㄴ 적이 있다/없다 expresses having or not having a particular experience in the past and corresponds to 'have done/had' in English. When the subject has had an experience, **–(으)ㄴ 적이 있다** is used, and when the subject has not had an experience, **–(으)ㄴ 적이 없다** is used. If the verb stem ends in a vowel, **–ㄴ 적이 있다/없다** is added, and if the verb stem ends in a consonant, **은 적이 있다/없다** is added. Although the form **–(으)ㄴ 일이 있다/없다** can also be used to express the same meaning, **–(으)ㄴ 적이 있다/없다** is used more often.

Stem Ending in Vowel	Stem Ending in Consonant
보다 + **–ㄴ 적이 있다** → 본 적이 있다	입다 + **–은 적이 있다** → 입은 적이 있다

Base Form	–ㄴ 적이 있다	Base Form	–은 적이 있다
타다	탄 적이 있다	읽다	읽은 적이 있다
만나다	만난 적이 있다	먹다	먹은 적이 있다
여행하다	여행한 적이 있다	받다	받은 적이 있다
*만들다	만든 적이 있다	*듣다	들은 적이 있다

* Irregular form

–(으)ㄴ 적이 있다 is commonly combined with –아/어 보다 to form –아/어 본 적이 있다, which means to have the experience of having tried something.

- 저는 미국에 가 본 적이 있어요. I have been (successfully tried to go) to the U.S.
- 한국 음식을 먹어 본 적이 없어요. I've never tried (had the experience) Korean food.

In Conversation

Track 132

A 어제 명동에서 연예인을 만났어요.
B 와, 난 지금까지 한 번도 연예인을 만난 적이 없어요.

A Yesterday, I met a celebrity in Myeongdong.
B Wow, I've never met a celebrity.

A 시장에서 물건값을 잘 깎아요?
B 아니요, 깎아 본 적이 없어요.

A Can you bargain well at the market?
B No, I've never been able to bargain.

Check It Out!

–(으)ㄴ 적이 있다 is not used when describing things that are often repeated or are everyday occurrences.

- 오늘 물을 마신 적이 있어요. (×) • 화장실에 간 적이 있어요. (×)

On Your Own

Look at the pictures and fill in the blanks using –(으)ㄴ 적이 있다/없다.

(1) 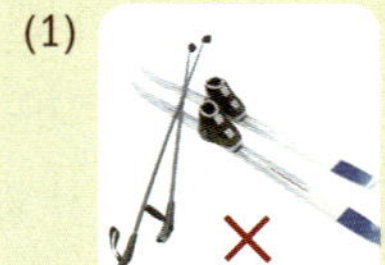 

A 이번 겨울에 스키를 탄 적이 있어요?
B 아니요, 스키를 ______________________.
그렇지만 스케이트는 ______________________.

(2)  

A 한국에 와서 병원에 간 적이 있어요?
B 아니요, 병원에 ______________________.
그렇지만 약국에는 ______________________.

(3)  

A 여권을 잃어버린 적이 있어요?
B 아니요, 여권을 ______________________.
그렇지만 우산은 ______________________.

Unit 12.

Asking Opinions and Making Suggestions

01 V-(으)ㄹ까요? ①

Track 133

같이 **농구할까요?**

Shall we play some basketball?

여기에서 좀 **쉴까요?**

Why don't we rest over here?

무슨 영화를 **볼까요?**

Which movie shall we see?

Grammar Focus

-(으)ㄹ까요? is used when the speaker wants to either suggest doing something together with the listener or ask about the listener's preference regarding something. The subject of these sentences is 우리, which is often omitted. The English equivalent is 'Shall we...?' or 'Why don't we...?' When answering, the suggestive form -(으)ㅂ시다 or -아/어요 is used. (See also Unit 12. Asking Opinions and Making Suggestions 03 V-(으)ㅂ시다) When the stem ends in a vowel or ㄹ, -ㄹ까요? is used, and when it ends in a consonant, -을까요? is used.

Stem Ending in Vowel or ㄹ	Stem Ending in Consonant
가다 + **-ㄹ까요?** → 갈까요?	먹다 + **-을까요?** → 먹을까요?

Base Form	-ㄹ까요?	Base Form	-을까요?
사다	살까요?	닫다	닫을까요?
여행하다	여행할까요?	*듣다	들을까요?
*열다	열까요?	*걷다	걸을까요?

* Irregular form

(Compare with Unit 12. Asking Opinions and Making Suggestions 02 V-(으)ㄹ까요? ②, Unit 17. Conjecture 03 A/V-(으)ㄹ까요? ③)

In Conversation

Track 134

A 주말에 같이 노래방에 갈까요?
B 네, 좋아요. 같이 가요.

A Shall we go sing karaoke over the weekend?
B Okay, sounds good. Let's go.

A 퇴근 후에 술 한잔할까요?
B 미안해요. 오늘 약속이 있어요. 다음에 같이해요.

A Would you like to go for a drink after work?
B Sorry. Today I have other plans. Let's do it next time.

On Your Own

The following is a conversation between Budi and Wang Jing. Look at the pictures and fill in the blanks using -(으)ㄹ까요? and -아/어요.

보기
부디: 왕징 씨, 우리 내일 뭐 할까요? (하다)
왕징: 영화 봐요. (보다)

부디: 무슨 영화를 (1)______________? (보다)
왕징: 한국 영화를 (2)______________. (보다)
부디: 그럼 어디에서 (3)______________? (만나다)
왕징: 학교 앞에서 (4)______________. (만나다)
부디: 3시 영화가 있어요.
왕징: 그럼, 영화 시작하기 전에 만나서 같이 점심을 (5)______________? (먹다)
부디: 네, 좋아요.
왕징: 영화 보고 나서 남대문시장에 가서 (6)______________? (쇼핑하다)
부디: 저는 쇼핑을 안 좋아해요. 커피 마시면서 (7)______________. (이야기하다)
왕징: 그럼, 그렇게 해요.

02 V–(으)ㄹ까요? ②

Track 135

창문을 **열까요?**

Shall I open the window?

내일 무엇을 **입을까요?**

What shall I wear tomorrow?

커피를 **드릴까요**, 주스를 **드릴까요?**

Would you like (me to get you) some coffee or juice?

Grammar Focus

–(으)ㄹ까요? is used when the speaker wants to make a suggestion to the listener or to ask the listener for his or her opinion. The subject is normally **제가** or **내가** and may be omitted. In English, this expression corresponds to 'Shall I...?' or 'Do you want me to...?' When responding, the imperative forms **–(으)세요** or **–지 마세요** can be used. When the verb stem ends in a vowel or ㄹ, **–ㄹ까요?** is used, and when the verb stem ends in a consonant, **–을까요?** is used.

Stem Ending in Vowel or ㄹ	Stem Ending in Consonant
사다 + **–ㄹ까요?** → 살까요?	닫다 + **–을까요?** → 닫을까요?

Base Form	–ㄹ까요?	Base Form	–을까요?
가다	갈까요?	읽다	읽을까요?
오다	올까요?	놓다	놓을까요?
*만들다	만들까요?	*듣다	들을까요?

* Irregular form

(Compare with Unit 12. Asking Opinions and Making Suggestions 01 V–(으)ㄹ까요? ①, Unit 17. Conjecture 03 A/V–(으)ㄹ까요? ③)

In Conversation

Track 136

A 내일 언제 전화할까요?
B 저녁에 전화하세요.

A When shall I call you tomorrow?
B Please call me in the evening.

A 가족들과 부산에 갈 거예요. 어느 호텔을 예약할까요?
B 이 호텔을 예약하세요. 가족들과 가기에 아주 좋아요.

A I'm going to Busan with my family. Which hotel should I make a reservation at?
B Make a reservation at this hotel. It's great for going with family.

A 이 컴퓨터를 어디에 놓을까요?
B 책상 위에 놓으세요.

A Where should I put this computer?
B Please put it on the desk.

On Your Own

Use -(으)ㄹ까요? to ask your partner for advice, and then use -(으)세요 or -지 마세요 to complete the appropriate response.

가다	가져가다	먹다	보다

(1)
A 오늘 날씨가 흐려요? 우산을 ________________?
B 네, ________________. 비가 곧 오겠어요.

(2)
A 외국 친구와 점심 약속이 있어요. 무슨 음식을 ____________?
B 잡채를 ____________. 외국 사람들은 잡채를 좋아해요.

(3)
A 미국에서 친구가 와요. 친구와 어디에 ____________?
B 민속촌에 ____________. 한국의 전통문화를 알 수 있어요.

(4)
A 내일 여자 친구와 데이트가 있어요. 이 영화를 ____________?
B 이 영화를 ____________. 사람들이 이 영화가 재미없대요.

03 V–(으)ㅂ시다

Track 137

한식을 **먹읍시다**.

Let's eat Korean food.

버스를 타지 마요. 지하철을 **탑시다**.

Let's not take the bus. Let's take the subway.

영화를 **보지 맙시다**.

Let's not see a movie.

Grammar Focus

–(으)ㅂ시다 is used to suggest or propose doing something with the listener and corresponds to 'Let's' or 'Shall we' in English. The same meaning can also be expressed by **–아/어요**. When the stem ends in a vowel, **–ㅂ시다** is used, and when it ends in a consonant, **–읍시다** is used. When suggesting not to do something, however, either **–지 맙시다** or **–지 마요** is used.

Stem Ending in Vowel	Stem Ending in Consonant
가다 + **–ㅂ시다** → 갑시다	먹다 + **–읍시다** → 먹읍시다

Base Form	–(으)ㅂ시다	–지 맙시다
오다	옵시다	오지 맙시다
만나다	만납시다	만나지 맙시다
여행하다	여행합시다	여행하지 맙시다
*만들다	만듭시다	만들지 맙시다
*걷다	걸읍시다	걷지 맙시다

* Irregular form

In Conversation

Track 138

A 언제 출발할까요?
B 10분 후에 출발합시다.

A When shall we depart?
B Let's leave in 10 minutes.

A 주말에 클럽에 갈까요?
B 월요일에 시험이 있으니까 클럽에 가지 맙시다. 같이 공부합시다.

A Shall we go to a club on the weekend?
B We have a test on Monday, so let's not go to a club. Let's study together.

A 오늘 등산 갈까요?
B 어제 비가 와서 미끄러워요. 다음 주에 가요.

A Why don't we go hiking today?
B It rained yesterday, so the ground is slippery. Let's go next week.

Check It Out!

-(으)ㅂ시다 can be used in formal situations in which the speaker is suggesting or inviting a group of people to do something or when the listener is younger or of lower status than the speaker. It cannot be used toward someone older or of higher status than the speaker. In such cases, 같이 -(으)세요 is appropriate.

❶ When suggesting or inviting a group of people to do something.

- 여러분, 우리 모두 공부 열심히 합시다. Everyone, let's all study hard.
- 점심시간입니다. 모두들 점심 식사합시다. It's lunchtime. Let's all have lunch.

❷ When the listener is younger or of a similar age or status as the speaker.

- 사장님: 토요일에 같이 점심 식사합시다. Company Director: Let's have lunch together on Saturday.
- 사원: 네, 좋습니다. Employee: Okay, that sounds good.

- 재준: 요코 씨, 주말에 같이 등산 갑시다. Jaejun: Yoko, let's go hiking over the weekend.
- 요코: 그래요, 재준 씨. Yoko: Sure, Jaejun.

❸ When the listener is older or of a higher status than the speaker.

- 선생님, 노래방에 같이 갑시다. (×)
  → 선생님, 노래방에 같이 가세요. (○) Teacher, please go sing karaoke together with us.
- 교수님, 저희와 같이 점심 먹읍시다. (×)
  → 교수님, 저희와 같이 점심 드세요. (○) Professor, please have lunch together with us.

On Your Own

Jisu is planning a trip for summer vacation with her friend, Carol. Use –(으)ㅂ시다 or –아/어요 to complete their dialogue in which they plan their trip.

지수: 캐럴 씨, 이번 여름에 휴가를 같이 갈까요?

캐럴: 네, 좋아요. 같이 (1) ______________. (가다)

지수: 어디로 갈까요? 해외로 갈까요, 국내로 갈까요?

캐럴: 저는 한국 여행을 많이 못했으니까 국내로 가고 싶어요.
국내 (2) ______________. (여행하다)

지수: 그래요. 아! 설악산에 가면 산과 바다에 갈 수 있어요. 설악산이 어때요?

캐럴: 설악산이 좋겠어요! 설악산에 (3) ______________. (가다)
바다에 가면 우리 수영도 하고 (4) ______________. (선탠도 하다)

지수: 와, 재미있겠어요.
산에도 갈 거니까 운동화나 등산화도 (5) ______________. (가져가다)

캐럴: 네, 알겠어요.

지수: 참, 거기에는 생선회가 유명해요. 캐럴 씨, 생선회 먹을 수 있어요?

캐럴: 물론이에요. 우리 생선회도 (6) ______________. (먹다)

04 V-(으)시겠어요?

Track 139

도넛 좀 **드시겠어요?**

Would you like a donut?

방을 **예약하시겠어요?**

Would you like to reserve a room?

커피에 설탕을 **넣으시겠어요?**

Would you like sugar in your coffee?

Grammar Focus

-(으)시겠어요? is used when politely suggesting something to the listener or when asking about the listener's preference or intention. It corresponds to 'Would you (mind/like to)...?' or 'Why not...?' in English and conveys a much more formal and polite feeling than -(으)ㄹ래요?/-(으)실래요?. When the stem ends in a vowel, -시겠어요? is used, and when it ends in a consonant, -으시겠어요? is used.

Stem Ending in Vowel	Stem Ending in Consonant
가다 + **-시겠어요?** → 가시겠어요?	읽다 + **-으시겠어요?** → 읽으시겠어요?

Base Form	-시겠어요?	Base Form	-으시겠어요?
오다	오시겠어요?	앉다	앉으시겠어요?
만나다	만나시겠어요?	받다	받으시겠어요?
구경하다	구경하시겠어요?	입다	입으시겠어요?
*만들다	만드시겠어요?	*듣다	들으시겠어요?

* Irregular form

In Conversation

Track 140

A 내일 몇 시에 오시겠어요?
B 3시까지 갈게요.

A What time will you come tomorrow?
B I will be there by three o'clock.

A 여보세요, 조엘 씨, 저 리라예요.
지금 통화 괜찮아요?
B 미안해요. 지금 회의 중이에요.
30분 후에 다시 전화해 주시겠어요?

A Hello, Joel. This is Lila.
Can you talk now?
B Sorry. I'm in the middle of a meeting.
Would you mind calling me in 30 minutes?

A 한국의 전통 기념품을 사고 싶어요.
B 그럼, 인사동에 가 보시겠어요?

A I want to buy a traditional Korean souvenir.
B In that case, why don't you go to Insadong?

On Your Own

Find the most appropriate response from the choices given, as shown in the example.

보기 김 선생님 계세요?	ⓐ 그럼 같이 영화 보러 가시겠어요?
(1) 머리를 어떻게 하시겠어요?	ⓑ 미안해요. 저도 잘 모르겠어요.
(2) 주말에 심심해요.	ⓒ 지금 수업 중이세요. 잠깐만 기다리시겠어요?
(3) 내일 제 생일 파티가 있어요. 와 주시겠어요?	ⓓ 짧게 잘라 주세요.
(4) 이 문제가 어려워요. 좀 가르쳐 주시겠어요?	ⓔ 네, 좋아요. 꼭 갈게요.

05 V-(으)ㄹ래요? ①

Track 141

등산 같이 **갈래요?**

Do you want to go hiking?

커피 **한잔하실래요?**

Would you like to have a cup of coffee?

한강에서 배를 **타지 않을래요?**

Would you like to go ride a boat on the Han River?

Grammar Focus

-(으)ㄹ래요? is used when asking about the listener's preference or intention or when gently making a request. It is used often in spoken language among close friends and thus does not convey as polite a feeling as -(으)시겠어요?. It corresponds to 'Want to...?' or 'How about...?' in English. When asking a question in the form of -(으)ㄹ래요?, the answer can be given in the form of -(으)ㄹ래요? or -(으)ㄹ게요. -(으)ㄹ래요? can also be replaced with **-지 않을래요?** (안 -(으)ㄹ래요?), which means the same as -(으)ㄹ래요? even though it is a negative form. When the relationship with the listener is close but the speaker still wants to show respect, -(으)실래요? can be used. When the verb stem ends in a vowel or ㄹ, -ㄹ래요? is used, and when it ends in a consonant, -을래요? is used.

Stem Ending in Vowel or ㄹ	Stem Ending in Consonant
가다 + **-ㄹ래요?** → 갈래요?	받다 + **-을래요?** → 받을래요?

Base Form	-ㄹ래요?	Base Form	-을래요?
보다	볼래요?	먹다	먹을래요?
사다	살래요?	앉다	앉을래요?

운동하다	운동할래요?	*듣다	들을래요?
*놀다	놀래요?	*걷다	걸을래요?

* Irregular form

(Compare with Unit 13. Intentions and Plans 03 V-(으)ㄹ래요 ②)

In Conversation

Track 142

A 저는 된장찌개를 먹을래요.
하미 씨는 뭐 드실래요?

B 저는 갈비탕을 먹을래요.

A I'll have doenjang stew.
What will you have, Hami?

B I'll have beef rib soup.

A 유키 씨, 우리 시험 끝나고 뭐 할래요?

B 영화 볼까요?

A Yuki, what do you want to do after we finish our tests?

B Shall we go see a movie?

A 서울의 야경이 보고 싶어요.

B 그럼 저녁에 N서울타워에 같이 갈래요?

A I want to see a night view of Seoul.

B In that case, how about going to N Seoul Tower this evening?

On Your Own

Choose the appropriate word from below to fill in each blank using -(으)ㄹ래요?.

걷다 | 보지 않다 | 쇼핑하다 | 앉다 | 타다

(1) A 흐엉 씨, 다리 아파요? 저기 의자에 ______________?
B 아니요, 괜찮아요.

(2) A 와, 눈이 많이 왔어요. 우리 스키 ______________?
B 네, 좋아요.

(3) A 요즘 백화점에서 세일해요.
B 그럼 오늘 백화점에서 같이 ______________?

(4) A 날씨가 정말 좋아요.
B 그래요? 그럼 밖에 나가서 좀 ______________?

(5) A 요즘 재미있는 영화가 많이 있어요. 같이 영화 ______________?
B 미안해요. 요즘 바빠서 시간이 없어요.

Unit 13.

Intentions and Plans

01 A/V-겠어요 ①
02 V-(으)ㄹ게요
03 V-(으)ㄹ래요 ②

01 A/V-겠어요 ①

Track 143

올해에는 담배를 꼭 **끊겠습니다**.

This year, I'm going to stop smoking.

제가 출장을 **가겠습니다**.

I'll go on the business trip.

잠시 후에 인천공항에 **도착하겠습니다**.

We will soon arrive at Incheon Airport.

Grammar Focus

1 **-겠어요** is added to the ends of verbs to express the intention or will of the speaker. It corresponds to '(I) will/am going to' or '(I) plan to' in English. It is made by adding **-겠어요** to the verb stem. The negative form is made by adding **-지 않겠어요** or **안 -겠어요**.

- 아침마다 운동하겠어요.
  I plan to exercise every morning.
- 이제 술을 마시지 않겠어요.
  I won't drink alcohol any more.

When **-겠어요** is used to express intention or will, the subject cannot be in the third person.

- 카일리 씨는 내일부터 다이어트를 하겠어요. (×)
  → 카일리 씨는 내일부터 다이어트를 할 거예요. (○)
  Kylie will start her diet (from) tomorrow.
  → 저는 내일부터 다이어트를 하겠어요. (○)
  I'll start my diet (from) tomorrow.

2 **–겠어요** can also be used to convey information that something is about to occur. In this case, it corresponds to 'should' or 'will' in English.

- (기차역 안내 방송) 기차가 곧 도착하겠습니다. (Train station announcement) The train will arrive shortly.
- (일기예보에서) 내일은 비가 오겠습니다. (Weather forecast) There is a good chance of rain tomorrow.

가다 + **–겠어요** → 가겠어요　　　먹다 + **–겠어요** → 먹겠어요

Base Form	–겠어요	Base Form	–겠어요
오다	오겠어요	읽다	읽겠어요
만나다	만나겠어요	만들다	만들겠어요
전화하다	전화하겠어요	듣다	듣겠어요

(Compare with Unit 17. Conjecture 01 A/V–겠어요 ②)

In Conversation

Track 144

A 왕단 씨, 지각하지 마십시오!
B 죄송합니다.
내일부터는 일찍 오겠습니다.

A Wang Dan, let's not be late to class!
B I'm sorry. I'll arrive early starting tomorrow.

A 외국 손님들이 오셔서 통역이 필요합니다.
B 부장님, 그럼 제가 통역을 하겠습니다.

A Some foreign guests are here, so I need someone to interpret.
B In that case, Chief, I will interpret for you.

A 잠시 후에는 안준호 교수님께서 한국 경제에 대해 강의를 하시겠습니다.
B 안녕하십니까? 안준호입니다.

A Professor An Junho will give a lecture on the Korean economy shortly.
B Good afternoon. I'm An Junho.

Check It Out!

❶ –겠– is used idiomatically in the following cases.

- 처음 뵙겠습니다. 이민우입니다. It's a pleasure to meet you. (We meet for the first time.) I'm Lee Minu.
- 잘 먹겠습니다. Thank you for preparing this food. (I will enjoy this food.)
- 어머니, 학교 다녀오겠습니다. Mother, I'm off to school.

❷ –겠– is also used when the speaker wants to be less assertive and more gentle and polite when expressing a thought.

A 여러분, 여기까지 알겠어요? Everyone, do you understand (what I've discussed) so far?
B 아니요, 잘 모르겠어요. No, I don't quite understand.

On Your Own

1 What have the following people decided to do in the new year? Look at the pictures and fill in the blanks using –겠어요.

(1) 올해에는 열심히 ______________________.
(공부하다)

(2)

올해에는 아이와 더 많이 ______________________.
(놀아 주다)

(3) 올해에는 ___________________________________.
(컴퓨터게임을 하다 ×)

2 The weather forecast is being shown on television. Look at the weather map below and fill in the blanks using –겠습니다.

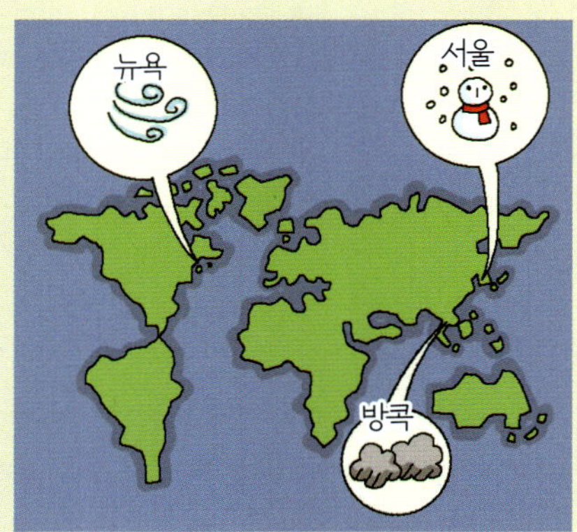

내일 세계의 날씨를 보시겠습니다. (1) 내일 서울은 ______________________.
(2) 뉴욕은 ______________________. (3) 방콕은 ______________________.

02 V-(으)ㄹ게요

Track 145

제가 전화 **받을게요**.

I'll answer the phone.

죄송합니다. 일이 있어서 먼저 **갈게요**.

Sorry. I have work to do, so I'll be leaving now.

저녁에 **전화할게요**.

I'll call you in the evening.

Grammar Focus

-(으)ㄹ게요 is used when the speaker wants to express a decision or intention to another person, similar to a promise, and also when actually making a promise to do something with the other person. It is also used simply to express that the speaker will do something. It thus corresponds to '(I) will (do)' in English. This expression is used in colloquial language mainly among intimates. When the verb stem ends in a vowel or ㄹ, then -ㄹ게요 is used, and when it ends in a consonant, -을게요 is used.

Stem Ending in Vowel or ㄹ	Stem Ending in Consonant
가다 + **-ㄹ게요** → 갈게요	찾다 + **-을게요** → 찾을게요

Base Form	-ㄹ게요	Base Form	-을게요
오다	올게요	끊다	끊을게요
타다	탈게요	*듣다	들을게요
공부하다	공부할게요	*걷다	걸을게요
*열다	열게요	*돕다	도울게요

* Irregular form

This expression can be used only with verbs that express the will of the subject.

- 오늘 오후에는 바람이 불게요. (×)
  (The blowing of the wind is not due to the will or intention of the wind.)
- 저는 이제부터 날씬할게요. (×)
  (It cannot be used with adjectives.)

Only subjects in the first person can be used.

- 부디 씨가 저녁에 전화할게요. (×)
  → 부디 씨가 저녁에 전화할 거예요. (○)
  Budi will call in the evening.
  → 제가 저녁에 전화할게요. (○)
  I'll call in the evening.

This expression cannot be used in questions.

- 리라 씨, 이제 늦지 않을게요? (×)
  → 리라 씨, 이제 늦지 않을 거예요? (○)
  Lila, you won't be late in the future, will you?

In Conversation

Track 146

A 제 책 가지고 왔어요?
B 미안해요. 잊어버렸어요.
내일은 꼭 가지고 올게요.

A Did you bring my book?
B Sorry. I forgot.
I'll definitely bring it tomorrow.

A 에릭 씨, 카일리 씨의 이메일 주소 아세요?
B 네, 알아요. 제가 종이에 써 드릴게요.

A Eric, do you know Kylie's email address?
B Yes, I do. I'll write it down (on paper) for you.

What's the Difference?

–(으)ㄹ게요	–(으)ㄹ 거예요
A relationship exists with the listener, and the subject's intention or thought is expressed while taking the listener into consideration. A 몸에 안 좋으니까 담배를 피우지 마세요. B 네, 담배를 안 피울게요. (Speaker B hears what Speaker A says and states the intention to follow the advice.) A 그럼, 안녕히 가세요. B 네, 제가 밤에 전화할게요. (Speaker B intends to call under the assumption that Speaker A expects it.)	No relationship exists with the listener, and the subject's thought, intention, or plan is expressed unidirectionally. A 이제부터 담배를 안 피울 거예요. B 잘 생각하셨어요. (Speaker A had already been planning to stop smoking, which was a decision unrelated to the relationship with Speaker B.) A 그럼, 안녕히 가세요. B 네, 제가 밤에 전화할 거예요. (Speaker B plans to call Speaker A irrespective of Speaker A's wishes.)

On Your Own

Look at the pictures and fill in the blanks as shown in the example.

보기

A 이거 너무 어려워요. 가르쳐 줄 수 있어요?
B 그럼요. __제가 가르쳐 줄게요__.
(가르쳐 주다)

(1)

A 웨슬리 씨가 점심을 샀으니까 제가 커피를 ________________.
(사다)
B 고마워요. 잘 마실게요.

(2)

A 티루엔 씨, 이 서류를 팩스로 보내 주시겠어요?
B 네, 바로 ________________.
(보내 드리다)

(3)

A 이거 비밀이니까 다른 사람한테 이야기하면 안 돼요.
B 알겠어요. ________________.
(이야기하다 ×)

(4)

A 내일 일찍 일어나야 하니까 오늘 늦게 자면 안 돼요.
B 네, 알겠어요. 오늘 ________________.
(늦게 자다 ×)

03 V-(으)ㄹ래요 ②

Track 147

너무 배가 불러요. 그만 **먹을래요**.

I'm so full. I'm not going to eat any more.

커피 **마실래요**.

I'll drink coffee.

이번 방학에는 여행을 **할래요**.

This vacation, I'm going on a trip.

Grammar Focus

-(으)ㄹ래요 expresses the fact that the speaker has the will or intention to do something. It is used often in colloquial language among intimates, and does not confer a feeling of politeness. This meaning corresponds to 'be going to' or 'will' in English. Used in questions, it is a way to ask the other person his or her intention (See also Unit 12. Asking Opinions and Making Suggestions 05 V-(으)ㄹ래요? ①) When the verb stem ends in a vowel or ㄹ, **-ㄹ래요** is used, and when it ends in a consonant, **-을래요** is used.

Stem Ending in Vowel or ㄹ	Stem Ending in Consonant
가다 + **-ㄹ래요** → 갈래요	먹다 + **-을래요** → 먹을래요

Base Form	-ㄹ래요	Base Form	-을래요
오다	올래요	받다	받을래요
타다	탈래요	있다	있을래요
공부하다	공부할래요	*듣다	들을래요
*놀다	놀래요	*걷다	걸을래요

* Irregular form

1 This expression can be used only with verbs.

- 저는 키가 클래요. (×)
  → 저는 키가 컸으면 좋겠어요. (○)
  I wish I were tall.
- 저는 예쁠래요. (×)
  → 저는 예뻤으면 좋겠어요. (○)
  I wish I were pretty.

(See also Unit 8. Expressions of Hope 02 A/V-았/었으면 좋겠다)

2 Only subjects in the first person can be used.

- 호앙 씨는 다음 주에 고향에 갈래요. (×)
  → 호앙 씨는 다음 주에 고향에 갈 거예요. (○)
  Hoang will go to his hometown next week.
  → 저는 다음 주에 고향에 갈래요. (○)
  I'll go to my hometown next week.

(Compare with Unit 12. Asking Opinions and Making Suggestions 05 V-(으)ㄹ래요? ①)

In Conversation

Track 148

A 하미 씨, 이따가 액션 영화 볼래요, 공포 영화 볼래요?
B 저는 공포 영화는 싫어요. 액션 영화 볼래요.

A Hami, do you want to see an action movie or a horror movie later?
B I don't like horror movies. I want to see an action movie.

A 뭐 드실래요?
B 저는 커피를 마실래요.

A What would you like to drink?
B I'd like to drink some coffee.

A 오늘 리라 씨의 생일 파티에 안 가요?
B 네, 안 갈래요. 피곤해서 집에서 쉴래요.

A Aren't you going to Lila's birthday party today?
B No, I'm not going. I'm tired, so I plan on resting at home.

On Your Own

Look at the pictures and fill in the blanks using -(으)ㄹ래요.

(1)

A 캐럴 씨는 빨간색이 잘 어울리니까 오늘 빨간색 옷을 입으세요.

B 지난번에 빨간색을 입었으니까 오늘은 검은색 옷을 ______________. (입다)

(2)

A 12시예요. 점심 안 드세요?

B 아침을 늦게 먹어서 저는 이따가 ______________. (먹다)

(3)

A 방학 때 피아노 배울래, 기타 배울래?

B 기타를 ______________. (배우다)

(4)

A 날씨가 더우니까 아이스크림 먹을래요?

B 저는 배가 아파서 ______________. (먹다 ×)

Unit 14.

Background Information and Explanations

01 A/V-(으)ㄴ/는데 ②

02 V-(으)니까 ②

01 A/V-(으)ㄴ/는데 ②

Track 149

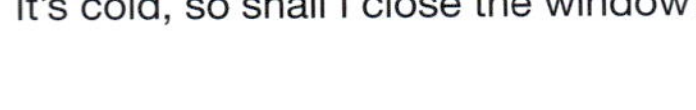

추운데 창문을 닫을까요?

It's cold, so shall I close the window?

백화점에 **가는데** 같이 갈래요?

I'm going to a department store, do you want to join me?

제 동생은 **학생인데** 공부를 아주 잘해요.

My little sister is a student, and she studies really hard.

많이 **샀는데** 이제 갈까요?

You've bought a lot already, so shall we go?

Grammar Focus

-(으)ㄴ/는데 is used when the first clause expresses the reason or background situation for the second clause and also when the first clause provides content introducing the second clause. It corresponds to 'so/therefore' or 'and' in English. When added to adjectives, -ㄴ데 is added to stems ending in a vowel, and -은데 is added to stems ending in a consonant. When added to verbs, -는데 is added to the stem.

Adjectives and Present Tense 이다		Present Tense Verbs 있다/없다	Past Tense Verbs and Adjectives
No Final Consonant	Final Consonant		
-ㄴ데	-은데	-는데	-았/었는데
바쁜데 학생인데	많은데 적은데	보는데 먹는데 있는데 없는데	봤는데 바빴는데 의사였는데 학생이었는데

Base Form	-(으)ㄴ/는데	Base Form	-(으)ㄴ/는데
작다	작은데	오다	오는데
높다	높은데	기다리다	기다리는데
편리하다	편리한데	찾다	찾는데
*귀엽다	귀여운데	듣다	듣는데
*하얗다	하얀데	*살다	사는데
아팠다	아팠는데	받았다	받았는데
경찰이었다	경찰이었는데	결혼했다	결혼했는데

* Irregular form

(Compare with Unit 4. Listing and Contrast 04 A/V-(으)ㄴ/는데 ①)

In Conversation

Track 150

A 요코 씨가 회사원이에요?

B 아니요, 아직 학생인데 올해 졸업할 거예요.

A Yoko, do you work for a company?

B No, I'm still a student, but I will graduate this year.

A 학교 근처에 어느 식당이 괜찮아요?

B 학교 옆에 '만나식당'이 괜찮은데 거기 한번 가 보세요.

A Where's a good restaurant near the school?

B The restaurant Manna right next to school is pretty good, so I suggest you go there.

A 이 옷을 어제 샀는데 마음에 안 들어요.

B 왜요? 지수 씨한테 잘 어울려요.

A I bought these clothes yesterday, but I'm not pleased with them.

B Why? They look fine on you (Jisu).

On Your Own

Look at the pictures and choose the appropriate word from below to fill in each blank using -(으)ㄴ/는데.

고프다	없다	오다	친구이다

(1)

A 이 사람이 누구예요?

B 제 ____________ 지금 미국에 있어요.

(2)

A 배가 ____________ 식당에 갈까요?

B 네, 좋아요.

(3)

A 비가 ____________ 택시를 탑시다.

B 네, 그러는 게 좋겠어요.

(4)

A 주스 한 잔 주시겠어요?

B 주스가 ____________ 커피 드릴까요?

02 V–(으)니까 ②

Track 151

집에 **들어오니까** 맛있는 냄새가 나요.
I arrived home to (discover) the smell of something tasty.

아침에 **일어나니까** 선물이 있었어요.
When I woke up in the morning, the gift had already arrived.

집에 **오니까** 밤 12시였어요.
When I arrived home, it was midnight.

Grammar Focus

–(으)니까 expresses the discovery of the fact described in the second clause as the result of performing the action described in the first clause. It corresponds to 'when' or '(do something) only to discover'. If the verb stem ends in a vowel, –니까 is used, and if it ends in a consonant, –으니까 is used. This form of –(으)니까 denoting discovery attaches only to verbs.

Verb Ending in Vowel	Verb Ending in Consonant
가다 + **–니까** → 가니까	받다 + **–으니까** → 받으니까

Base Form	–니까	Base Form	–으니까
오다	오니까	먹다	먹으니까
배우다	배우니까	읽다	읽으니까
일어나다	일어나니까	있다	있으니까
전화하다	전화하니까	*듣다	들으니까
*만들다	만드니까	*걷다	걸으니까

* Irregular form

When **–(으)니까** expresses the result of an action (discovery), **–았–** and **–겠–** cannot precede it.

- 아침에 회사에 갔으니까 아무도 없었어요. (×)
  → 아침에 회사에 가니까 아무도 없었어요. (○)
  I arrived at the office only to discover that nobody was there.
- 저녁에 집에 왔으니까 어머니가 계셨어요. (×)
  → 저녁에 집에 오니까 어머니가 계셨어요. (○)
  When I arrived home in the evening, my mother was there.

(Compare with Unit 9. Reasons and Causes 02 A/V–(으)니까 ①)

In Conversation

Track 152

A 제이슨 씨한테 전화해 봤어요?
B 네, 그런데 전화하니까 안 받아요.

A Did you call Jason on the phone?
B Yes, I called but he did not answer.

A 그 모자 얼마예요?
B 만 원이요. 어제 백화점에 가니까 세일을 하고 있었어요.

A How much was that hat?
B 10,000 won. When I went to the department store yesterday, they were having a sale.

On Your Own

Connect each phrase on the left to the most appropriate phrase on the right, and write sentences using the phrases as shown in the example.

보기 친구 집에 전화하다 •	• ⓐ 한국 생활이 재미있어요.
(1) 지하철을 타 보다 •	• ⓑ 생선회가 싸고 맛있었어요.
(2) 한국에서 살아 보다 •	• ⓒ 할머니가 전화를 받으셨어요.
(3) 부산에 가다 •	• ⓓ 빠르고 편해요.
(4) 동생의 구두를 신어 보다 •	• ⓔ 작았어요.

보기 친구 집에 전화하니까 할머니가 전화를 받으셨어요.

(1) ______________________________.

(2) ______________________________.

(3) ______________________________.

(4) ______________________________.

Unit 15.

Purpose and Intention

01 V-(으)러 가다/오다
02 V-(으)려고
03 V-(으)려고 하다
04 N을/를 위해(서), V-기 위해(서)
05 V-기로 하다

01 V-(으)러 가다/오다

Track 153

옷을 **사러** 동대문시장에 **가요.**

We're going to Dongdaemun Market to buy clothes.

한국 팬들을 **만나러** 한국에 **왔어요.**

I came to Korea to see my Korean fans.

은행에 돈을 **찾으러 가요.**

I'm going to the bank to withdraw some money.

Grammar Focus

-(으)러 가다/오다 expresses going or coming to a place to perform an action, with the action stated first and the place second. It corresponds to '(in order) to' in English. When the verb stem ends in a vowel or ㄹ, then **-러 가다/오다** is used, and when it ends in a consonant, **-으러 가다/오다** is used.

Stem Ending in Vowel or ㄹ	Stem Ending in Consonant
사다 + **-러 가다** → 사러 가다	먹다 + **-으러 가다** → 먹으러 가다

Base Form	-러 가요/와요	Base Form	-으러 가요/와요
보다	보러 가요/와요	받다	받으러 가요/와요
배우다	배우러 가요/와요	찾다	찾으러 가요/와요
공부하다	공부하러 가요/와요	*듣다	들으러 가요/와요
*놀다	놀러 가요/와요	*짓다	지으러 가요/와요
*살다	살러 가요/와요	*돕다	도우러 가요/와요

* Irregular form

Only movement verbs such as **가다** (to go), **오다** (to come), and **다니다** (to attend/commute) are used after **–(으)러**.

- 옷을 사러 시장에 가요. (◯) (I) go to the market to buy clothes.
- 옷을 사러 돈을 찾아요. (×)
  → 옷을 사려고 돈을 찾아요. (◯) (I) withdrew money to buy clothes.

Furthermore, the following verbs that express movement cannot be used before **–(으)러**: **가다** (to go), **오다** (to come), **올라가다** (to go up), **내려가다** (to go down), **들어가다** (to enter), **나가다** (to leave), **여행하다** (to travel), and **이사하다** (to move/change residences).

- 가러 가다 (×), 오러 가다 (×), 올라가러 가다 (×), 나가러 가다 (×)

In Conversation

Track 154

A 이사했어요?
B 네, 지난주에 했어요.
주말에 우리 집에 놀러 오세요.

A Did you move (change residences)?
B Yes, I moved last week.
Please come to visit over the weekend.

A 요즘 바빠요?
B 네, 조금 바빠요.
한국 춤을 배우러 학원에 다녀요.

A Are you busy these days?
B Yes, I'm a bit busy.
I'm attending an academy to learn Korean dance.

On Your Own

Look at the pictures and fill in the blanks using –(으)러 가다/오다.

(1)

A 어떻게 오셨습니까?
B 사장님을 ______________ 왔습니다.
(만나다)

(2)

A 어디에 가요?
B ______________ 나가요. 남자 친구하고 약속이 있어요.
(데이트하다)

(3)

A 음식이 나왔는데 어디에 가요?
B 손을 ______________ 화장실에 가요.
(씻다)

02 V-(으)려고

Track 155

살을 **빼려고** 매일 세 시간씩 운동을 해요.

I exercise three hours a day to try to lose weight.

아내에게 **주려고** 선물을 샀어요.

I bought a present to give to my wife.

잠을 **자지 않으려고** 커피를 5잔이나 마셨어요.

I drank five cups of coffee so that I wouldn't go to sleep.

Grammar Focus

-(으)려고 expresses the intention or plan of the speaker. Specifically, it indicates the speaker will do what is stated in the second clause to accomplish what is stated in the first clause. It corresponds to '(in order) to' or 'so that' in English. When the verb stem ends in a vowel or ㄹ, then **-려고** is used, and when it ends in a consonant, **-으려고** is used.

Stem Ending in Vowel or ㄹ	Stem Ending in Consonant
보다 + **-려고** → 보려고	먹다 + **-으려고** → 먹으려고

Base Form	-려고	Base Form	-으려고
가다	가려고	찍다	찍으려고
만나다	만나려고	읽다	읽으려고
이야기하다	이야기하려고	찾다	찾으려고
*놀다	놀려고	*듣다	들으려고
*벌다	벌려고	*짓다	지으려고

* Irregular form

In Conversation

Track 156

A 정아 씨, 요즘 학원에 다녀요?
B 네, 컴퓨터를 배우려고 학원에 다니고 있어요.

A Jeonga, do you attend an academy these days?
B Yes, I go to an academy to learn how to use computers.

A 아까 만났는데 왜 또 전화했어요?
B 당신 목소리를 들으려고 전화했어요.

A We just met a little while ago, so why are you calling again?
B I called so that I could hear your voice.

A 자려고 누웠는데 잠이 안 와요.
B 그러면 따뜻한 우유를 한 잔 마셔 보세요.

A Even though I've lain down in bed, I can't go to sleep.
B In that case, try drinking a glass of warm milk.

What's the Difference?

–(으)러

❶ Used with movement verbs, such as 가다, 오다, 다니다, 올라가다, and 나가다.
- 친구를 만나러 커피숍에서 친구를 기다려요. (×)
- 친구를 만나러 커피숍에 가요. (○)
  (I) go to the coffee shop to meet my friend.

❷ Present, past, and future tense verbs can all follow –(으)러.
- 친구를 만나러 커피숍에 가요. (○)
  (I) go to the coffee shop to meet my friend.
- 친구를 만나러 커피숍에 갔어요. (○)
  (I) went to the coffee shop to meet my friend.
- 친구를 만나러 커피숍에 갈 거예요. (○)
  (I) will go to the coffee shop to meet my friend.

❸ –(으)ㅂ시다 and –(으)세요 can be used in combination with this expression.
- 밥을 먹으러 식당에 갑시다. (○)
  Let's go to the restaurant to have a meal.
- 밥을 먹으러 식당에 가세요. (○)
  Please go to the restaurant to have a meal.

–(으)려고

❶ Can be used with all verbs.
- 친구를 만나려고 커피숍에 가요. (○)
  (I) go to the coffee shop to meet my friend.
- 친구를 만나려고 커피숍에서 친구를 기다려요. (○)
  (I) am waiting at the coffee shop to meet my friend.

❷ Present and past tense verbs can follow –(으)려고, but the meaning becomes awkward when used with a verb in the future tense.
- 친구를 만나려고 커피숍에 가요. (○)
  (I) go to the coffee shop to meet my friend.
- 친구를 만나려고 커피숍에 갔어요. (○)
  (I) went to the coffee shop to meet my friend.
- 친구를 만나려고 커피숍에 갈 거예요. (×)

❸ –(으)ㅂ시다 and –(으)세요 sound awkward when used with this expression.
- 밥을 먹으려고 식당에 갑시다. (×)
- 밥을 먹으려고 식당에 가세요. (×)

Why are the following people studying Korean? Write the answers in the blanks as shown in the example.

보기 한국 대학교에 입학하려고 한국말을 배워요.

(1) ______________________ 한국말을 배워요.

(2) ______________________ 한국말을 배워요.

(3) ______________________ 한국말을 배워요.

(4) ______________________ 한국말을 배워요.

(5) ______________________ 한국말을 배워요.

03 V-(으)려고 하다

Track 157

여름휴가 때 여행을 **하려고 해요**.

I plan to travel during the summer vacation.

결혼하면 아이를 두 명 **낳으려고 해요**.

I intend to have two children once I'm married.

방학 동안 운전을 **배우려고 했어요**.
그런데 팔을 다쳐서 못 배웠어요.

I had planned on learning how to drive during the vacation.
But I injured my arm and wasn't able to.

Grammar Focus

-(으)려고 하다 expresses the subject's intention or plan that has yet to be acted upon. It means 'plan to' or 'intend to' in English. When the verb stem ends in a vowel or ㄹ, **-려고 하다** is used, and when the stem ends in a consonant, **-으려고 하다** is used. Moreover, while **-(으)려고 했다** is the past tense form of **-(으)려고 하다**, it is only used when the intended action or plan did not materialize as expected.

Stem Ending in Vowel or ㄹ	Stem Ending in Consonant
가다 + **-려고 하다** → 가려고 하다	먹다 + **-으려고 하다** → 먹으려고 하다

Base Form	-려고 해요	Base Form	-으려고 해요
보다	보려고 해요	받다	받으려고 해요
사다	사려고 해요	씻다	씻으려고 해요
만나다	만나려고 해요	*듣다	들으려고 해요
취직하다	취직하려고 해요	*묻다	물으려고 해요
*놀다	놀려고 해요	*돕다	도우려고 해요

* Irregular form

In Conversation

Track 158

A 보너스를 받으면 뭐 할 거예요?
B 새 차를 사려고 해요.

A What will you do once you get your bonus?
B I plan to buy a new car.

A 대학교를 졸업하면 무엇을 할 거예요?
B 대학원에서 공부를 더 하려고 해요.
A 저는 회사에 취직하려고 해요.

A What do you plan to do after you graduate?
B I intend to continue my studies at graduate school.
A I plan on getting a job at a company.

On Your Own

Carol plans to travel during her vacation. Look at the contents of Carol's suitcase and write what you think she intends to do during her trip as shown in the example.

보기 호주에 가려고 해요.

(1) 어머니께 엽서를 ______________________.

(2) 비행기 안에서 한국어를 ______________________.

(3) 비행기 안에서 음악을 ______________________.

(4) 호주에 있는 친구에게 선물을 ______________________.

(5) 호주에서 골프를 ______________________.

(6) 호주에서 사진을 ______________________.

(7) 바다에서 수영을 ______________________.

 N을/를 위해(서), V-기 위해(서)

건강**을 위해서** 매일 비타민을 먹고 있습니다.

I take vitamins daily for my health.

군인은 나라**를 위해서** 일하는 사람입니다.

Soldiers are people who work for their country.

훌륭한 스케이트 선수가 **되기 위해** 열심히 연습을 합니다.

I practice hard to become a great skater.

Grammar Focus

This pattern is used when performing an action for the sake of something or to accomplish something. Specifically, it indicates the speaker will do what is stated in the second clause for the sake of what is stated in the first clause. In the case of a noun being the reason for the action, **을/를 위해서** is used. **위해서** is the shortened form of **위하여서**. Further, **서** can also be omitted, leaving **위해**. It corresponds to 'for the sake of' or '(in order) to' in English. When used with a verb, **-기 위해서** is added to the verb stem.

Noun + 을/를 위해서		Verb Stem + -기 위해서
Word Ending in Vowel	Word Ending in Consonant	
나라 + **를 위해서** → 나라를 위해서	가족 + **을 위해서** → 가족을 위해서	가다 + **-기 위해서** → 가기 위해서

N 을/를 위해서	Base Form	V-기 위해서
나라를 위해서	보다	보기 위해서
회사를 위해서	만나다	만나기 위해서

친구를 위해서	받다	받기 위해서
사랑을 위해서	입학하다	입학하기 위해서
남편을 위해서	벌다	벌기 위해서
건강을 위해서	듣다	듣기 위해서
가족을 위해서	돕다	돕기 위해서

–기 위해서 cannot be added directly to adjectives. However, if **–아/어지다** has been added to an adjective, making it a verb, then it can be used with **–기 위해서**.

- 건강하기 위해서 운동을 합니다. (×)
  → 건강해지기 위해서 운동을 합니다. (○)
  (I) exercise to be healthy.

In Conversation

Track 160

A 잘 부탁드립니다. 신입사원 이민우입니다.
B 반갑습니다. 회사를 위해서 열심히 일해 주십시오.

A It's nice to meet you. I'm new recruit Lee Minu.
B Pleased to meet you. I trust you'll work hard for the company.

A 가족을 위해서 무엇을 하세요?
B 저는 가족을 위해서 매일 기도하고 있어요.

A What do you do for your family?
B I pray for my family every day.

A 아파트 산 것을 축하합니다.
B 감사합니다. 이 집을 사기 위해서 우리 부부가 열심히 돈을 모았어요.

A Congratulations on buying an apartment.
B Thank you. We both worked hard to save money to buy this home.

What's the Difference?

–(으)려고

Cannot be used with –아/어야 해요, –(으)ㅂ시다, –(으)세요, or –(으)ㄹ까요?

- 대학교에 입학하려고 열심히 공부했어요. (○)
  (I) studied hard to enter the university.
- 대학교에 입학하려고 열심히 공부해야 해요. (×)
- 대학교에 입학하려고 열심히 공부합시다. (×)
- 대학교에 입학하려고 열심히 공부하세요. (×)

–기 위해서

Can be used with –아/어야 해요, –(으)ㅂ시다, –(으)세요, and –(으)ㄹ까요?

- 대학교에 입학하기 위해서 열심히 공부했어요. (○)
  (I) studied hard to enter the university.
- 대학교에 입학하기 위해서 열심히 공부해야 해요. (○)
  (I) have to study hard to enter the university.
- 대학교에 입학하기 위해서 열심히 공부합시다. (○)
  Let's study hard to enter the university.
- 대학교에 입학하기 위해서 열심히 공부하세요. (○)
  (You) study hard to enter the university.

Look at the pictures and choose the appropriate word from below to fill in each blank using either 을/를 위해(서) or –기 위해(서).

건강	당신	만나다	취직하다

(1)

A 매일 아침에 조깅을 해요?

B 네, 저는 ________________ 매일 아침에 조깅을 해요.

(2)

A 와, 맛있겠어요. 무슨 날이에요?

B 오늘이 당신 생일이라서 ________________ 내가 만들었어요.

(3)

A 왜 한국말을 배워요?

B 한국 회사에 ________________ 한국말을 배워요.

(4)

A 왜 한국에 왔어요?

B 한국 친구를 ________________ 왔어요.

05 V-기로 하다

Track 161

건강 때문에 올해부터 담배를 **끊기로 했어요.**

I made the decision to stop smoking for my health starting this year.

주말에 친구하고 같이 **등산하기로 했어요.**

I decided to go hiking with my friend over the weekend.

우리는 3년 후에 **결혼하기로 했습니다.**

We've decided to get married three years from now.

Grammar Focus

1 **-기로 하다** expresses the making of a promise with another person and is made by adding **-기로 했다** to the verb stem.

A 정아 씨, 사랑해요. 우리 내년에 결혼합시다.
Jeonga, I love you. Let's get married next year.

B 좋아요. 내년에 결혼해요. Okay. Let's get married next year.
→ 정아 씨와 나는 서로 사랑하고 있어요. 우리는 내년에 결혼하**기로 했어요.**
Jeonga and I love each other. We decided to get married next year.

2 **-기로 하다** can also express the making of a promise with oneself. That is, it can express a decision or resolution to do something. It is made by adding **-기로 했다** to the verb stem.

- 나는 올해부터 매일 운동하**기로 했어요.**
  I resolved to exercise every day starting this year.

가다 + **-기로 했다** → 가기로 했어요　　먹다 + **-기로 했다** → 먹기로 했어요

Base Form	-기로 했어요	Base Form	-기로 했어요
만나다	만나기로 했어요	입다	입기로 했어요
공부하다	공부하기로 했어요	찍다	찍기로 했어요
놀다	놀기로 했어요	듣다	듣기로 했어요
살다	살기로 했어요	돕다	돕기로 했어요

In Conversation

Track 162

A 재준 씨, 오늘 왜 이렇게 기분이 좋아요?
B 이번 주말에 캐럴 씨와 데이트하기로 했어요.

A Jaejun, why are you in such a good mood today?
B Carol and I have decided to go on a date this weekend.

A 내일 등산 갈 때 누가 카메라를 가져와요?
B 부디 씨가 가져오기로 했어요.

A Who will bring the camera tomorrow when we go hiking?
B Budi decided to bring one.

A 새해에 무슨 계획이 있어요?
B 새해에는 자기 전에 꼭 일기를 쓰기로 했어요.

A What plans do you have for the new year?
B I've decided to write in my journal every day before going to sleep.

Check It Out!

While -기로 하다 is mainly used in its past tense forms of -기로 했어요/했습니다, it is sometimes used in its present tense form of -기로 해요. In such cases, it refers to the speaker and listener making a promise to do something.

A 내일 뭐 할까요?　　What shall we do tomorrow?
B 등산하기로 해요. (= 등산하기로 합시다.) Let's (decide to) go hiking.

What have the following people resolved to do in the new year? Look at the pictures and choose the appropriate word from below to fill in each blank using -기로 하다.

공부하다	끊다	배우다	사다	하지 않다

(1) 이민우 씨는 새해에 차를 ______________________.

(2) 부디 씨는 술을 ______________________.

(3) 캐럴 씨는 태권도를 ______________________.

(4) 왕징 씨는 열심히 ______________________.

(5) 티루엔 씨는 컴퓨터게임을 ______________________.

Unit 16.

Conditions and Suppositions

01 A/V-(으)면
02 V-(으)려면
03 A/V-아/어도

01 A/V-(으)면

Track 163

컴퓨터를 많이 **하면** 눈이 아파요.

If you spend too much time on the computer, you'll hurt your eyes.

나는 기분이 **좋으면** 춤을 춰요.

I dance when I'm in a good mood.

돈을 많이 **벌면** 집을 살 거예요.

If I make a lot of money, I'm going to buy a house.

Grammar Focus

-(으)면 is used when stating a condition about some fact, daily occurrence, or some repetitive action mentioned later in the sentence, or when supposing an uncertain situation or a situation that has not yet been realized. It means 'if', 'when', or 'once' in English. When expressing a supposition, adverbs such as **혹시** and **만일** can also be used. When the verb stem ends in a vowel or ㄹ, **-면** is used, and when it ends in a consonant, **-으면** is used.

Stem Ending in Vowel or ㄹ	Stem Ending in Consonant
가다 + **-면** → 가면	먹다 + **-으면** → 먹으면

Base Form	-면	Base Form	-으면
바쁘다	바쁘면	받다	받으면
만나다	만나면	있다	있으면
졸업하다	졸업하면	*듣다	들으면
*살다	살면	*덥다	더우면
*만들다	만들면	*낫다	나으면

* Irregular form

Information about something that happened in the past cannot come before **–(으)면** in a sentence. Furthermore, when an action only occurs once, **–(으)ㄹ 때** is used.

- 어제 영화를 보면 울었어요. (×)
  → 어제 영화를 볼 때 울었어요. (○)
  Yesterday, when I watched a movie, I cried.
- 동생이 집에 없으면 친구가 왔어요. (×)
  → 동생이 집에 없을 때 친구가 왔어요. (○)
  Yesterday, my friend came by when my younger brother/sister was not at home.

In Conversation

Track **164**

A 주말에 보통 뭐 해요?
B 날씨가 좋으면 등산을 해요. 그렇지만 비나 눈이 오면 집에서 텔레비전을 봐요.

A What do you normally do on the weekend?
B If the weather's nice, I go hiking. But if it rains or snows, then I watch TV at home.

A 다음 주에 고향에 돌아가요.
B 그래요? 섭섭해요. 고향에 돌아가면 연락하세요.

A I'm going back to my hometown next week.
B Really? That's too bad. Please stay in touch when you're back home.

A 결혼하면 어디에서 살 거예요?
B 회사 근처 아파트에서 살려고 해요.

A Where will you live once you get married?
B We plan to live in an apartment near the company.

Check It Out!

When the subjects of the first and second clauses are different, the particle following the subject of the first clause changes from 은/는 to 이/가.

- 동생**은** 이야기하면 친구들이 웃어요. (×) →동생**이** 이야기하면 친구들이 웃어요. (○)
  When my brother tells a story, his friends laugh.
- 티루엔 씨**는** 회사에 안 오면 사무실이 조용해요. (×)
  → 티루엔 씨**가** 회사에 안 오면 사무실이 조용해요. (○) When Tiruen does not come to work, the office is quiet.

On Your Own

Connect the pictures that go together, and then select the words from below to fill in the blanks using –(으)면.

가다	먹다	오지 않다	출발하다

(1)  • • ⓐ 

(2)  • • ⓑ 

(3)  • • ⓒ 

(4)  • • ⓓ 

(1) 아이스크림을 많이 __________ 살이 쪄요.

(2) 지금 __________ 3시에 도착할 수 있어요.

(3) 밤에 잠이 __________ 텔레비전을 봐요.

(4) 동대문시장에 __________ 옷이 싸요.

02 V-(으)려면

Track 165

농구를 **잘하려면** 점프를 잘해야 돼요.

If you want to play basketball well, you have to be able to jump high.

동대문에 **가려면** 지하철 4호선을 타세요.

If you're trying to get to Dongdaemun, then please take subway line 4.

이 선생님을 **만나려면** 월요일에 학교로 가세요.

If you want to meet with Ms. Lee then come to school on Monday.

Grammar Focus

-(으)려면 is the shortened form of **-(으)려고 하면**. It is used with verbs to express a plan or intention to do something in the first clause, with the condition required to fulfill that plan or intention given in the second clause. For this reason, it is common for the following grammatical forms to be used in the second clause: **-아/어야 해요/돼요**, **-(으)면 돼요**, **-(으)세요**, **이/가 필요해요**, and **-는 게 좋아요**. This expression means 'if you want to' or 'if your intention is to' in English. When the verb stem ends in a vowel or ㄹ, **-려면** is used, and when it ends in a consonant, **-으려면** is used.

Stem Ending in Vowel or ㄹ	Stem Ending in Consonant
가다 + **-려면** → 가려면	먹다 + **-으려면** → 먹으려면

Base Form	-려면	Base Form	-으려면
만나다	만나려면	받다	받으려면
취직하다	취직하려면	끊다	끊으려면
부르다	부르려면	*듣다	들으려면
*살다	살려면	*돕다	도우려면

* Irregular form

In Conversation

Track 166

A 한국말을 잘하고 싶어요.
B 한국말을 잘하려면 매일 한국말로만 이야기하세요.

A I want to be able to speak Korean well.
B If you want to speak Korean well, then only speak Korean every day.

A 펜을 자주 잃어버려요.
B 잃어버리지 않으려면 펜에 이름을 쓰세요.

A I often lose my pen.
B If you don't want to lose your pen, then write your name on it.

A 사장님, 이 회사에서 일하고 싶습니다.
B 우리 회사에서 일하려면 한국말도 잘하고 컴퓨터도 잘해야 합니다.

A Mr. President, I want to work at your company.
B If you intend to work at our company, you have to be able to speak Korean and use computers well.

On Your Own

Look at the pictures and connect them with the appropriate sentences.

(1)  • • ⓐ 이 문을 열려면 비밀번호를 알아야 해요.

(2)  • • ⓑ 감기에 걸리지 않으려면 코트를 입으세요.

(3)  • • ⓒ 공주와 결혼하려면 금사과를 가져와야 해요.

(4)  • • ⓓ 식사하시려면 예약을 하셔야 합니다.

03 A/V-아/어도

Track 167

크게 **말해도** 할머니가 못 들어요.

Grandma can't hear you even if you speak loudly.

이 옷이 마음에 들어요. **비싸도** 사고 싶어요.

I like these clothes. I want to buy them even if they are expensive.

뉴스를 **들어도** 이해하지 못해요.

Even if I listen to the news, I can't understand it.

Grammar Focus

-아/어도 indicates that the situation in the second clause occurs regardless of the action or state described in the first clause. It means 'even if' or 'regardless whether' in English. When the verb stem ends in ㅏ or ㅗ, **-아도** is used, and when the verb stem ends in any other vowel, **-어도** is used. For verbs that end in **하다**, the form changes to **해도**.

Stem Ending in ㅏ or ㅗ	Stem Ending in Vowel Other than ㅏ or ㅗ	Verb Ending in 하다
가다 + **-아도** → 가도	먹다 + **-어도** → 먹어도	피곤하다 → 피곤해도

Base Form	-아/어도	Base Form	-아/어도
보다	봐도	켜다	켜도
찾다	찾아도	씻다	씻어도
닦다	닦아도	*듣다	들어도
공부하다	공부해도	*맵다	매워도
*바쁘다	바빠도	*부르다	불러도

* Irregular form

In Conversation

Track 168

A 3시까지 명동에 가야 해요. 택시를 탑시다.

B 지금 2시 50분이에요. 택시를 타도 3시까지 못 가요.

A 요즘 바빠서 아침을 못 먹어요.

B 바빠도 아침 식사를 꼭 해야 해요. 아침 식사를 안 하면 건강에 안 좋아요.

A We have to be in Myeongdong by 3:00. Let's take a taxi.

B It's 2:50 right now. We won't make it by 3:00 even if we take a taxi.

A I'm so busy these days I don't have time to eat breakfast.

B You have to eat breakfast even if you're busy. It's unhealthy not to eat breakfast.

Check It Out!

The meaning of –아/어 can be emphasized by using 아무리 in front of the verb, giving the expression the meaning of 'no matter how (much)'.

- 나는 바빠도 아침을 꼭 먹어요. → 나는 아무리 바빠도 아침을 꼭 먹어요.
  Even if I'm busy I eat breakfast. → No matter how busy I am, I always eat breakfast.
- 그 옷이 비싸도 살 거예요. → 그 옷이 아무리 비싸도 꼭 살 거예요.
  I'll buy those clothes even if they're expensive. → No matter how expensive those clothes are, I will buy them.

On Your Own

Look at the pictures and choose the appropriate word from below to fill in each blank using –아/어도.

먹다	반대하다	보내다

(1) 

A 감기 다 나았어요?
B 아니요, 약을 ________ 안 나아요.

(2) 

A 두 사람이 정말 결혼할 거예요?
B 네, 부모님이 ____________ 꼭 결혼할 거예요.

(3) 

A 친구하고 자주 연락해요?
B 아니요, 문자를 _________ 친구가 답장을 안 해요.

Unit 17.

Conjecture

01 A/V-겠어요 ②

02 A/V-(으)ㄹ 거예요 ②

03 A/V-(으)ㄹ까요? ③

04 A/V-(으)ㄴ/는/(으)ㄹ 것 같다

01 A/V-겠어요 ②

Track 169

와, 맛있겠어요.

Wow, that looks delicious.

저 포스터를 보세요. 재미있겠어요!

Look at that poster. It looks interesting!

시원하겠어요.

That looks refreshing.

Grammar Focus

-겠어요 is an expression of supposition about a certain situation or state corresponding to 'looks like', 'sounds', or 'appears' in English. It is formed by adding **-겠어요** to the stems of verbs and adjectives. In the case of past tense supposition, **-았/었-** is added in front of **-겠어요** to form **-았/었겠어요**.

오다 + **-겠어요** → 오겠어요　　　덥다 + **-겠어요** → 덥겠어요

Base Form	-겠어요	Base Form	-겠어요
보다	보겠어요	좋다	좋겠어요
되다	되겠어요	예쁘다	예쁘겠어요
받다	받겠어요	재미있다	재미있겠어요
찾다	찾겠어요	시원하다	시원하겠어요
일하다	일하겠어요	편하다	편하겠어요

(Compare with Unit 13. Intentions and Plans 01 A/V-겠어요 ①)

In Conversation

Track 170

A 이번 주에 제주도로 여행 갈 거예요.
B 와, 좋겠어요. 저도 가고 싶어요.

A I'm planning to take a trip to Jeju Island this week.
B Wow, that sounds nice. I want to go, too.

A 요즘 퇴근하고 매일 영어를 배워요.
B 매일이요? 힘들겠어요.

A These days, I study English every day after getting off work.
B Every day? That sounds tough.

A 이게 요즘 제가 배우는 한국어책이에요.
B 어렵겠어요.

A This is the book I've been using to study Korean lately.
B It looks difficult.

On Your Own

Choose the appropriate word from below to fill in each blank using -겠어요.

기분이 좋다	바쁘다	일본 요리를 잘하다
배가 고프다	피곤하다	한국말을 잘하다

(1) A 어제 일이 많아서 잠을 못 잤어요.
B 그래요? ______________.

(2) A 저는 한국에서 5년 살았어요.
B 그럼 ______________________.

(3) A 어제 집에 손님들이 오셔서 음식을 많이 만들었어요.
B 어제 많이 ______________.

(4) A 이번 시험에서 1등을 했어요.
B ______________________.

(5) A 저는 학원에서 1년 동안 일본 요리를 배웠어요.
B 그래요? 그럼 ______________.

(6) A 오늘 하루 종일 밥을 못 먹었어요.
B ______________________.

02 A/V-(으)ㄹ 거예요 ②

Track 171

그 옷을 입으면 **더울 거예요.**

You'll be hot if you wear that.

하영 씨에게는 보라색 티셔츠가 잘 **어울릴 거예요.**

I think Hayeong will look good in a violet T-shirt.

7시니까 댄 씨는 벌써 **퇴근했을 거예요.**

I think Dane has already left work because it's 7:00.

Grammar Focus

-(으)ㄹ 거예요 expresses the speaker's supposition based on a personal experience or something seen or heard that provides a basis for the belief. It corresponds to 'think' or 'will' in English. When the verb or adjective stem ends in a vowel or ㄹ, **-ㄹ 거예요** is used, and when the stem ends in a consonant, **-을 거예요** is used. In the case of past tense supposition, **-았/었-** is added in front of **-(으)ㄹ 거예요** to form **-았/었을 거예요**.

Stem Ending in Vowel or ㄹ	Stem Ending in Consonant
사다 + **-ㄹ 거예요** → 살 거예요	먹다 + **-을 거예요** → 먹을 거예요

Base Form	-ㄹ 거예요	Base Form	-을 거예요
바쁘다	바쁠 거예요	입다	입을 거예요
시원하다	시원할 거예요	많다	많을 거예요
*만들다	만들 거예요	*가깝다	가까울 거예요
*길다	길 거예요	*덥다	더울 거예요

* Irregular form

When used to indicate supposition, **–을 거예요** cannot be used in questions. For questions, **–(으)ㄹ까요?** is used.

A 내가 이 옷을 입으면 멋있을까요? [이 옷을 입으면 멋있을 거예요? (×)]
Do you think these clothes will look good on me?

B 네, 멋있을 거예요.
Yes, I think you'll look nice in them.

(Compare with Unit 1. Tenses 04 V–(으)ㄹ 거예요 ①)

In Conversation

Track 172

A 여기에서 학교까지 버스가 있어요?
B 네, 그렇지만 자주 안 와서 지하철이 더 편할 거예요.

A Is there a bus that goes from here to school?
B Yes, there is, but it doesn't come very often, so the subway may be more convenient.

A 댄 씨에게 음악 CD를 주면 좋아할까요?
B 매일 음악을 들으면서 다니니까 좋아할 거예요.

A Do you think Dane would like it if I gave him a music CD?
B He listens to music every day on the way to school, so I think he'd like it.

A 요코 씨가 결혼했어요?
B 왼손에 반지를 끼었으니까 결혼했을 거예요.

A Is Yoko married?
B She has a ring on her left hand, so I think she's married.

On Your Own

Choose the appropriate word from below to fill in each blank using -(으)ㄹ 거예요.

가다	걸리다	문을 닫다	바쁘다
예쁘다	오다	알다	자다

(1) A 민우 씨가 오늘 파티에 와요?
B 출장 준비를 해야 하니까 아마 못 ________________.

(2) A 햄버거를 먹고 싶어요. 햄버거 가게가 문을 열었을까요?
B 지금 밤 11시니까 ______________________.

(3) A 미국에 가려고 하는데 어디가 좋아요?
B 댄 씨 고향이 미국이니까 잘 ______________. 댄 씨에게 물어보세요.

(4) A 티루엔 씨가 왜 회의에 안 왔어요?
B 몸이 안 좋아서 일찍 집에 ________________.

(5) A 어제 캐럴 씨가 전화를 안 받았어요.
B 어제 일이 많아서 ________________.

(6) A 부디 씨가 아침부터 계속 졸고 있어요.
B 어젯밤에 파티를 해서 못 ________________.

(7) A 거기까지 시간이 많이 걸릴까요?
B 지금 퇴근 시간이니까 시간이 좀 ________________.

(8) A 내일 돌잔치에 무슨 옷을 입고 갈까요?
B 한복을 입으면 ________________.

03 A/V-(으)ㄹ까요? ③

Track 173

주말에 날씨가 **더울까요?**

Do you think the weather will be hot this weekend?

캐럴 씨가 오늘 **나올까요?**

Will Carol show up today?

댄 씨가 이 책을 **읽었을까요?**

Do you think Dane has read this book?

Grammar Focus

-(으)ㄹ까요? expresses in question form the supposition of an action or state that has yet to happen. It corresponds to 'I wonder if...' or 'Do you think...?' in English. In response, **-(으)ㄹ 거예요** and **-(으)ㄴ/는 것 같아요** are often used. When the verb or adjective stem ends in a vowel or ㄹ, **-ㄹ까요?** is used, and when the stem ends in a consonant, **-을까요?** is used. In the case of a past tense supposition, **-았/었-** is added in front of **-(으)ㄹ까요?** to form **-았/었을까요?**.

Stem Ending in Vowel	Stem Ending in Consonant
가다 + **-ㄹ까요?** → 갈까요?	먹다 + **-을까요?** → 먹을까요?

Base Form	-ㄹ까요?	Base Form	-을까요?
예쁘다	예쁠까요?	괜찮다	괜찮을까요?
친절하다	친절할까요?	*듣다	들을까요?
*살다	살까요?	*춥다	추울까요?

* Irregular form

(Compare with Unit 12. Asking Opinions and Making Suggestions 01 V-(으)ㄹ까요? ①, 02 V-(으)ㄹ까요? ②)

In Conversation

Track 174

A 요즘 꽃이 비쌀까요?

B 졸업식 때니까 비쌀 거예요.

A Do you think flowers are expensive these days?

B It's graduation time, so I think they're probably expensive.

A 이번에 누가 승진을 할까요?

B 댄 씨가 일을 잘하니까 이번에 승진할 거예요.

A Who do you think will get promoted this time?

B Dane is a hard worker, so I think he'll be promoted this time.

A 지금 가면 길이 막힐까요?

B 아니요, 이 시간에는 길이 안 막혀요.

A Do you think there will be much traffic if we go now?

B No. There's not much traffic this time of day.

On Your Own

Choose the appropriate word from below to fill in each blank using -(으)ㄹ까요?.

도착하다	돈이 많다	돌아오다	막히다	바쁘다

(1) A 웨슬리 씨가 ______________?

B 네, 아버지가 부자니까 웨슬리 씨도 돈이 많을 거예요.

(2) A 버스를 타면 __________?

B 지금 퇴근 시간이니까 지금 버스를 타면 막힐 거예요.

(3) A 나탈리아 씨가 집에 ______________?

B 1시간 전에 출발했으니까 지금쯤 도착했을 거예요.

(4) A 김 과장님이 ___________?

B 요즘 연말이라서 바쁘실 거예요.

(5) A 선생님이 몇 시쯤 ___________?

B 2시쯤 돌아오실 거예요.

04 A/V-(으)ㄴ/는/(으)ㄹ 것 같다

Track 175

어제 비가 **온 것 같아요**.

(It) looks like it rained yesterday.

지금 비가 **오는 것 같아요**.

(It) looks like it's raining right now.

비가 **올 것 같아요**.

(It) looks like it's going to rain.

Grammar Focus

1 This expression is used when supposing that something happened in the past or when supposing the occurrence of an action or situation that has yet to occur. It corresponds to 'looks/sounds like' or 'appears that' in English. For present tense adjectives and past tense verbs, -(으)ㄴ is added to the stem, for present tense verbs, -는 is added, and for future tense verbs, -(으)ㄹ is added.

A 댄 씨, 오늘 기분이 좋은 것 같아요. 무슨 좋은 일 있어요?
Dane, you look like you're in a good mood today. Did something good happen?

B 네, 어제 아내가 딸을 낳았어요.
Yes, yesterday my wife had our daughter.

2 It is also used to express the speaker's opinion or thought about something indirectly in a polite, nonassertive, and gentle manner.

A 음식 맛이 어때요? How does the food taste?

B 좀 짠 것 같아요. It seems a little salty.

Present Tense Adjectives		Past Tense Verbs		Present Tense Verbs	Future Tense Verbs	
No Final Consonant	Final Consonant	No Final Consonant	Final Consonant		No Final Consonant	Final Consonant
-ㄴ 것 같다	-은 것 같다	-ㄴ 것 같다	-은 것 같다	-는 것 같다	-ㄹ 것 같다	-을 것 같다
바쁜 것 같다	많은 것 같다	간 것 같다	먹은 것 같다	가는 것 같다 먹는 것 같다	갈 것 같다	먹을 것 같다

	Base Form	Past Tense	Present Tense	Future Tense
Adjectives	예쁘다	–	예쁜 것 같다	예쁠 것 같다
	작다	–	작은 것 같다	작을 것 같다
	친절하다	–	친절한 것 같다	친절할 것 같다
	*춥다	–	추운 것 같다	추울 것 같다
Verbs	가다	간 것 같다	가는 것 같다	갈 것 같다
	찾다	찾은 것 같다	찾는 것 같다	찾을 것 같다
	결혼하다	결혼한 것 같다	결혼하는 것 같다	결혼할 것 같다
	*만들다	만든 것 같다	만드는 것 같다	만들 것 같다
	*듣다	들은 것 같다	듣는 것 같다	들을 것 같다
이다	학생이다	–	학생인 것 같다	학생일 것 같다

* Irregular form
(※The past tense forms of adjectives are introduced at the advanced level.)

In Conversation

Track 176

A 일주일이 빨리 가는 것 같아요.
B 정말 그래요. 벌써 금요일이에요.

A It seems like the week is just flying by.
B You're so right. It's already Friday.

A 그 식당 주인이 친절한 것 같아요.
B 네, 항상 밥도 많이 주고 서비스도 좋아요.

A That restaurant owner seems nice.
B Yeah, she always gives us lots of rice, and the service is good, too.

A 더 드세요.
B 죄송해요. 배가 불러서 더 못 먹을 거 같아요.

A Please have some more to eat.
B I'm sorry. I'm quite full and don't think I'll be able to eat any more.

Check It Out!

–(으)ㄴ 것 같다 is a more direct expression and thus is used when the speaker has a clear and definite basis for the supposition. –(으)ㄹ 것 같다, on the other hand, is more indirect and therefore is used when making a vague supposition.

- 오늘 날씨가 더운 것 같아요. It looks like the weather today is warm.
  (Supposition made after either seeing others experience the hot weather or after experiencing the heat directly.)
- 오늘 날씨가 더울 것 같아요. I guess the weather today will be warm.
  (Vague supposition made on the basis that yesterday was hot, so therefore today will likely be hot as well.)

What's the Difference?

–겠어요

Intuitive, instantaneous supposition made with no reason or basis.

A 이 식당의 음식이 맛있을까요?
Do you think this restaurant has good food?

B 맛있겠어요. (X)

A 제가 만들었어요. 맛있게 드세요.
I made it. Please give it a try.

B (맛있어 보이는 음식을 보는 순간) 와, 정말 맛있겠어요.
(At the same moment B sees the food) Wow, it really looks tasty.

–(으)ㄹ 거예요

Supposition based on information known only by the speaker.

A 이 식당의 음식이 맛있을까요?
Do you think this restaurant has good food?

B 이 식당은 손님이 많으니까 음식이 맛있을 거예요.
I imagine it's good because there are a lot of customers.

–(으)ㄴ/는/(으)ㄹ 것 같다

Supposition based on intuitive, subjective reasons that can be used in all cases, regardless of whether there is a reason or basis.

A 이 식당의 음식이 맛있을까요?
Do you think this restaurant has good food?

B ① (잘 모르겠지만 제 생각에는) 맛있을 것 같아요.
(I'm not sure, but in my view) It looks good.

B ② 사람이 많은 것을 보니까 맛있을 것 같아요.
Seeing how there are many customers, it seems to be good.

Used to state something indirectly in a non-assertive manner.

A 다음 주 제 생일 파티에 올 수 있어요?
Can you come to my birthday party next week?

B 가고 싶지만 다음 주에 출장이 있어서 못 갈 것 같아요. 죄송해요.
I want to go, but I don't think I can make it because I have a business trip next week. I'm sorry.

Look at the pictures and choose the appropriate word from below to fill in each blank using -(으)ㄴ/는/(으)ㄹ 것 같다.

맑다	가족이다	먹다	하다

(1) A 세 사람은 어떤 관계일까요?
B ____________________.

(2) A 고양이는 목욕을 했을까요?
B ____________________.

(3) A 오늘 날씨가 어떤 것 같아요?
B ____________________.

(4) A 강아지는 목욕이 끝난 후에 무엇을 할까요?
B ____________________.

Unit 18.

Changes in Parts of Speech

01 관형형 –(으)ㄴ/–는/–(으)ㄹ N
02 A/V–기
03 A–게
04 A–아/어하다

01 관형형 –(으)ㄴ/–는/–(으)ㄹ N

가방이 예뻐요. 그 가방을 사고 싶어요.

Track 177

That purse is pretty. I want to buy that purse.

→ **예쁜** 가방을 사고 싶어요.

I want to buy a pretty purse.

소파에서 사람이 자요. 그 사람이 누구예요?

There's someone sleeping on the sofa. Who is that person?

→ 소파에서 **자는** 사람이 누구예요?

Who is that person (who is) sleeping on the sofa?

오늘 저녁에 한국 음식을 먹을 거예요.
그 음식이 뭐예요?

We'll have a Korean dish for dinner today. What's the dish?

→ 오늘 저녁에 **먹을** 한국 음식이 뭐예요?

What's the Korean dish (that) we'll have for dinner today?

Grammar Focus

This pattern is added to verbs and adjectives to allow them to function as noun modifiers. The English equivalent is 'that' or 'who'. For present tense adjectives and past tense verbs, **–(으)ㄴ** is added to the stem, for present tense verbs, **–는** is added, and for future tense verbs, **–(으)ㄹ** is added. The negative forms are made by adding **–지 않은** to the stem for adjectives and past tense verbs, and **–지 않는** to the stem for verbs.

Present Tense Adjectives		Past Tense Verbs		Present Tense Verbs, 있다/없다	Future Tense Verbs	
No Final Consonant	Final Consonant	No Final Consonant	Final Consonant		No Final Consonant	Final Consonant
–ㄴ N	–은 N	–ㄴ N	–은 N	–는 N	–ㄹ N	–을 N
예쁜 날씬한	높은 낮은	간 본	읽은 먹은	가는 읽는 있는 없는	갈 볼	읽을 먹을

Base Form	Past	Present	Future
넓다	–	넓은 방	–
친절하다	–	친절한 사람	–
읽다	읽은 책	읽는 책	읽을 책
먹다	먹은 빵	먹는 빵	먹을 빵
공부하다	공부한 사람	공부하는 사람	공부할 사람
*만들다	만든 요리	만드는 요리	만들 요리
*듣다	들은 음악	듣는 음악	들을 음악

* Irregular form
(※ The past tense forms of adjectives are introduced at the advanced level.)

In Conversation

Track 178

A 어떤 영화를 좋아해요?
B 재미있는 영화를 좋아해요.

A What kind of movies do you like?
B I like funny movies.

A 지금 커피를 마시는 사람이 누구예요?
B 제 친구예요.

A Who is the person (who is) drinking coffee?
B My friend.

A 어제 간 식당이 어땠어요?
B 친절한 서비스 때문에 기분이 좋았어요.

A How was the restaurant (that) you went to yesterday?
B It was nice because of the good service.

A 주말에 왜 못 만나요?
B 할 일이 너무 많아서 못 만나요.

A Why can't you meet up during the weekend?
B I have so many things (that I have) to do that I can't meet up.

Check It Out!

When two or more adjectives are used in succession, only the final adjective is conjugated to a noun modifier form.

- 착해요. 그리고 예뻐요. 그런 여자를 좋아해요. (Someone who is) sincere. And pretty. I like that kind of girl.
  → 착한 예쁜 여자를 좋아해요. (×)
  착하고 예쁜 여자를 좋아해요. (○) I like a girl who is sincere and pretty.

On Your Own

1 Look at the pictures and fill in the blanks using -(으)ㄴ/-는/-(으)ㄹ.

(1)

A 어떤 음식을 먹고 싶어요?

B ______________________________.
(맵다, 뜨겁다)

(2)

A 내일 영화 봐요? 무슨 영화를 볼 거예요?

B 내일 ______________________________.
(보다, 해리포터)

2 Read the following passage and fill in the blanks using -(으)ㄴ/-는/-(으)ㄹ.

> 어제는 날씨가 아주 보기 <u>추웠어요</u>. 저는 학교 앞에서 친구를 만났어요. 배가 고파서 친구와 같이 식당에 갔어요. 저는 김치찌개를 먹었어요. 김치찌개는 아주 (1)<u>매웠어요</u>. 친구는 불고기를 먹었어요. 불고기는 맛있고 (2)<u>맵지 않았어요</u>. 밥을 먹고 친구와 영화를 봤어요. 그 영화는 정말 (3)<u>재미있었어요</u>. 영화를 보고 친구하고 커피숍에 갔어요. 저와 친구는 커피를 마셨어요. 커피가 아주 (4)<u>뜨거웠어요</u>. 친구와 이야기를 많이 하고 집에 왔어요. 내일은 친구와 월드컵경기장에 (5)<u>갈 거예요</u>.

↓

> 어제는 아주 보기 <u>추운</u> 날씨였어요. 저는 학교 앞에서 친구를 만났어요. 배가 고파서 친구와 같이 식당에 갔어요. 저는 아주 (1)__________ 김치찌개를 먹었어요. 친구는 맛있고 (2)__________ 불고기를 먹었어요. 밥을 먹고 친구와 정말 (3)__________ 영화를 봤어요. 영화를 보고 친구하고 커피숍에 갔어요. 저와 친구는 (4)__________ 커피를 마셨어요. 친구와 이야기를 많이 하고 집에 왔어요. 내일 친구와 (5)__________ 곳은 월드컵경기장이에요.

02 A/V-기

Track 179

한국말을 **공부하기**가 어려워요.
Studying Korean is difficult.

제 취미는 **요리하기**예요.
My hobby is cooking.

다리가 아파서 **걷기**가 힘들어요.
My legs hurt, so walking is difficult.

Grammar Focus

-기 functions to turn verbs and adjectives into nouns and corresponds roughly to '-ing' in English. In a sentence, this form can be used to represent various parts of speech, including subjects and objects. The noun form is made by adding -기 to the stems of verbs and adjectives.

1 Examples of single verbs and adjectives used as nouns.

말하다 → 말하기 to speak speaking	크다 → 크기 big size	세다 → 세기 strong strength
듣다 → 듣기 to listen listening	밝다 → 밝기 bright brightness	뛰다 → 뛰기 jump jumping
쓰다 → 쓰기 to write writing	굵다 → 굵기 thick thickness	달리다 → 달리기 run running
읽다 → 읽기 to read reading	빠르다 → 빠르기 quick quickness	던지다 → 던지기 throw throwing

2 Examples of entire phrases used as nouns.

- 집이 멀어서 학교에 오기가 힘들어요. My house is far way, so coming to school is difficult.
- 한국 노래 듣기를 좋아해요. I like listening to Korean songs.
- 혼자 밥 먹기를 싫어해요. I don't like eating meals by myself.

달리다 + **-기** → 달리기 받다 + **-기** → 받기

Base Form	-기	Base Form	-기
보다	보기	입다	입기
배우다	배우기	살다	살기
만나다	만나기	먹다	먹기
기다리다	기다리기	찾다	찾기

In Conversation

Track 180

A 한국어 공부할 때 뭐가 제일 어려워요?
B 말하기가 제일 어려워요.

A What's the most difficult part of studying Korean?
B Speaking is most difficult.

A 왜 이 옷을 안 사요?
B 그 옷은 입기가 불편해요. 그래서 안 사요.

A Why won't you buy this outfit?
B Wearing it is uncomfortable. So I'm not going to buy it.

A 우리 버스를 탈까요?
B 아니요, 여기는 버스 타기가 불편해요. 지하철을 탑시다.

A Shall we take the bus?
B No, taking the bus from here is inconvenient. Let's take the subway.

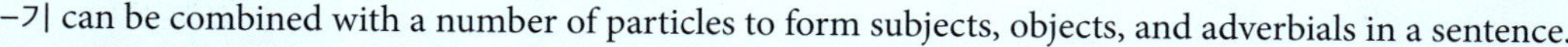

Check It Out!

-기 can be combined with a number of particles to form subjects, objects, and adverbials in a sentence.

- -기(를) 좋아하다/싫어하다
- -기(를) 바라다/원하다
- -기(를) 시작하다/끝내다/그만두다
- -기(가) 쉽다/어렵다/좋다/싫다/나쁘다/재미있다/편하다/불편하다/힘들다
- -기(에) 좋다/나쁘다

- 한국말을 잘하면 한국에서 살기가 편해요. If you can speak Korean well, then living in Korea is easy.
- 댄 씨, 대학에 꼭 합격하기를 바라요. Dane, I wish for your successful admission into university.
- 이 책은 글씨가 커서 보기에 좋아요. The printed text of this book is large, which makes reading it easy.

On Your Own

Look at the pictures and fill in the blanks using -기.

(1)

A 취미가 뭐예요?

B 제 취미는 ______________ 예요.
(우표 모으다)

(2)

A 요리를 자주 하세요?

B 아니요. 저는 ______________ 를 싫어해요.
(요리하다)

(3)

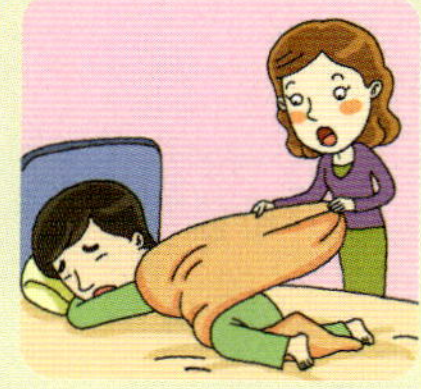

A 여보, 일어나세요. 회사에 갈 시간이에요.

B 아, 오늘은 피곤해서 ______________ 가 싫어요.
(회사에 가다)

(4)

A 태권도 재미있어요?

B 네, 재미있는데 ______________ 가 어려워요.
(배우다)

03 A-게

Track 181

머리를 **짧게** 잘랐어요.

I cut my hair short.

오늘 아침에 **늦게** 일어났어요.

I woke up late today.

크게 읽으세요.

Please read it loudly.

Grammar Focus

-게 functions as an adverb in a sentence and expresses the purpose, basis, degree, method of, or some thought about the action that follows. It corresponds to 'in a... manner' or '-ly' in English. The adverb form is made by adding **-게** to the stems of adjectives.

예쁘다 + **-게** → 예쁘게　　　길다 + **-게** → 길게

Base Form	-게	Base Form	-게
크다	크게	가깝다	가깝게
작다	작게	멀다	멀게
쉽다	쉽게	귀엽다	귀엽게
어렵다	어렵게	편하다	편하게
짧다	짧게	깨끗하다	깨끗하게

In Conversation

Track 182

A 여보, 이제 무엇을 할까요?
B 화장실 청소를 해 주세요.
깨끗하게 해 주세요.

A Dear, what should I do now?
B Please tidy up the bathroom.
Make it clean.

A 넥타이가 아주 멋있어요.
B 고마워요. 세일해서 싸게 샀어요.

A Your necktie really looks nice.
B Thanks. I bought it cheap on sale.

A 엄마, 오늘 날씨가 추워요?
B 응, 추우니까 따뜻하게 입어.

A Mom, will the weather be cold today?
B Yes, it's going to be cold, so dress warmly.

Check It Out!

❶ Although the adverbial form of an adjective is made by adding –게 to the stem, in the case of 많다 and 이르다, the forms 많이 and 일찍 are used in favor of 많게 and 이르게.

많다 → 많이

A 잘 먹겠습니다. Thank you for the food (idiomatic).
B 많이 드세요. Please eat a lot.

이르다 → 일찍

A 늦어서 죄송합니다. I'm sorry for being late.
B 내일은 일찍 오세요. Please come early tomorrow.

❷ There are also cases in which both the adverbial form –게 and a different form are used.

빠르다 → 빠르게/빨리

- 비행기가 빠르게 지나가요.
  The plane goes by fast.
- 이쪽으로 빨리 오세요.
  Come this way quick.

적다 → 적게/조금

- 소금은 적게 넣으세요.
  Only a little salt, please.
- 커피 조금 더 드실래요?
  Won't you have a little more coffee?

느리다 → 느리게/천천히

- 시계가 느리게 가요.
  My watch is slow.
- 천천히 드세요.
  Please take your time eating (eat slowly).

On Your Own

Look at the pictures and choose the appropriate word from below to fill in each blank using –게.

맛있다	예쁘다	재미있다	행복하다

(1) 

A 요즘 어떻게 지내요?
B ________ 지내요.

(2) 

A ________ 드세요.
B 잘 먹겠습니다.

(3) 

A 제가 주말에 제주도에 가요.
B 와, 좋겠어요. ________ 놀고 오세요.

(4) 

A 자, 사진 찍습니다. ________ 웃으세요.
B 김~치.

04 A-아/어하다

Track 183

아이들이 **배고파해요**.

The children are hungry.

요즘 아버지가 **피곤해하세요**.

Recently, my father has been tired.

아이가 **심심해해요**.

The child is bored.

Grammar Focus

-아/어하다 is added to the end of some adjectives to change them into verbs to express the speaker's feeling or observation about some action or outward appearance. It corresponds to 'appears (to be)' or 'seems' in English. If the stem ends in the vowel ㅏ or ㅗ, then **-아하다** is used. Otherwise **-어하다** is used. As for verbs ending in **하다**, the form changes to **-해하다**.

Stem Ending in Vowel ㅏ or ㅗ	Stem Ending in Vowel Other than ㅏ or ㅗ	Verb Ending in 하다
좋다 + **-아하다** → 좋아하다	예쁘다 + **-어하다** → 예뻐하다	미안하다 + **-해하다** → 미안해하다

Base Form	-아/어하다	Base Form	-아/어하다
아프다	아파하다	피곤하다	피곤해하다
싫다	싫어하다	*무섭다	무서워하다
*밉다	미워하다	*어렵다	어려워하다
*덥다	더워하다	*즐겁다	즐거워하다

* Irregular form

When adding **–지 마세요** to the adjective stem, the pattern becomes **–아/어하지 마세요**.

- 무서워하지 마세요. (◯) Don't be afraid. 무섭지 마세요. (×)
- 어려워하지 마세요. (◯) Please don't take it so hard. 어렵지 마세요. (×)

In Conversation

Track 184

A 왜 부디 씨는 롤러코스터를 안 타요?
B 부디 씨는 롤러코스터를 무서워해요.

A Why isn't Budi riding the roller coaster?
B Budi is afraid of roller coasters.

A 아이들이 이 게임을 좋아해요?
B 네, 재미있어해요.

A Do children like this game?
B Yes, they find it amusing.

Check It Out!

When –아/어하다 is added to 예쁘다 and 귀엽다 to form 예뻐하다 and 귀여워하다, the meaning becomes 'to hold dear' or 'to treat with love and affection'.

- 할아버지는 나를 귀여워하세요. My grandfather treats me with much affection.
- 동생이 강아지를 예뻐해요. My little brother/sister adores our dog.

On Your Own

Circle the appropriate words as you read the following passage.

우리 집에는 강아지 한 마리가 있는데 이름은 바비예요. 바비는 아주 (1) (귀여워요/귀여워해요). 그래서 우리 가족들은 모두 바비를 (2) (좋아요/좋아해요). 바비는 하루에 두 번 밥을 먹어요. 그런데 밥 먹는 시간이 지나면 아주 (3) (배고파서/배고파해서) 밥을 빨리 줘야 해요. 또 겨울에 밖에 나갈 때 바비는 많이 (4) (추워서/추워해서) 옷이 필요해요. 강아지를 키우기가 조금 힘들지만 바비가 없으면 저는 정말 슬플 거예요.

Unit 19.

Expressions of State

01 V-고 있다 ②

Track 185

목걸이와 귀걸이를 **하고 있어요.**

I'm wearing a necklace and earrings.

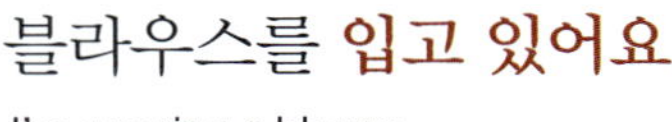

블라우스를 **입고 있어요.**

I'm wearing a blouse.

치마를 **입고 있어요.**

I'm wearing a skirt.

부츠를 **신고 있어요.**

I'm wearing boots.

안경을 **쓰고/끼고 있어요.**

I'm wearing glasses.

장갑을 **끼고 있어요.**

I'm wearing gloves.

양복을 **입고 있어요.**

I'm wearing a suit.

가방을 **들고 있어요.**

I'm carrying a briefcase.

구두를 **신고 있어요.**

I'm wearing shoes.

Grammar Focus

When used with verbs that express putting on or taking off something, such as **입다** (to wear clothes), **신다** (to wear shoes/socks), **쓰다** (to wear a hat/glasses), **끼다** (to wear a ring/gloves), and **벗다** (to take off), **-고 있다** means the result of the action has continued in that state until the present.

It corresponds to 'is -ing' in English. The same meaning can also be expressed by using the past tense form **-았/었어요** to indicate a state of completed action.

- 치마를 입고 있어요. = 치마를 입었어요. I'm wearing a skirt.
- 안경을 쓰고 있어요. = 안경을 썼어요. I'm wearing glasses.

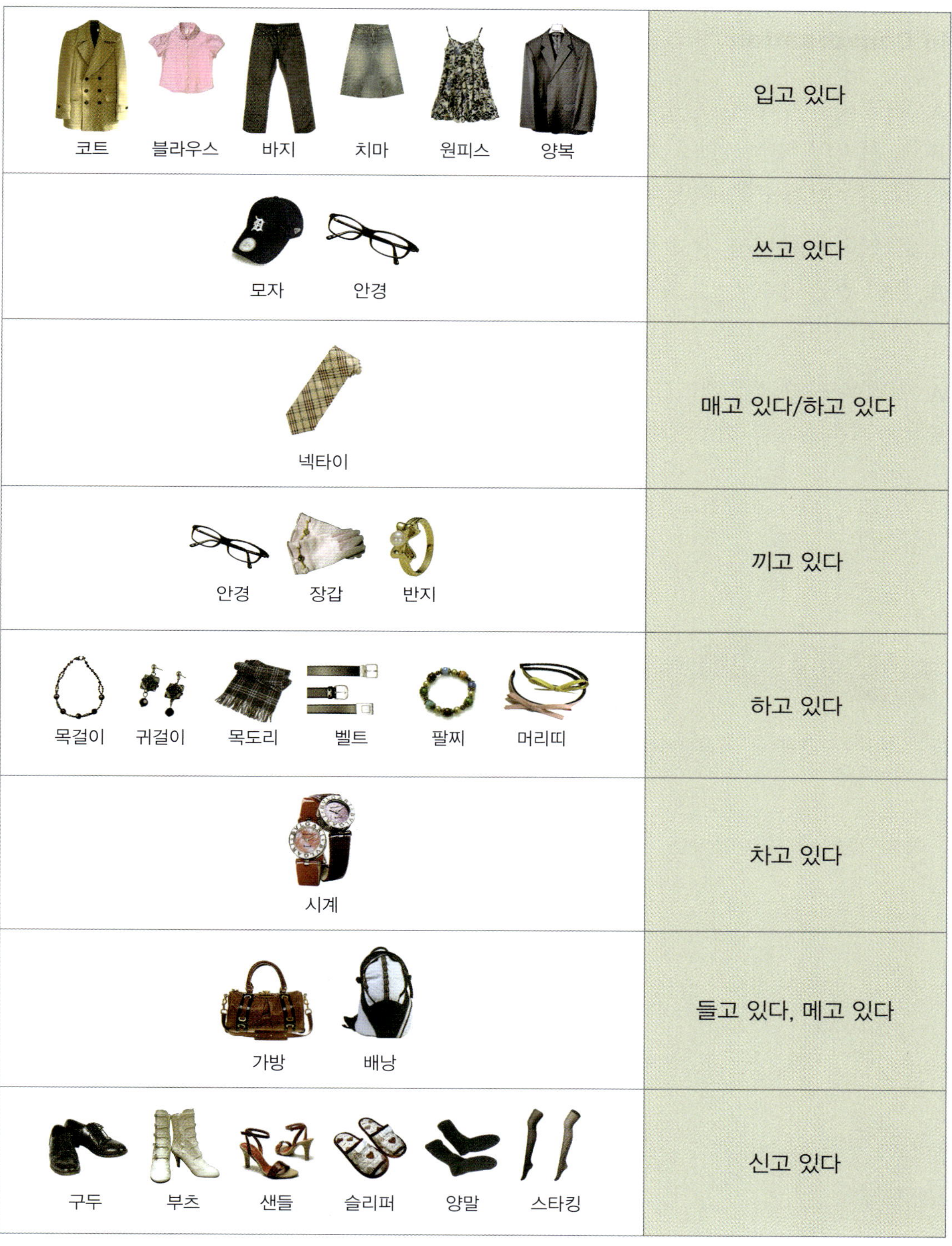

코트 블라우스 바지 치마 원피스 양복	입고 있다
모자 안경	쓰고 있다
넥타이	매고 있다/하고 있다
안경 장갑 반지	끼고 있다
목걸이 귀걸이 목도리 벨트 팔찌 머리띠	하고 있다
시계	차고 있다
가방 배낭	들고 있다, 메고 있다
구두 부츠 샌들 슬리퍼 양말 스타킹	신고 있다

(Compare with Unit 1. Tense 05 V-고 있다 ①)

In Conversation

Track 186

A 하영 씨가 누구예요?
B 저 사람이 하영 씨예요. 빨간색 원피스를 입고 있어요.

A Who is Hayeong?
B That person (over there) is Hayeong. She's wearing a red dress.

A 왜 집에서 양말을 신고 있어요?
B 우리 집은 추워요. 그래서 양말을 신고 있어요.

A Why are you wearing socks inside your house?
B Our house is cold. So I'm wearing socks.

A 이민우 씨가 결혼했어요?
B 네, 결혼반지를 끼고 있어요.

A Is Lee Minu married?
B Yes, he's wearing a wedding ring.

On Your Own

What is the person in the picture below wearing? Look at the picture and fill in the blanks as shown in the example.

보기 모자를 쓰고 있어요.

(1) 안경을 ___________.

(2) 목도리를 ___________.

(3) 넥타이를 ___________.

(4) 재킷을 ___________.

(5) 바지를 ___________.

(6) 배낭을 ___________.

(7) 책을 ___________.

(8) 양말을 ___________.

(9) 운동화를 ___________.

02 V-아/어 있다

선생님이 서 있어요.

The teacher is standing.

Track 187

학생들이 앉아 있어요.

The students are sitting.

환자들이 병원에 누워 있어요.

The patients are lying down in the hospital.

우산에 이름이 쓰여 있어요.

His name is written on the umbrella.

Grammar Focus

-아/어 있다 expresses a continuing state of a completed action and corresponds to 'is -ed/-ing' in English. It is often used with passive verbs, such as **열리다** (to be opened), **닫히다** (to be closed), **켜지다** (to be turned on), **꺼지다** (to be turned off), **떨어지다** (to be dropped), and **놓이다** (to be put, to be placed).

Stem Ending in Vowel ㅏ or ㅗ	Stem Ending in Vowel Other than ㅏ or ㅗ	Verb Ending in 하다
앉다 + **-아 있다** → 앉아 있다	피다 + **-어 있다** → 피어 있다	하다 → 해 있다

Base Form	-아/어 있어요	Base Form	-아/어 있어요	Base Form	-어 있어요
가다	가 있어요	서다	서 있어요	잠기다	잠겨 있어요
오다	와 있어요	붙다	붙어 있어요	닫히다	닫혀 있어요
남다	남아 있어요	*쓰이다	쓰여 있어요	꺼지다	꺼져 있어요
켜지다	켜져 있어요	*눕다	누워 있어요	떨어지다	떨어져 있어요

* Irregular form

In Conversation

Track 188

A 지갑을 잃어버렸어요.
B 어떻게 해요? 지갑 안에 뭐가 들어 있었어요?
A 돈하고 카드가 들어 있었어요.

A I've lost my wallet.
B What will you do? Was there anything inside it?
A My money and cards were inside.

A 하숙집을 어떻게 찾았어요?
B 학교 앞에 광고가 붙어 있었어요.

A How did you find your boarding house?
B There was an advertisement put up in front of school.

A 왜 식당에 안 들어가요?
B 문이 닫혀 있어요.

A Why don't you go inside the restaurant?
B It's closed.

Check It Out!

❶ For verbs meaning 'to put on' or 'to wear', such as 입다, 신다, and 쓰다, –고 있다 is added to the stem to form 입고 있다, 신고 있다, and 쓰고 있다 instead of 입어 있다, 신어 있다, and 써 있다.

- 우리 동생은 코트를 입어 있어요. (×) → 코트를 입고 있어요. (○) (I) am wearing a coat.
- 운동화를 신어 있어요. (×) → 운동화를 신고 있어요. (○) (I) am wearing running shoes.
- 모자를 써 있어요. (×) → 모자를 쓰고 있어요. (○) (I) am wearing a hat.
- 가방을 들어 있어요. (×) → 가방을 들고 있어요. (○) (I) am holding a bag.
- 넥타이를 매 있어요. (×) → 넥타이를 매고 있어요. (○) (I) am wearing a necktie.

❷ –아/어 있다 is used only with verbs that do not require a direct object.

- 창문을 열었어요. 그래서 창문이 열려 있어요. (○) I opened the window. Therefore, the window is open.
- 창문을 열어 있어요. (×)

What's the Difference?

–고 있다	–아/어 있다
Expresses an action currently in progress. • 의자에 앉**고 있다** ([Somebody] is in the process of sitting in a chair.) • 꽃이 피**고 있다** (The flowers are in the process of blooming.) • 죽**고 있다** ([Something] is in a state of dying gradually.)	Expresses the continuing state of a completed action. • 의자에 앉**아 있다** ([Somebody] continues to sit in a chair.) • 꽃이 피**어 있다** (The flowers have bloomed and remain in that state.) • 죽**어 있다** ([Something] has died and remains dead.)

On Your Own

Look at the following pictures and choose the appropriate verb form for each sentence that follows.

(1) 칠판에 "생일 축하합니다!"라고 (쓰고/쓰여) 있습니다.

(2) 창문이 (열고/열려) 있습니다.

(3) 책상 위에는 케이크가 (놓이고/놓여) 있습니다.

(4) 케이크에 촛불이 (켜고/켜져) 있습니다.

(5) 왕징 씨는 열쇠를 (찾고/찾아) 있습니다.

(6) 열쇠가 의자 밑에 (떨어지고/떨어져) 있습니다.

(7) 티루엔 씨는 지금 카드를 (쓰고/쓰여) 있습니다.

(8) 요코 씨는 커피를 (마시고/마셔) 있습니다.

(9) 캐럴 씨는 노래를 (부르고/불러) 있습니다.

(10) 민우 씨가 (서고/서) 있습니다.

(11) 하영 씨가 (앉고/앉아) 있습니다.

03 A–아/어지다

Track 189

풍선이 **커졌어요**.

The balloon became bigger.

언니가 **날씬해졌어요**.

My elder sister became thinner.

피노키오는 거짓말을 하면 코가 **길어져요**.

Pinocchio's nose grows longer when he tells a lie.

Grammar Focus

–아/어지다 expresses a change in state over time and means 'become' or 'turn' in English. If the stem ends in the vowel ㅏ or ㅗ, then **–아지다** is used. Otherwise, **–어지다** is used. As for verbs ending in **하다**, the form changes to **해지다**.

Stem Ending in Vowel ㅏ or ㅗ	Stem Ending in Vowel Other than ㅏ or ㅗ	Verb Ending in 하다
작다 + **–아지다** → 작아지다	길다 + **–어지다** → 길어지다	하다 → 해지다

Base Form	–아/어져요	Base Form	–아/어져요
좋다	좋아져요	따뜻하다	따뜻해져요
*예쁘다	예뻐져요	건강하다	건강해져요
*덥다	더워져요	편하다	편해져요
*빨갛다	빨개져요	*다르다	달라져요

* Irregular form

In Conversation

Track 190

A 회사가 멀어요?

B 옛날에는 멀었는데 이사해서 가까워졌어요.

A Is your company far away?

B It used to be, but since I've moved it has become closer.

A 날씨가 많이 추워요?

B 비가 오고 나서 추워졌어요.

A Is the weather really cold?

B After it rained, the weather turned cold.

A 눈이 나빠요. 어떻게 해야 돼요?

B 당근을 많이 먹으면 눈이 좋아져요.

A My vision is bad. What should I do about it?

B If you eat a lot of carrots, your vision will get better.

Check It Out!

❶ This expression is always used with adjectives and cannot be used with verbs.

- 요코 씨가 예뻐졌습니다. (○) Yoko has become pretty.
- 요코 씨가 한국말을 잘해졌습니다. (×) → 요코 씨가 한국말을 잘하게 되었습니다. (○)
  Yoko has begun speaking Korean well.

(See also Unit 19. Expressions of State 04 V-게 되다)

❷ The past tense form -아/어졌어요 expresses a change resulting from an action performed in the past while the present tense form -아/어져요 is used to describe a change that generally occurs when a particular action is performed.

- 아이스크림을 많이 먹어서 뚱뚱해져요. (×) → 아이스크림을 많이 먹어서 뚱뚱해졌어요. (○)
  I ate a lot of ice cream, so I have become fat.
- 아이스크림을 많이 먹으면 뚱뚱해졌어요. (×) → 아이스크림을 많이 먹으면 뚱뚱해져요. (○)
  If you eat a lot of ice cream, you will become fat.

Look at the following pictures. What has changed? Choose the appropriate word from below to fill in each blank using –아/어지다.

건강하다	넓다	높다	많다	빨갛다
시원하다	예쁘다	적다	크다	

(1) 몸이 약했는데 지금은 ____________.

(2) 눈이 ____________.

(3) 얼굴이 ____________.

(4) 가을이 되어서 날씨가 ____________.

(5) 나뭇잎이 ____________.

(6) 바다에 사람들이 ____________.

(7) 길이 ____________.

(8) 차가 ____________.

(9) 빌딩이 ____________.

04 V-게 되다

Track 191

요리를 **잘하게 되었어요.**

I became good at cooking.

축구를 **좋아하게 되었어요.**

I came to like soccer.

외국으로 출장을 **가게 됐어요.**

(It's been decided) I will go abroad on a business trip.

Grammar Focus

-게 되다 expresses a change from one state to another or a change in a situation as a result of someone else's action or the environment, regardless of the will of the subject. It is made by adding **-게 되다** to the verb stem. It corresponds to 'became', 'came to (be/do)' and 'has been decided' in English.

- 옛날에는 축구를 싫어했는데 남자 친구가 생기고 나서부터 축구를 좋아하게 되었어요.
  I used to dislike soccer, but after I began dating my boyfriend I came to like it.
- 출장을 가기 싫었는데 사장님의 명령 때문에 출장을 가게 되었어요.
  I didn't want to go on the business trip, but I had to because my boss ordered me to go.

가다 + **-게 되다** → 가게 되었어요　　먹다 + **-게 되다** → 먹게 되었어요

Base Form	-게 되었어요	Base Form	-게 되었어요
보다	보게 되었어요	살다	살게 되었어요
마시다	마시게 되었어요	듣다	듣게 되었어요
잘하다	잘하게 되었어요	알다	알게 되었어요

In Conversation

Track 192

A 요즘 일찍 일어나요?

B 네, 회사에 다닌 후부터 일찍 일어나게 되었어요.

A 영화배우 장동건 씨를 알아요?

B 한국에 오기 전에는 몰랐는데 한국에 와서 알게 되었어요.

A Do you get up early these days?

B Yes, after starting to work at a company, I became an early riser (came to get up early).

A Do you know the movie star Jang Dong-gun?

B I hadn't heard of him before coming to Korea, but after coming here, I learned of him.

On Your Own

What changed after Lee Minu got married? Choose the appropriate word from below to fill in each blank using –게 되다.

가다　끊다　들어가다　마시다　만나다　먹다　저축하다

보기 술을 안 마시게 되었어요.

(1) 집에 일찍 ________________. 친구들을 자주 못 ________________.

(2) 담배를 ________________.

(3) 맛있는 음식을 ________________.

(4) 시장에 자주 ________________.

(5) ________________.

Unit 20.

Confirming Information

01 A/V-(으)ㄴ/는지

02 V-는 데 걸리다/들다

03 A/V-지요?

01 A/V-(으)ㄴ/는지

Track 193

명동에 어떻게 **가는지** 알아요?

Do you know how to get to Myeongdong?

저분이 **누구인지** 모르겠어요.

I don't know who that person is.

어제 무엇을 **했는지** 생각이 안 나요.

I can't remember what I did yesterday.

Grammar Focus

-(으)ㄴ/는지 is a connective ending used when connecting a clause requiring additional information to the following verb. It corresponds to 'who/what/where/when/how/whether + Clause' in English. It generally precedes one of the following verbs: **알다** (to know), **모르다** (not to know, be unaware of), **궁금하다** (to be anxious or curious about), **질문하다** (to ask a question, to inquire), **조사하다** (to investigate), **알아보다** (to look into, to recognize), **생각나다** (to recall, to remember), **말하다** (to speak, to say), and **가르치다** (to teach).

- 내일 날씨가 좋아요, 나빠요? + 알아요? → 내일 날씨가 좋은지 나쁜지 알아요?
  Will tomorrow's weather be good or bad? + Do you know?
  → Do you know whether tomorrow's weather will be good or bad?

- 명동에 어떻게 가요? + 가르쳐 주세요. → 명동에 어떻게 가는지 가르쳐 주세요.
  How do you get to Myeongdong? + Please tell me.
  → Please tell me how to get to Myeongdong.

For present tense adjectives, when the stem ends in a vowel or ㄹ, **-ㄴ지** is added, and when it ends in a consonant, **-은지** is added. For present tense verbs, **-는지** is added to the stem. For past tense adjectives and verbs, **-았/었는지** is added, while for future tense verbs, **-(으)ㄹ 건지** is added.

Present Tense Adjectives and 이다		Present Tense Verbs	Past Tense Verbs, Adjectives, 이다	Future Tense Verbs	
No Final Consonant	Final Consonant			No Final Consonant	Final Consonant
-ㄴ지	-은지	-는지	-았/었는지	-ㄹ 건지	-을 건지
큰지 인지	작은지	가는지 먹는지	갔는지 컸는지 의사였는지 학생이었는지	갈 건지	먹을 건지

Base Form	-(으)ㄴ/는지	Base Form	-(으)ㄴ/는지
예쁘다	예쁜지	만나다	만나는지
높다	높은지	입다	입는지
학생이다	학생인지	운동하다	운동하는지
*길다	긴지	청소하다	청소하는지
*춥다	추운지	*살다	사는지
더웠다	더웠는지	찍었다	찍었는지
교수였다	교수였는지	공부했다	공부했는지
선생님이었다	선생님이었는지	일했다	일했는지

* Irregular form

In Conversation

Track 194

A 제이슨 씨가 병원에 입원했어요. 어디가 아픈지 알아요?

B 글쎄요. 저도 어디가 아픈지 모르겠어요.

A Jason is in the hospital. Do you know what's wrong?

B Hmm. No, I don't know what's wrong.

A 여보, 우리 아들이 지금 공부하고 있어요?

B 방에 있는데 공부하는지 자는지 잘 모르겠어요.

A Dear, is our son studying now?

B He's in his room, but I don't know if he's studying or sleeping.

A 이거 제가 만들었어요. 드셔 보세요.

B 와, 맛있어요. 이거 어떻게 만들었는지 가르쳐 주세요.

A I made this. Please take a bite.

B Wow, this is delicious. Please tell me how you made it.

Check It Out!

–는지 is used in the following forms.

❶ Interrogative + Verb–(으)ㄴ/는지

- 우리 아이가 방에서 무엇을 하는지 모르겠어요. I don't know what our son/daughter is doing in his/her room.
- 그 사람이 어느 나라 사람인지 알아요? Do you know what country that person is from?

❷ Verb 1–(으)ㄴ/는지 Verb 2–(으)ㄴ/는지

- 우리 아이가 방에서 자는지 공부하는지 모르겠어요.
  I don't know if our son/daughter is sleeping or studying in his/her room.
- 그 사람이 일본 사람인지 중국 사람인지 알아요? Do you know if that person is Japanese or Chinese?

❸ Verb 1–(으)ㄴ/는지 안 Verb 1–(으)ㄴ/는지

- 우리 아이가 공부를 하는지 안 하는지 모르겠어요. I don't know if our son/daughter is studying (or not).
- 그 사람이 일본 사람인지 아닌지 모르겠어요. I don't know whether that person is Japanese (or not).

On Your Own

What do you know about this person? Use –(으)ㄴ/는지 to ask questions about him.

(1) A 이 사람이 ___________ 알아요?
B 네, 알아요. 제이슨 씨예요.

(2) A 제이슨 씨의 나이가 ___________ 모르겠어요.
B 제이슨 씨는 22살이에요.

(3) A 제이슨 씨가 _______________ 알아요?
B 네, 알아요. 작년에 한국에 왔어요.

(4) A ___________________________?
B 네, 알아요. 한국대학교에 다녀요.

(5) A 무엇을 ___________ 말해 주세요.
B 제이슨 씨는 노래하고 운동을 좋아해요.

(6) A 여자 친구가 있는지 ________ 궁금해요.
B 제이슨 씨는 여자 친구가 있어요.

02 V–는 데 걸리다/들다

Track 195

운전을 **배우는 데** 두 달 **걸렸어요.**

It took (me) two months to learn to drive.

숙제하는 데 한 시간 **걸려요.**

It took (me) an hour to finish my homework.

차를 **고치는 데** 30만 원 **들었어요.**

It cost (me) 300,000 won to repair my car.

Grammar Focus

–는 데 걸리다/들다 is added to the end of verbs to express how much money, time, or effort is involved in doing a task. It means 'takes/requires/costs ... to (do)' in English. This expression is made by adding **–는 데 걸리다/들다** to the stems of verbs. **–는 데 걸리다** is used when expressing an amount of time required, and **–는 데 들다** is used when expressing an amount of money required.

- 차를 고쳐요. 30만 원 들어요. → 차를 고치는 데 30만 원 들어요.
  I will repair my car. It costs 300,000 won. → It costs 300,000 won to repair my car.

가다 + **–는 데** → 가는 데 　　　　 짓다 + **–는 데** → 짓는 데

<table>
<tr><th>Base Form</th><th>–는 데</th><th></th></tr>
<tr><td>여행하다</td><td>여행하는 데</td><td rowspan="4">(Time) (Money) + 걸리다 들다</td></tr>
<tr><td>읽다</td><td>읽는 데</td></tr>
<tr><td>짓다</td><td>짓는 데</td></tr>
<tr><td>*만들다</td><td>만드는 데</td></tr>
</table>

* Irregular form

In Conversation

Track 196

A 여기에서 명동까지 가는 데 얼마나 걸려요?

B 버스로 가면 40분, 지하철로 가면 20분 걸려요.

A 지난주에 이사했어요? 이사하는 데 얼마 들었어요?

B 150만 원쯤 들었어요.

A How long does it take to get to Myeongdong from here?

B If you go by bus, it takes 40 minutes, and if you go by subway, 20 minutes.

A Did you move (change residences) last week? How much did it cost to move?

B It cost about 1,500,000 Won.

How much time or money does it take to do the following things? Look at the pictures and fill in the blanks using –는 데 걸리다/들다.

(1)

A 와, 맛있는 갈비예요.

B 갈비 ______________ 10시간이나 걸렸어요.
(만들다)

A 그래요? ______________ 10분밖에 안 걸려요.
(먹다)

(2)

A 한글 자음, 모음 다 외웠어요?

B 네, 자음, 모음 ______________ 일주일 걸렸어요.
(외우다)

(3)

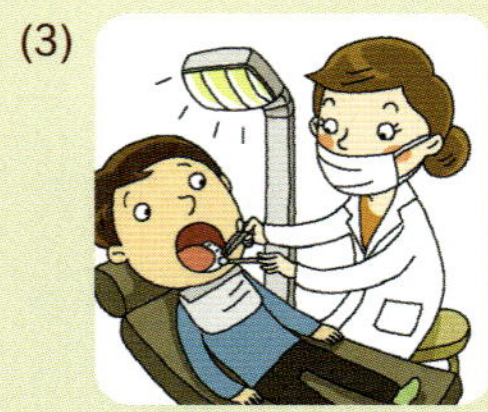

A 이를 ______________ 얼마나 들어요?
(치료하다)

B 이를 ______________ 보통 6만 원쯤 ______________.
(치료하다) (들다)

(4)

A 한국에서 머리를 자르고 싶어요. 돈이 얼마쯤 들어요?

B 머리 ______________ 20,000원 정도 ______________.
(자르다) (들다)

03 A/V-지요?

Track 197

중국 사람**이지요?**
You're Chinese, right?

불고기가 **맛있지요?**
Isn't bulgogi tasty?

한국어를 **배우지요?**
You study Korean, don't you?

Grammar Focus

-지요? is used when the speaker wants to confirm with the listener or to obtain the listener's agreement about something already known. It means 'Isn't/Aren't...?' or 'Don't/Doesn't...?' in English. For present tense adjectives and verbs, **-지요?** is added to the stem. For past tense adjectives and verbs, **-았/었지요?** is added; for future tense verbs, **-(으)ㄹ 거지요?** is added. In colloquial speech, **-지요?** is sometimes shortened to **-죠?**

크다 + **-지요?** → 크지요?　　　먹다 + **-지요?** → 먹지요?

Base Form	-지요?	Base Form	-지요?
싸다	싸지요?	가다	가지요?
많다	많지요?	읽다	읽지요?
춥다	춥지요?	듣다	듣지요?
멀다	멀지요?	공부하다	공부하지요?
맛있다	맛있지요?	재미없다	재미없지요?
학생이다	학생이지요?	학생이 아니다	학생이 아니지요?

In Conversation

Track 198

A 우리 아이가 벌써 10살이 되었어요. 세월이 참 빠르지요?
B 네, 정말 세월이 빨라요.

A Our son/daughter is already 10 years old. Doesn't time just fly by?
B Yes, time really does fly by.

A 호앙 씨, 어제 밤새웠지요?
B 어떻게 알았어요? 제가 피곤해 보여요?

A Hoang, you stayed up all night last night, didn't you?
B How did you know? Do I look tired?

A 내일 회의에 참석할 거지요?
B 네, 회의에 꼭 참석하겠습니다.

A You'll attend the meeting tomorrow, won't you?
B Yes, I will most definitely attend the meeting.

On Your Own

Look at the following drawing of Carol, and complete each of the questions based on what you see using –지요?.

(1) A 캐럴 씨, 백화점에서 __________?
B 네, 한국백화점에서 쇼핑했어요.

(2) A 요즘 한국백화점에서 __________?
B 네, 다음 주까지 세일을 해요.

(3) A 세일 기간이라서 백화점에 사람이 __________?
B 정말 많았어요. 복잡했어요.

(4) A 남자 구두를 __________?
B 네, 남자 구두를 샀어요.

(5) A 그 구두를 남자 친구에게 __________?
B 아니요, 아버지께 드릴 거예요.

Unit 21.

Discovery and Surprise

01 A-군요, V-는군요

02 A/V-네요

01 A-군요, V-는군요

Track 199

눈이 **나쁘군요**.

Your vision is bad indeed.

아이스크림을 **좋아하는군요**.

You really like ice cream!

감기에 **걸렸군요**.

I see you've caught a cold.

Grammar Focus

-군요/는군요 is used to express surprise or wonder upon learning something new either by direct observation or experience or by hearing about it from someone else. It corresponds to 'I see (that)', 'indeed', 'how', or simply an exclamation point (!) in English. For adjectives, **-군요** is added to the stem, while for verbs, **-는군요** is added. This expression can also attach to nouns by adding **-(이)군요**. To express the past tense, it is added to the past tense ending to form **-았/었군요**.

Adjective + -군요	Verb + -는군요
크다 + **-군요** → 크군요	먹다 + **-는군요** → 먹는군요

Base Form	-군요	Base Form	-는군요
학생이다	학생이군요	가다	가는군요
의사이다	의사(이)군요	사다	사는군요
피곤하다	피곤하군요	운동하다	운동하는군요
덥다	덥군요	*만들다	만드는군요

* Irregular form

In Conversation

Track 200

A 부디 씨가 이번에 차를 또 바꿨어요.
B 그래요? 부디 씨는 정말 돈이 많군요.

A Budi has changed vehicles again.
B Really? Budi really does have a lot of money!

A 댄 씨, 인사하세요, 이분이 우리 회사 사장님이세요.
B 아, 사장님이시군요. 안녕하세요.

A Dane, please say hello. This is our company president.
B Oh, the company president! Nice to meet you.

A 우산 있어요? 지금 밖에 비가 와요.
B 정말 비가 오는군요. 우산이 없는데 어떻게 하죠?

A Do you have an umbrella? It's raining outside now.
B Wow, it's really raining! I don't have an umbrella, so what shall I do?

Check It Out!

In the informal plain style, -군요 changes to -구나/-군 in the case of adjectives, -는구나/-는군 in the case of verbs, and (이)구나/(이)군 in the case of nouns.

A 저 아이가 제 동생이에요.
B (혼잣말로) 아, 저 아이가 민우 씨의 동생이구나.

That boy/girl is my little brother/sister.
(To oneself) Oh, so that's Minu's little brother/sister.

A 엄마, 오늘 학교에서 일이 있어서 늦게 왔어요.
B 응, 그래서 늦었구나.

Mom, today I was busy at school, and that's why I'm late.
Okay, so (I see) that's why you're late.

On Your Own

Read the following dialogues and fill in the blanks using -군요/-는군요.

(1) A 오늘 아침에 출근하는 데 한 시간이나 걸렸어요.
B 그래요? 월요일이어서 길이 많이 ___________. (막히다)

(2) A 제 여자 친구 사진이에요.
B 여자 친구가 ___________. (예쁘다)

(3) A 요즘 사람들이 노란색 옷을 많이 입어요.
B 요즘 노란색이 ___________. (유행하다)

(4) A 점심시간인데 밥 안 먹어요?
B 아, 벌써 _______________. (점심시간이다)

02 A/V-네요

Track 201

벌써 **여름이네요**.

Wow, it's already summer.

가족이 **많네요**.

You certainly have a large family.

글씨를 잘 **쓰네요**.

You really have good handwriting.

책을 많이 **읽었네요**.

You really have read a lot of books.

Grammar Focus

-네요 is used to express surprise or wonder upon learning something through direct experience or when agreeing with something said by someone else. It is made by adding **-네요** to the stems of adjectives and verbs. It corresponds to 'really', 'certainly', 'wow', or 'My(!)' in English.

1 Expressing surprise or wonder upon learning something through direct experience:

A 한국말을 정말 잘하시네요. You really do speak Korean well! (While witnessing a friend speak Korean)

B 아니에요. 더 많이 공부해야 돼요. Not really. I have to study a lot more.

2 Agreeing with something said by someone else:

A 오늘 날씨가 춥지요? Isn't it cold today?

B 네, 정말 춥네요. Yes, it really is cold.

오다 + **–네요** → 오네요 가깝다 + **–네요**→ 가깝네요

Base Form	–네요	Base Form	–네요
책상이다	책상이네요	춥다	춥네요
아니다	아니네요	찍다	찍네요
예쁘다	예쁘네요	듣다	듣네요
친절하다	친절하네요	요리하다	요리하네요
주다	주네요	*멀다	머네요
마시다	마시네요	*살다	사네요

* Irregular form

(Compare with Unit 21. Discovery and Suprise 01 A–군요, V–는군요)

What's the Difference?

–군요

❶ Used mostly in books and other written texts.

❷ Used to express surprise or wonder upon learning something new either by direct experience or by hearing about it from someone else.

A 이 식당에서 갈비 먹어 봤어요? 정말 맛있어요.
Have you ever had galbi at this restaurant? It's really delicious.

B 그래요? 이 집 갈비가 맛있군요. (○)
Really? The galbi at this restaurant must be delicious.

(Can be used because the sentence refers to what is learned from someone else even though the speaker has yet to actually try the restaurant's galbi.)

–네요

❶ Used mostly in daily conversation.

❷ Cannot be used to express something not learned directly by the speaker's own experience.

A 이 식당에서 갈비 먹어 봤어요? 정말 맛있어요.
Have you ever had galbi at this restaurant? It's really delicious.

B 그래요? 이 집 갈비가 맛있네요. (×)
(Cannot be used because the speaker did not try galbi personally.)

In Conversation

Track 202

A 남편이 키가 크시네요.
B 네, 187cm(센티미터)예요.

A Your husband is really tall!
B Yes, he's 187cm tall.

A 제 선물이에요. 빨리 열어 보세요.
B 예쁜 목도리네요. 고마워요.
겨울에 잘 할게요.

A It's a present (I got for you). Go ahead and open it.
B What a beautiful scarf! Thank you.
I'll wear it often in winter.

A 우리 딸이 그린 그림인데 어때요?
B 정말 잘 그렸네요. 언제부터 그림을
배웠어요?

A What do you think of this painting by my daughter?
B My, she really painted well! When did she start learning to paint?

On Your Own

Look at the pictures and fill in the blanks using either –네요 or –군요.

(1)

A 우리 동네 근처에 있는 시장에 가봤어요? 물건이 싸고 좋아요.
B 그래요? 그 시장 물건이 ____________.

(2)

A 오늘 하늘 좀 보세요. 정말 아름다워요.
B 네, 하늘이 정말 ____________.

(3)

A 짜장면 배달 왔습니다.
B 오늘 짜장면이 빨리 ________.

(4)

A 요코 씨가 병원에 입원했어요.
B 요코 씨가 많이 ____________.
(아프다)

Unit 22.

Additional Endings

01 A-(으)ㄴ가요?, V-나요?

02 A/V-(으)ㄴ/는데요

01 A–(으)ㄴ가요?, V–나요?

Track 203

한국 친구가 **많은가요?**

Do you have a lot of Korean friends?

나를 **사랑하나요?**

Do you love me?

주말에 재미있게 **보내셨나요?**

Did you have a pleasant weekend?

Grammar Focus

–(으)ㄴ가요? and **–나요?** are used to politely and gently ask somebody a question and correspond to 'Is/Were there…?', 'Is/Was it…?', 'Are/Were you…?', or 'Do/Did you…?' in English. For adjectives, when the stem ends in a vowel, **–ㄴ가요?** is used, and when it ends in a consonant, **–은가요?** is used. For verbs, **–나요?** is added to the stem.

Present Tense Adjective		Present Tense Verb	Past Tense Adjective, Verb	Future Tense Verb	
No Final Consonant	Final Consonant			No Final Consonant	Final Consonant
–ㄴ가요?	–은가요?	–나요?	–았/었나요?	–ㄹ 건가요?	–을 건가요?
아픈가요? 학생인가요?	많은가요? 적은가요?	가나요? 있나요?	갔나요? 적었나요?	갈 건가요? 볼 건가요?	먹을 건가요? 있을 건가요?

Base Form	–(으)ㄴ가요?	Base Form	–나요?
빠르다	빠른가요?	오다	오나요?
친절하다	친절한가요?	찾다	찾나요?

의사이다	의사인가요?	아팠다	아팠나요?
작다	작은가요?	받았다	받았나요?
*무섭다	무서운가요?	*만들다	만드나요?
*멀다	먼가요?	*살다	사나요?

* Irregular form

In Conversation

Track 204

A 오늘 시간이 있나요?
B 네, 있는데 왜 그러세요?

A Do you have time today?
B Yes, I do, but why do you ask?

A 요즘 바쁜가요?
B 아니요, 그렇게 많이 바쁘지 않아요.

A Are you busy these days?
B No, I'm not that busy.

A 댄 씨 어머님이 언제 서울에 오시나요?
B 다음 주에 오실 거예요.

A Dane, when is your mom coming to Seoul?
B She's coming next week.

A 몇 시에 집에서 출발할 건가요?
B 9시쯤 출발할 거예요.

A What time will you leave your house?
B I'll leave at around 9.

On Your Own

Fill in the blanks as shown in the example.

보기 A 오늘 날씨가 좋은가요?
B 네, 날씨가 좋아요.

(1) A 티루엔 씨, 요즘 회사에서 자꾸 자는데 ____________?
B 네, 피곤해요.

(2) A 여권을 만드는 데 며칠이 ____________?
B 아마 일주일쯤 걸릴 거예요.

(3) A 댄 씨, 한국에 ____________? 한국말을 잘하세요.
B 작년에 왔어요.

(4) A 캐럴 씨와 ____________?
B 물론이에요. 결혼할 거예요.

02 A/V-(으)ㄴ/는데요

저는 **재미있는데요**.

I think it's interesting.

민우 씨는 지금 자리에 **없는데요**.

Minu is not at his desk right now.

정말 **높은데요**!

We're really high up!

Grammar Focus

1 -(으)ㄴ/는데요 is used to express one's disagreement with or opposition to what somebody says. It corresponds to 'Well (in my case)' in English. For adjectives, when the stem ends in a vowel, -ㄴ데요 is used, and when it ends in a consonant -은데요 is used. For verbs, -는데요 is added to the stem.

A 오늘 날씨가 안 추워요. The weather's not cold today.

B 저는 추운데요. Well, I feel cold.

2 -(으)ㄴ/는데요 is also used to express the expectation of, or waiting for, a response from the other person and corresponds to '...and?' or '...but?' in English.

A 여보세요, 거기 하영 씨 댁이지요? Hello, is this the home of Hayeong?

B 네, 맞는데요. (누구세요? / 무슨 일이세요?)
Yes, it is... (And you are? / What is the reason for your call?)

3 **-(으)ㄴ/는데요** is also used to express the speaker's surprise at discovering or feeling something unexpected when observing a situation. It corresponds to '(I'm surprised to learn that)... is so...' in English.

- (친구가 만든 옷을 보면서) 옷이 정말 예쁜데요!
  Wow, your clothes look really nice! (said while seeing the clothes your friend made)
- (외국인을 보면서) 한국말을 아주 잘하시는데요.
  (I'm surprised to see that) he (she) speaks Korean really well. (said while observing a foreigner)

Present Tense Adjective, 이다		Present Tense Verb 있다/없다	Past Tense Verb and Adjective
No Final Consonant	Final Consonant		
-ㄴ데요	-은데요	-는데요	-았/었는데요
바쁜데요 의사인데요	많은데요 높은데요	사는데요 읽는데요 있는데요 없는데요	샀는데 바빴는데요 의사였는데요 학생이었는데요

Base Form	-(으)ㄴ/는데요	Base Form	-(으)ㄴ/는데요
예쁘다	예쁜데요	보다	보는데요
작다	작은데요	듣다	듣는데요
피곤하다	피곤한데요	일하다	일하는데요
*힘들다	힘든데요	*만들다	만드는데요
*덥다	더운데요	*살다	사는데요
친절했다	친절했는데요	받았다	받았는데요
편했다	편했는데요	찾았다	찾았는데요

* Irregular form

In Conversation

Track 206

A 내일 저녁에 시간 있어요?
B 내일은 시간이 없는데요.

A Do you have time tomorrow evening?
B Well, tomorrow I don't have any time.

A 이 그림 어때요?
B 와, 멋있는데요.

A What do you think of this painting?
B Wow, it's really nice.

A 와, 댄 씨, 공부 열심히 하는데요.
B 아니에요. 그냥 책을 읽고 있어요.

A Wow, Dane, you really are studying hard.
B Not really. I'm just reading a book.

On Your Own

Look at the pictures and choose the appropriate word from below to fill in each blank using –(으)ㄴ/는데요.

대단하다	먹다	불다	없다

(1) 

A 저 선수 좀 보세요.
B 와, 정말 ________________.

(2) 

A 같이 저녁 먹을까요?
B 저는 벌써 ________________.

(3) 

A 웨슬리 씨, 돈 좀 빌려주세요.
B 죄송해요. 지금 돈이 ________________.

(4) 

A 우리 산책하러 갈까요?
B 지금 바람이 많이 ________________.

Unit 23.

Quotations

01 Direct Quotations
02 Indirect Quotations
03 Indirect Quotation Contracted Forms

01 Direct Quotations

에디슨은 "실패는 성공의 어머니입니다." **라고 했어요.**

To paraphrase Edison, "Failure is the mother of success".

예수님은 "서로 사랑하세요."**라고 말씀했어요.**

Jesus said, "Love each other".

왕징 씨는 저에게 "내일 몇 시에 와요?" **하고 물어봤어요.**

Wang Jing asked me, "What time will you come tomorrow?"

부디 씨는 '문제가 너무 어려워.' **하고 생각했어요.**

"This problem is too hard", Budi thought.

Grammar Focus

A direct quotation refers to the word-for-word quoting, using quotation marks, of what someone wrote, said, or thought. In Korean, '**하고/라고** Verb' follows the quotation marks. When asking a question about what someone wrote or said, however, **뭐라고** is used instead of **무엇을**: "**카일리 씨가 뭐라고 말했어요?**" (What did Kyle say?) **하고/라고** is often followed by **이야기하다**, **물어보다**, **말하다**, **생각하다**, or **쓰다**, but these verbs can be substituted with **하다** or **그러다**.

"Quoted Speech"	하고 라고	(말)하다 (to speak) / 이야기하다 (to talk/converse) / 그러다 (to say/to indicate) 물어보다 (to ask) 생각하다 (to think) 부탁하다 (to request) 쓰다 (to write) 듣다 (to listen) 써 있다 (to be written)

In Conversation

Track 208

A 민우 씨하고 얘기했어요?

B 네, 민우 씨가 "요즘 너무 바빠서 만날 수 없어요."라고 그랬어요.

A Did you speak with Minu?

B Yes, Minu said, "I've been too busy recently to be able to meet you."

A 여보, "여기에 주차하지 마세요."라고 쓰여 있는데요.

B 그래요? 다른 곳에 주차할게요.

A Dear, it says, "No parking here."

B Really? I'll park somewhere else then.

Check It Out!

❶ 하고 했어요 is not used after a quotation when the part inside the quotation marks ends in 하다. It is also common practice to avoid using 하다 as the verb directly following 하고. These conventions exist because it sounds awkward when 하다 is repeated consecutively.

- 민우 씨는 "운동하세요." 하고 했어요. (×)
  → 민우 씨는 "운동하세요."라고 (말)했어요. (○)
  → 민우 씨는 "운동하세요." 하고 말했어요. (○)
  Minu said to me, "Please exercise".
- 하영 씨는 "내일 만나요." 하고 했어요. (×)
  → 하영 씨는 "내일 만나요."라고 (말)했어요. (○)
  → 하영 씨는 "내일 만나요." 하고 말했어요. (○)
  Hayeong said to me, "See you tomorrow".

❷ Although both 하고 and 라고 are used after a quotation in a sentence, they convey slightly different meanings. 하고 conveys a feeling of including not just the cited text but also the original intonation, emotion, and feeling of the cited words. This is why 하고 is used when something must be conveyed vividly, such as in fairy tales, children's stories, and onomatopoeia. In the case of everyday conversations and speech, however, 라고 is used often.

- 준호 씨가 초인종을 누르니까 "딩동" 하고 소리가 났어요. Junho rang the bell, and it chimed "ding-dong".
- 그 남자는 "살려 주세요!" 하고 소리쳤어요. The boy yelled out, "Help me!"
- 왕비는 "거울아, 거울아, 세상에서 누가 제일 예쁘니?" 하고 물어봤어요.
  The queen asked, "Mirror, mirror on the wall, who is the fairest one of all?"
  (The 'ding-dong' sound and the accent, intonation, and feeling of the words of the boy and queen are conveyed.)

On Your Own

Change what each of the following people say into direct quotations.

(1)

A 여자가 남자에게 뭐라고 말했어요?
B 여자는 남자에게 ______________________.

(2)

A 재준 씨가 무엇을 물어봤어요?
B 재준 씨는 ______________________.

(3)

A 카드에 뭐라고 썼어요?
B 카드에 ______________________.

(4)

A 성경에 뭐라고 쓰여 있어요?
B 성경에 ______________________.

(5)

A 선물을 주니까 부디 씨가 뭐라고 했어요?
B 부디 씨는 ______________________.

02 Indirect Quotations

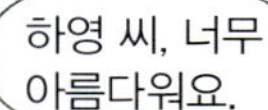

Track 209

민우 씨가 저에게 정말 **아름답다고 했어요**.

Minu said I was really beautiful.

하영 씨가 저에게 **사랑한다고 그랬어요**.

Hayeong said she loves me.

민우 씨가 **결혼하자고 했어요**.

Minu said we should get married.

Grammar Focus

An indirect quotation refers to the citing, without the use of quotation marks, of what someone wrote or said. Further, the form of the expression can change depending on the type of quotation, verb tense, and parts of speech involved. Thus, the forms of indirect quotations are more varied and complex than those of direct quotations. After changing the form of the content to be quoted, **–고** is attached and used along with a verb such as **말하다** (to speak, to say), **물어보다** (to ask, to inquire), **전하다** (to tell, to convey) or **듣다** (to listen, to hear). These verbs can be substituted with **하다** or **그러다**.

Sentence Type	Tense	Contracted Form	Examples
Declarative	Present	Vst + **–(느)ㄴ다고 하다**	만난다고 합니다 먹는다고 합니다
		Ast + **–다고 하다**	바쁘다고 합니다
		Noun + **(이)라고 하다**	의사라고 합니다 회사원이라고 합니다
	Past	V/Ast + **–았/었/였다고 하다**	만났다고 합니다 먹었다고 합니다
	Future	V/Ast + **–(으)ㄹ 거라고 하다**	만날 거라고 합니다 먹을 거라고 합니다

Interrogative	Ast + **–(으)냐고 합니다**	춥냐고 합니다 = 추우냐고 합니다
	Vst + **–(느)냐고 하다**	먹냐고 합니다 = 먹(느)냐고 합니다
	Noun + **(이)냐고 하다**	의사냐고 합니다 회사원이냐고 합니다
Suggestive	Vst + **–자고 하다**	가자고 합니다
Imperative	Vst + **–(으)라고 하다**	가라고 합니다 입으라고 합니다
	–아/어 주다 → Vst + **–아/어/여 달라고 하다** Vst + **–아/어/여 주라고 하다**	도와 달라고 합니다 도와주라고 합니다

* Vst means 'Verb stem', and Ast means 'Abjective stem'.

The negative forms of suggestive and imperative quotations are **–지 말자고 하다** and **–지 말라고 하다**, respectively.

1 Suggestive Sentences

- 민우 씨는 "내일 산에 가지 **맙시다**."라고 말했어요.
  Minu said, "Let's not go to the mountain tomorrow."
  → 민우 씨는 내일 산에 가지 **말자고** 했어요. Minu said we shouldn't go to the mountain tomorrow.

2 Imperative Sentences

- 의사 선생님이 "담배를 피우지 **마세요**."라고 하셨어요. The doctor said, "Don't smoke."
  → 의사 선생님이 담배를 피우지 **말라고** 하셨어요. The doctor said not to smoke.

When the first person pronoun **나/내** or **저/제** appears inside an indirect quotation, it changes to **자기**.

- 왕징 씨가 "저한테 얘기하세요."라고 말했어요. Wang Jing said, "Please tell me."
  → 왕징 씨가 자기한테 말하라고 했어요. Wang Jing said to tell her.
- 리처드 씨가 "제 고향은 뉴욕이에요."라고 말했어요. Richard said, "My hometown is New York."
  → 리처드 씨가 자기(의) 고향은 뉴욕이라고 말했어요. Richard said his hometown is New York.

In Conversation

Track 210

A 제이슨 씨 여기 있어요?
B 없는데요.
A 제이슨 씨가 오면 식당으로 오라고 전해 주세요.

A Is Jason here?
B No, he's not (here).
A When he gets here, please tell him to come to the cafeteria.

A 삼계탕 먹어 봤어요?
B 아니요, 그렇지만 먹어 본 친구들이 맛있다고 해요.

A Have you tried samgyetang?
B No, but my friends who have tried it said it was delicious.

Check It Out!

When indirect quotations are made from sentences that originally end in 주세요 or –아/어 주세요, these parts change to 달라고 하다 and –아/어 달라고 하다, or 주라고 하다 and –아/어 주라고 하다, respectively. Specifically, when the speaker is making the request directly to the listener, then 달라고 하다 and –아/어 달라고 하다 are used, but when the speaker is asking the listener to help a third party, then 주라고 하다 and –아/어 주라고 하다 are used.

The speaker makes a direct request of the listener. **달라고 하다, –아/어 달라고 하다**	The speaker makes a request on behalf of a third person. **주라고 하다, –아/어 주라고 하다**
물 좀 주세요. 재준 씨는 물을 달라고 했어요. (달라고 is used because Jaejun is requesting something for himself.)	웨슬리 씨에게 이 물을 주세요. / 웨슬리 캐럴 씨는 웨슬리 씨에게 물을 주라고 했어요. (주라고 is used because Carol is requesting that something be done for Wesley [a third person].)
저를 도와주세요. 재준 씨는 왕징 씨에게 도와 달라고 했어요. (달라고 is used because the speaker [Jaejun] and the recipient of the help [Jaejun] are the same person.)	왕징 씨를 도와주세요. 재준 씨는 댄 씨에게 왕징 씨를 도와주라고 했어요. (주라고 is used because the speaker [Jaejun] and the recipient of the help [Wang Jing] are not the same person.)

On Your Own

Change the following direct quotations to indirect quotations.

보기 제니퍼 씨가 "비행기 표가 너무 비싸요."라고 말했어요.
→ 제니퍼 씨가 비행기 표가 너무 비싸다고 했어요.

(1) 요코 씨가 "어제 쇼핑했어요."라고 했어요.
→ ______________________.

(2) 란란 씨가 "빨간색 가방은 제 것이에요."라고 했어요.
→ ______________________.

(3) 민우 씨가 "언제 고향에 가요?"라고 물어봤어요.
→ ______________________.

(4) 마틴 씨가 "허리가 아프면 수영을 하세요."라고 했어요.
→ ______________________.

03 Indirect Quotation Contracted Forms

요코 씨는 한국어가 **재미있대요**.
Yoko said Korean is interesting.

티루엔 씨는 다음 달에 **결혼한대요**.
Tiluen said she's getting married next month.

웨슬리 씨는 저녁에 **전화하래요**.
Wesley said to call this evening.

재준 씨는 내일 같이 테니스를 **치재요**.
Jaejun said we should play tennis tomorrow.

부디 씨는 뭐 먹고 **싶내요**.
Budi wants to know what (you/we) want to eat.

Grammar Focus

Indirect quotations are often used in contracted forms, particularly in colloquial speech.

Sentence Type	Tense	Contracted Form	Examples
Declarative	Present	Vst + -(느)ㄴ다고 해요 → **-(느)ㄴ대요**	만난대요/먹는대요
		Ast + -다고 해요 → **-대요**	바쁘대요
		Noun + (이)라고 해요 → **(이)래요**	변호사래요 선생님이래요
	Past	A/Vst + -았/었/였다고 해요 → **-았/었/였대요**	만났대요 먹었대요
	Future	A/Vst + -(으)ㄹ 거라고 해요 → **-(으)ㄹ 거래요**	만날 거래요 먹을 거래요

Interrogative	Present	Noun + (이)냐고 해요 → **(이)내요**	변호사내요 선생님이내요
		Vst + -(느)냐고 해요 → **-내요** Ast + -(으)냐고 해요 → **-(으)내요**	가내요/먹내요 춥내요 (= 추우내요)
	Past	A/Vst + -았/었(느)냐고 하다 → **-았/었내요**	갔었내요/먹었내요 추웠내요
	Future (Supposition)	A/Vst + -(으)ㄹ 거냐고 하다 → **-(으)ㄹ 거내요**	갈 거내요/먹을 거내요 추울 거내요
Suggestive		Vst + -자고 해요 → **-재요**	가재요/입재요
Imperative		Vst + -(으)라고 해요 → **-(으)래요**	가래요/입으래요
		Vst + -아/어 달라고 하다 → **-아/어 달래요** Vst + -아/어/여 주라고 하다 → **-아/어 주래요**	도와 달래요 도와주래요

* Vst means 'Verb stem', and Ast means 'Adjective stem'.

In Conversation

Track 212

A 에릭 씨가 요즘 어떻게 지내는지 알아요?
B 네, 요즘 한국어를 배운대요.

A Do you know how Eric is doing these days?
B Yes, he said he's been studying Korean.

A 지수 씨가 주말에 같이 등산 가재요. 시간 있어요?
B 네, 있어요. 같이 가요.

A Jisu said we should go hiking this weekend. Do you have time?
B Yes, I have time. Let's go.

A 사람들이 내일 몇 시에 모이내요.
B 9시까지 학교 앞으로 오라고 해 주세요.

A People are asking what time we'll meet up tomorrow.
B Please tell them to come to the front of the school by 9 o'clock.

A 재준 씨, 어디에 가요?
B 유키 씨가 숙제를 좀 도와 달래요. 그래서 유키 씨를 만나러 가요.

A Jaejun, where are you going?
B Yuki said she wants help on her homework. So I'm going to meet her.

What did Tiluen say to Budi? As shown in the example, change each quotation into its appropriate indirect quotation in contracted form.

보기 부디 씨, 주말에 시간 있어요?
→ 티루엔 씨가 부디 씨에게 주말에 시간 있냬요.

티루엔 씨는 부디 씨에게 시간 있으면 (1) ________________. 티루엔 씨는 부디 씨에게 무슨 영화를 (2) ________________. 티루엔 씨는 공포 영화를 (3) ________________. 코미디 영화가 (4) ________________. 그래서 코미디 영화를 (5) ________________. 영화를 본 후에 (6) ________________. 티루엔 씨는 파란색 옷을 (7) ________________. 티루엔 씨는 부디 씨도 (8) ________________. 같이 (9) ________________. 티루엔 씨는 자기와 부디 씨는 정말 (10) ________________.

Unit 24.

Irregular Conjugations

01 '—' 불규칙 (Irregular Conjugation)

Track **213**

민우 씨는 요즘 많이 **바빠요**.

Minu is really busy these days.

불 좀 **꺼** 주세요.

Please turn off the lights.

배가 **고파요**.

(I'm) hungry.

Grammar Focus

For verb and adjective stems that end in —, — is omitted without exception when adding an ending that begins with 아/어. Then, the vowel that preceded — determines whether 아 or 어 is used in the ending. That is, when the vowel is ㅏ or ㅗ, ㅏ is used, otherwise ㅓ is used. In the case of single-syllable stems in which — is the only vowel, ㅓ is added after — is omitted.

바쁘다 + **-아요** → 바빠요.

(ㅏ is the vowel preceding —, so therefore -아요 is added.)

예쁘다 + **-어서** → 예뻐서

(ㅖ is the vowel preceding —, so therefore -어서 is added.)

크다 + **-었어요** → 컸어요

(The stem 크 is a single syllable, so therefore -었어요 is added.)

Base Form	-(스)ㅂ니다	-고	-아/어요	-았/었어요	-아/어서	-아/어도
예쁘다 to be pretty	예쁩니다	예쁘고	예뻐요	예뻤어요	예뻐서	예뻐도
바쁘다 to be busy	바쁩니다	바쁘고	바빠요	바빴어요	바빠서	바빠도
아프다 to be sick	아픕니다	아프고	아파요	아팠어요	아파서	아파도
(배가) 고프다 to be hungry	(배가) 고픕니다	(배가) 고프고	(배가) 고파요	(배가) 고팠어요	(배가) 고파서	(배가) 고파도
크다 to be big	큽니다	크고	커요	컸어요	커서	커도
나쁘다 to be bad	나쁩니다	나쁘고	나빠요	나빴어요	나빠서	나빠도
쓰다 to write, use	씁니다	쓰고	써요	썼어요	써서	써도
끄다 to turn off	끕니다	끄고	꺼요	껐어요	꺼서	꺼도

In Conversation

Track 214

A 하미 씨, 지금 울어요?
B 네, 영화가 너무 슬퍼서 울고 있어요.

A Hami, are you crying?
B Yes, I'm crying because the movie was so sad.

A 주말에 소풍 잘 갔다 왔어요?
B 아니요, 날씨가 나빠서 소풍을 못 갔어요.

A Did you have a nice picnic over the weekend?
B No, the weather was bad, so I couldn't go.

A 어제 왜 학교에 안 왔어요?
B 배가 많이 아팠어요. 그래서 학교에 못 왔어요.

A Why didn't you come to school yesterday?
B I had a bad stomachache. So I couldn't come to school.

On Your Own

Change the words in parentheses to their appropriate forms as shown in the example.

보기 시험을 못 봐서 기분이 나빠요. (나쁘다)
-아/어요

(1) 공연을 볼 때는 핸드폰을 ______ 주세요. (끄다)
-아/어

(2) 오늘 너무 ______ 저녁 약속을 취소했어요. (바쁘다)
-아/어서

(3) 제 여자 친구는 저보다 키가 ______. (크다)
-아/어요

(4) 요코 씨는 아이들이 세 명 있는데 모두 ______. (예쁘다)
-아/어요

(5) 호앙 씨는 몸이 ______ 항상 운동을 해요. (아프다)
-아/어도

(6) 남자 친구한테서 프러포즈를 받고 너무 ______. (기쁘다)
-았/었어요

(7) A 어제 오후에 뭐 했어요?

B 부모님께 편지를 ______. (쓰다)
-았었어요

(8) A 배가 ______? (고프다)
-아/어요?

B 아니요, 배가 ______. (고프다)
-지 않아요

(9) A 주희 씨는 참 예쁘지요?

B 얼굴은 ______ 성격이 별로 안 좋아요. (예쁘다)
-지만

02 'ㄹ' 불규칙 (Irregular Conjugation)

Track 215

아이가 혼자서 잘 **놉니다**.

The girl plays well by herself.

백화점이 몇 시에 **여는지** 알고 싶어요.

I'd like to know what time the department store opens.

지금 **만드는** 게 뭐예요?

What are you making?

Grammar Focus

For verb and adjective stems that end in ㄹ, ㄹ is omitted without exception when adding an ending that begins with ㄴ, ㅂ, or ㅅ. However, when an ending that begins with –으 is added to such a stem, even though ㄹ remains as a final consonant, it is treated as a vowel, and therefore –으 is omitted.

만들다 + **–(으)세요** → 만드세요 〔만들으세요 (×)〕
알다 + **–(스)ㅂ니다** → 압니다 〔알습니다 (×)〕
살다 + **–는** → 사는 〔살는 (×)〕

Base Form	–아/어요	–(으)러	–(스)ㅂ니다	–(으)세요	–(으)ㅂ시다	–(으)니까	Noun Modifier (Present) –(으)ㄴ/는
살다 to live	살아요	살러	삽니다	사세요	삽시다	사니까	사는
팔다 to sell	팔아요	팔러	팝니다	파세요	팝시다	파니까	파는

만들다 to make	만들어요	만들러	만듭니다	만드세요	만듭시다	만드니까	만드는
열다 to open	열어요	열러	엽니다	여세요	엽시다	여니까	여는
놀다 to play	놀아요	놀러	놉니다	노세요	놉시다	노니까	노는
알다 to know	알아요	–	압니다	아세요	압시다	아니까	아는
멀다 to be far	멀어요	–	멉니다	머세요	–	머니까	먼
달다 to be sweet	달아요	–	답니다	다세요	–	다니까	단

When –(으)ㄹ is added to stems ending in ㄹ, such as **(으)ㄹ 때**, **–(으)ㄹ게요**, and **–(으)ㄹ 래요?**, –(으)ㄹ is omitted, and the stem attaches directly to the ending.

살다 + –(으)ㄹ 때 → 살 때 　　　 만들다 + –(으)ㄹ래요? → 만들래요?

In Conversation

Track 216

A 살을 좀 빼고 싶어요.
B 그러면 케이크나 초콜릿 같은 단 음식을 먹지 마세요.

A I want to lose some weight.
B In that case, stop eating sweets like cake and chocolate.

A 노트북을 어디에서 싸게 파는지 아세요?
B 용산에서 전자 제품을 싸게 파니까 가 보세요.

A Do you know where I can get a laptop for a good price?
B Go to Yongsan. They sell electronics cheap there.

A 우리 집은 머니까 학교 다니기 힘들어요.
B 학교 근처로 이사 오는 게 어때요?

A Our house is far from school, so it's hard to commute.
B Then why don't you move someplace closer to school?

On Your Own

Change the words in parentheses to their appropriate form, as shown in the example.

보기 재준 씨가 어디에서 사는지 알아요? (살다)
-(으)ㄴ/는지

(1) 바람이 많이 ____________ 창문을 좀 닫아 주세요. (불다)
-(으)니까

(2) 저기 ____________ 아이가 제 동생이에요. (울다)
-(으)ㄴ/는

(3) 저 식당에서 우리나라 음식을 ____________ , 같이 먹으러 갈래요. (팔다)
-(으)ㄴ/는데

(4) 질문이 있으면 손을 ____________ . (들다)
-(으)세요

(5) 저는 학교 근처에서 ____________ . (살다)
-(스)ㅂ니다

(6) 외국 생활은 ____________ 재미있어요. (힘들다)
-지만

(7) A 옆 반에 혹시 ____________ 사람이 있어요? (알다)
-(으)ㄴ/는

B 제 고등학교 때 친구가 옆 반에 있는데, 왜요?

(8) A 에릭 씨를 언제 만났어요?

B 한국에 ____________ 만났어요. (살다)
-(으)ㄹ 때

(9) A 이 치마 어때요? 하영 씨에게 잘 어울릴 것 같아요.

B 저는 ____________ 치마를 안 좋아해요. (길다)
-(으)ㄴ/는

03 'ㅂ' 불규칙 (Irregular Conjugation)

Track 217

커피가 **뜨거우니까** 조심하세요.

The coffee's hot, so be careful.

날씨가 **추워서** 집에 있었어요.

It's cold outside, so I stayed home.

저는 **매운** 음식을 좋아해요.

I like spicy food.

Grammar Focus

For a few verb and adjective stems that end in ㅂ, ㅂ changes to 오 or 우 when added to an ending that begins with a vowel. 돕다 (to assist) and 곱다 (lovely/charming) are the only two words that change to 오, while all others change to 우.

쉽다 + **-어요** → 쉬우 + **-어요** → 쉬워요

돕다 + **-아요** → 도오 + **-아요** → 도와요

Base Form	-(스)ㅂ니다	-고	-아/어요	-아/어서	-(으)면	Noun Modifier -(으)ㄴ/는
쉽다 to be easy	쉽습니다	쉽고	쉬워요	쉬워서	쉬우면	쉬운
어렵다 to be difficult	어렵습니다	어렵고	어려워요	어려워서	어려우면	어려운

맵다 to be spicy	맵습니다	맵고	매워요	매워서	매우면	매운
덥다 to be hot	덥습니다	덥고	더워요	더워서	더우면	더운
춥다 to be cold	춥습니다	춥고	추워요	추워서	추우면	추운
무겁다 to be heavy	무겁습니다	무겁고	무거워요	무거워서	무거우면	무거운
*돕다 to help	돕습니다	돕고	**도와요**	**도와서**	도우면	도운

Although the stems of **좁다** (to be narrow), **입다** (to wear), **씹다** (to chew), and **잡다** (to catch) end in ㅂ, they are conjugated regularly.

Base Form	-(스)ㅂ니다	-고	-아/어요	-아/어서	-(으)면	Noun Modifier -(으)ㄴ/는
입다 to wear	입습니다	입고	입어요	입어서	입으면	입는
좁다 to be narrow	좁습니다	좁고	좁아요	좁아서	좁으면	좁은

In Conversation

Track 218

A 어떤 영화를 좋아하세요?
B 저는 무서운 영화를 좋아해요.

A What kind of movies do you like?
B I like scary movies.

A 음식이 싱거운데 소금 좀 주세요.
B 여기 있습니다.

A The food is a little bland, so could I have some salt?
B Here you go.

A 아이가 누구를 닮았어요? 정말 귀여워요.
B 감사합니다. 엄마를 많이 닮았어요.

A Who does the baby resemble most? She/He's adorable.
B Thank you. She/He resembles his/her mother.

On Your Own

Change the words in parentheses to their appropriate forms as shown in the example.

보기 A 왜 음악을 껐어요?

B 시끄러워서 껐어요. (시끄럽다)
-아/어서

(1) A 가방이 무거워요?

B 아니요, ________________. (가볍다)
-아/어요

(2) A 숙제가 ________________ 좀 도와주시겠어요? (어렵다)
-(으)ㄴ/는데

B 네, 알겠어요.

(3) A 날씨가 ________________ 따뜻한 음식을 먹으러 가요. (춥다)
-(으)니까

B 네, 좋아요.

(4) A 기사 아저씨, 저기 앞에서 세워 주실 수 있어요?

B 저기는 길이 ________________ 자동차가 못 들어가요. (좁다)
-아/어서

(5) A 이 음식이 정말 맵지요?

B 음식이 ________________ 맛있어요. (맵다)
-지만

(6) A 한국어 배우기가 어때요?

B 생각보다 ________________ 재미있어요. (쉽다)
-고

(7) A 그 옷을 ________________ 멋있네요. (입다)
-(으)니까

B 그래요? 감사합니다.

'ㄷ' 불규칙 (Irregular Conjugation)

Track 219

음악을 **들으면서** 운동해요.

I listen to music while I exercise.

돈이 없어서 **걸어서** 갔어요.

I had no money, so I went by foot.

그 여자에게 전화번호를 **물어봤어요**.

I asked her for her phone number.

Grammar Focus

For a few verb stems that end in ㄷ, ㄷ changes to ㄹ when added to an ending that begins with a vowel.

듣다 + **-어요** → 들어요   걷다 + **-을 거예요** → 걸을 거예요

Base Form	-(스)ㅂ니다	-고	-아/어요	-았/었어요	-(으)세요	-(으)ㄹ까요?	-(으)면
듣다 to listen	듣습니다	듣고	들어요	들었어요	들으세요	들을까요?	들으면
묻다 to ask	묻습니다	묻고	물어요	물었어요	물으세요	물을까요?	물으면
걷다 to walk	걷습니다	걷고	걸어요	걸었어요	걸으세요	걸을까요?	걸으면

Although the stems of **닫다** (to close), **받다** (to receive), and **믿다** (to believe) end in ㄷ, they are conjugated regularly.

Base Form	-(스)ㅂ니다	-고	-아/어요	-았/었어요	-(으)세요	-(으)ㄹ까요?	-(으)면
닫다	닫습니다	닫고	닫아요	닫았어요	닫으세요	닫을까요?	닫으면
받다	받습니다	받고	받아요	받았어요	받으세요	받을까요?	받으면

In Conversation

Track 220

A 캐럴 씨, 날씨가 좋은데 밖에 나가서 좀 걸을까요?
B 네, 좋아요.

A Carol, the weather's nice, so why don't we go for a walk outside?
B Okay, that sounds nice.

A 이 노래 들어 봤어요? 정말 좋아요.
B 그래요? 누구 노래인데요?

A Have you heard this song? It's really good.
B Really? Who sings it?

On Your Own

Change the words in parentheses to their appropriate forms as shown in the example.

보기 A 학교에 어떻게 가요?
B 걸어서 가요. (걷다)
-아/어서

(1) A 내일 같이 영화 볼까요?
B 좋아요. 제가 에릭 씨에게도 내일 시간이 있는지 ________ 볼게요. (묻다)
-아/어

(2) A 어떻게 하면 한국어 듣기가 좋아질까요?
B 한국 드라마와 영화도 많이 보고, 한국 음악도 많이 ________. (듣다)
-(으)세요

(3) A 어제 많이 ________ 다리 안 아파요? (걷다)
-았/었는데
B 평소에 많이 ________ 괜찮아요. (걷다)
-아/어서

(4) A 백화점이 몇 시에 문을 ________? (닫다)
-아/어요
B 보통은 8시에 ________ 세일 기간에는 9시까지 열어요. (닫다)
-(으)ㄴ/는데

 '르' 불규칙 (Irregular Conjugation)

Track 221

댄 씨는 노래를 잘 **불러서** 인기가 많아요.

Dane is popular because he can sing well.

출근 시간에는 지하철이 버스보다 **빨라요**.

The subway is faster than the bus during rush hour.

저는 영어를 **몰라요**.

I don't speak English.

Grammar Focus

For most verb and adjective stems that end in 르, the ㅡ of 르 is omitted, and an additional ㄹ is added to form ㄹㄹ.

다르다 + -아요 → 다르다 + ㄹ + 아요 → 달라요
부르다 + -어요 → 부르다 + ㄹ + 어요 → 불러요

Base Form	-(스)ㅂ니다	-고	-(으)면	-아/어요	-았/었어요	-아/어서
다르다 to be different	다릅니다	다르고	다르면	달라요	달랐어요	달라서
빠르다 to be fast	빠릅니다	빠르고	빠르면	빨라요	빨랐어요	빨라서
자르다 to cut	자릅니다	자르고	자르면	잘라요	잘랐어요	잘라서

모르다 to know	모릅니다	모르고	모르면	몰라요	몰랐어요	몰라서
부르다 to call, sing	부릅니다	부르고	부르면	불러요	불렀어요	불러서
기르다 to grow, raise	기릅니다	기르고	기르면	길러요	길렀어요	길러서

In Conversation

Track 222

A 준호 씨, 머리 잘랐어요? 멋있네요.
B 그래요? 고마워요.

A Junho, did you cut your hair? It's stylish.
B Really? Thanks.

A 에릭 씨와 제이슨 씨는 쌍둥이인데 얼굴이 안 닮았어요.
B 네, 성격도 많이 달라요.

A Eric and Jason are twins, but they don't resemble each other.
B Right, and their personalities are really different, too.

On Your Own

Change the words in parentheses to their appropriate forms as shown in the example.

보기 A 더 드세요.
B 배가 불러서 (-아/어서) 더 못 먹겠어요. (부르다)

(1) A 이 노래 부를 수 있어요?
B 아니요, 노래가 너무 ______ (-아/어서) 못 불러요. (빠르다)

(2) A 중국의 결혼식은 한국과 비슷해요?
B 아니요, 많이 ______ (-아/어요). (다르다)

(3) A 한국말을 잘하시네요.
B 아니에요, 아직도 한국말이 ______ (-아/어서) 실수를 많이 해요. (서투르다)

(4) A 초인종을 여러 번 ______ (-았/었는데) 아무도 안 나와요. (누르다)
B 이상하네요. 소냐 씨가 오늘 집에 있겠다고 했는데…….

06 'ㅎ' 불규칙 (Irregular Conjugation)

Track 223

백설공주는 머리는 **까맣고** 피부는 **하얘요**.

Snow White has black hair and a white complexion.

왕비는 백설공주에게 **빨간** 사과를 줬어요.

The queen gave Snow White a red apple.

왕자는 크고 **파란** 눈으로 공주를 봤어요.

The prince looked at Snow White with his big blue eyes.

Grammar Focus

When an adjective stem ending in ㅎ is added to an ending that begins with a vowel, ㅎ is omitted.

1 When endings beginning in –으 are added to adjective stems ending in ㅎ, ㅎ and 으 are omitted.

하얗다 + **–(으)ㄴ** → 하얀　　　까맣다 + **–(으)니까** → 까마니까

2 When endings beginning in –아/어 are added to adjective stems ending in ㅎ, ㅎ is omitted and ㅣ is added.

까맣다 + **–아서** → 까마 + ㅣ + **–아서** → 까매서
하얗다 + **–아요** → 하야 + ㅣ + **–아요** → 하얘요

Base Form	-(스)ㅂ니다	-고	-(으)면	-(으)ㄴ/는	-아/어요	-았/었어요	-아/어서
까맣다 to be black	까맣습니다	까맣고	까마면	까만	까매요	까맸어요	까매서
노랗다 to be yellow	노랗습니다	노랗고	노라면	노란	노래요	노랬어요	노래서
파랗다 to be blue	파랗습니다	파랗고	파라면	파란	파래요	파랬어요	파래서
빨갛다 to be red	빨갛습니다	빨갛고	빨가면	빨간	빨개요	빨갰어요	빨개서
하얗다 to be white	하얗습니다	하얗고	하야면	하얀	하얘요	하 어요	하얘서
이렇다 to be like this	이렇습니다	이렇고	이러면	이런	이래요	이랬어요	이래서
그렇다 to be like that	그렇습니다	그렇고	그러면	그런	그래요	그랬어요	그래서
저렇다 to be like that	저렇습니다	저렇고	저러면	저런	저래요	저랬어요	저래서
어떻다 to be how, to be like what	어떻습니다	어떻고	어떠면	어떤	어때요	어땠어요	어때서

Although the stems of **좋다** (to be good), **많다** (many), **낳다** (to bear, to give birth to), and **넣다** (to put in, to insert) etc. end in ㅎ, they are conjugated regularly.

Base Form	-(스)ㅂ니다	-고	-(으)면	-(으)ㄴ/는	-아/어요	-았/었어요	-아/어서
낳다	낳습니다	낳고	낳으면	낳는	낳아요	낳았어요	낳아서
좋다	좋습니다	좋고	좋으면	좋은	좋아요	좋았어요	좋아서

In Conversation

Track 224

A 보세요! 가을 하늘이 정말 파래요.
B 하늘은 파랗고 구름은 하얘서 그림 같아요.

A Look! The autumn sky is really blue.
B The sky is blue and the clouds are white, just like a painting.

A 얼굴이 많이 까매졌네요.
B 휴가 때 바다에 갔다 와서 그래요.

A Your face has tanned really brown (black).
B That's because I went to the beach during vacation.

A 파란 티셔츠 입은 남자가 누군지 아세요?

B 네, 제 동생이에요. 관심 있어요?

A Do you know who that boy wearing the blue T-shirt is?

B Yes, that's my little brother. Are you interested in him?

Check It Out!

When the stems of 이렇다, 그렇다, 저렇다, and 어떻다 are added to endings that begin with -아/어, they conjugate to 이래, 그래, 저래, and 어때 instead of 이레, 그레, 저레, and 어떼.

- 날씨가 어떼요? (×) → 날씨가 어때요? (○) How is the weather?
- 이번 성적이 너무 안 좋구나. 성적이 그레서 대학에 갈 수 있겠니? (×)
  이번 성적이 너무 안 좋구나. 성적이 그래서 대학에 갈 수 있겠니? (○)
  You didn't get a good result this time. Can you attend a university?

On Your Own

Look at the pictures and fill in the blanks appropriately.

(1) 

A 혹시 티루엔 씨가 누군지 아세요?

B 네, 저기 ___________ 정장을 입은 사람이에요. (노랗다)
-(으)ㄴ/는

(2) 

A 댄 씨가 술을 많이 마신 것 같아요.

B 맞아요. 지금 얼굴이 ___________. (빨갛다)
-아/어요

(3) 

A 눈이 많이 왔네요!

B 네, 눈 때문에 세상이 다 ___________. (하얗다)
-아/어요

(4) 

A 어머, 캐럴 씨 머리 바꿨네요.

B 네, 요즘 ___________ 머리가 유행이에요. (이렇다)
-(으)ㄴ/는

(5) 

A ___________ 색을 좋아해요? (어떻다)
-(으)ㄴ/는

B 저는 ___________ 색을 좋아해요. (까맣다)
-(으)ㄴ/는

07 'ㅅ' 불규칙 (Irregular Conjugation)

Track 225

모기가 물어서 눈이 **부었어요**.

A mosquito bit me, so my eye became swollen.

컵에 커피와 크림, 설탕을 넣고 **저어요**.

I put coffee, cream, and sugar in the cup and stir it all together.

어느 옷이 더 **나아요**?

Which outfit is better?

Grammar Focus

For a few verb and adjective stems that end in ㅅ, ㅅ is omitted when added to an ending that begins with a vowel.

잇다 + **-어요** → 이어요　　　　짓다 + **-을 거예요** → 지을 거예요

Base Form	-(스)ㅂ니다	-고	-아/어요	-았/었어요	-아/어서	-(으)면
잇다 to connect, to link	잇습니다	잇고	이어요	이었어요	이어서	이으면
낫다 ① to be cured ② to be better	낫습니다	낫고	나아요	나았어요	나아서	나으면
붓다 ① to swell ② to pour	붓습니다	붓고	부어요	부었어요	부어서	부으면

긋다 to draw (a line)	긋습니다	긋고	그어요	그었어요	그어서	그으면
젓다 to stir, to whip	젓습니다	젓고	저어요	저었어요	저어서	저으면
짓다 to name, to build, to write	짓습니다	짓고	지어요	지었어요	지어서	지으면

Although the stems of **벗다** (to take off), **웃다** (to laugh), and **씻다** (to wash) end in ㅅ, they are conjugated regularly.

Base Form	-(스)ㅂ니다	-고	-아/어요	-았/었어요	-아/어서	-(으)면
웃다	웃습니다	웃고	웃어요	웃었어요	웃어서	웃으면
씻다	씻습니다	씻고	씻어요	씻었어요	씻어서	씻으면

In Conversation

Track 226

A 아이 이름을 누가 지었어요?
B 할아버지가 지어 주셨어요.

A Who named your baby?
B His/Her grandfather named him/her.

A 감기 다 나았어요?
B 네, 이제 괜찮아요.

A Did you get over your cold?
B Yes, I'm fine now.

A 이 단어는 중요하니까 단어 밑에 줄을 그으세요.
B 네, 알겠습니다.

A This word is important, so please underline it.
B Okay, I will.

Check It Out!

In Korean, vowels will often combine when they meet. For example, 배우+어요 combine to become 배워요. However, in the case of irregular ㅅ stems, even though vowels may meet after the ㅅ is deleted, they do not combine.

- 짓다 + **-어요** → 지어요 (○) / 져요 (×) (져요 is the combined form of 지다 + -어요.)
- 낫다 + **-아요** → 나아요 (○) / 나요 (×) (나요 is the combined form of 나다 + -아요.)

On Your Own

Change the words in parentheses to their appropriate forms as shown in the example.

> 보기 이 노래를 누가 지었어요 ? (짓다)
> -았/었어요

(1) 어제 밤에 라면을 먹고 자서 얼굴이 많이 ______________. (붓다)
-았/었어요

(2) 커피를 잘 ______________ 드세요. (젓다)
-아/어서

(3) 지금 회사보다 더 ______________ 곳에서 일하고 싶어요. (낫다)
-(으)ㄴ/는

(4) 저기 지금 ______________ 있는 건물이 뭐예요? (짓다)
-고

(5) 제니퍼 씨는 ______________ 때 참 예뻐요. (웃다)
-(으)ㄹ

(6) 피터 씨의 한국말보다 요코 씨의 한국말이 더 ______________. (낫다)
-아/어요

(7) 저는 중요한 문장에 밑줄을 ______________ 공부를 합니다. (긋다)
-(으)면서

(8) 과일을 ______________ 드세요. (씻다)
-아/어서

(9) 옷을 ______________ 후에 저 옷걸이에 거세요. (벗다)
-(으)ㄴ

(10) 커피 잔에 물을 ______________. (붓다)
-(으)세요

Appendix

- Good Things to Know
- Answer Key
- Grammar Explanations in Korean
- Grammar Index

Good Things to Know

1. Demonstrative Pronouns

A 이것이 무엇입니까?
What is this?

B 이것은 연필입니다.
This is a pencil.

A 그것이 무엇입니까?
What is that?

B 이것은 가방입니다.
That's a bag.

A 저것이 무엇입니까?
What is that (over there)?

B 저것은 시계입니다.
That's a clock.

When indicating an object or location, **이/그/저** is used in front of the noun representing it. Of these, **이** is used when the noun is close to the speaker, **그** is used when it is close to the listener, and **저** is used when it is located away from both the speaker and listener.

	Close to Speaker	Close to Listener	Away from Both Speaker and Listener
	이	그	저
Thing	이것	그것	저것
Person	이 사람/이 분	그 사람/그 분	저 사람/저 분
Place	이곳 (여기)	그곳 (거기)	저곳 (저기)

When the particle **이** is added to **이것**, **그것**, and **저것**, the result is **이것이**, **그것이**, and **저것이**. However, in conversation these forms are contracted to **이게**, **그게**, and **저게**. The particles 은 and 을 are also contracted in the same way.

이것이 → 이게	**이것은** → 이건	**이것을** → 이걸
그것이 → 그게	**그것은** → 그건	**그것을** → 그걸
저것이 → 저게	**저것은** → 저건	**저것을** → 저걸

A **이건** 뭐예요? — What is this?
B **이건** 꽃이에요. — This is a flower.

A 너무 커요. **이걸** 어떻게 먹어요? — It's too big. I can't eat this. (How is one to eat this?)
B 그럼 **저게** 작으니까 **저걸** 드세요. — Then eat that one (over there) because it's smaller.

Demonstrative pronouns are also used to refer to something already mentioned in a particular context.

어제 동대문시장에 갔어요.
거기는 예쁜 옷이 아주 많았어요.
(= 동대문시장)

Yesterday, I went to Namdaemun Market.
There were lots of pretty clothes **there**.
(= Namdaemun Market)

지난주에 댄 씨를 만났어요
그분은 아주 친절했어요.
(= 댄 씨)

I met Dane last week.
He (that person) was very kind.
(= Dane)

2. Temporal Adverbs

아직 (not) yet, still / **이미** already (previously) / **벌써** already (so soon)

● 아직 (not) yet, still, only

(1) **아직** indicates that more time must pass before something can happen or some state can be reached. It is used together with negative expressions.

A 밥 먹었어요? — Have you eaten yet?

B 아니요, **아직** 안 먹었어요. — No, I haven't eaten yet.

(2) **아직** can also indicate that something or some state still continues without ending.

A 숙제 다 했어요? — Did you finish your homework?

B 아니요, **아직** 하고 있어요. 조금만 더 하면 끝나요. — No, I'm still doing it. Just a little more and I'll be done.

이미 Already (Previously)	**벌써** Already (So soon)
Indicates something that has completely finished or already passed by.	Sooner than expected.
A 지금 가면 영화를 볼 수 있을까요? Do you think we can see the movie if we go now? B 아니요, 지금 6:40분이에요. **이미** 늦었으니까 9시 영화를 봅시다. No, it's 6:40 now. It's already too late, so let's see the 9:00 movie.	A 저녁에 뭐 먹고 싶어요? What do you want to eat for dinner? B 저녁 먹었는데요. I've eaten dinner. A 5시인데 **벌써** 먹었어요? It's 5:00, and you've already eaten?

A 댄 씨를 만나고 싶은데 지금 한국에 있어요? I'd like to meet with Dane. Is he in Korea now? B **이미** 미국으로 떠났어요. He's already left for the U.S. (Dane has gone to the U.S., and thus there is no way to meet him even if one wanted to.)	A 댄 씨를 만나고 싶은데 지금 한국에 있어요? I'd like to meet with Dane. Is he in Korea now? B 지난주에 미국으로 떠났어요. He left for the U.S. last week. A **벌써** 떠났어요? He's already left? (Dane left for the U.S. sooner than expected.)

지금 (right) now / 이제 (from) now / 요즘 recently

지금 (Right) Now	**이제** (From) Now
The precise moment when the speaker is speaking.	Can mean 'now' but has a sense of separation from the past and includes a sense of 'from now'.
A **지금** 뭐하고 있어요? What are you doing (right) now? B 음악을 듣고 있어요. Listening to music.	A **이제** 그 식당에 안 갈 거예요. I won't go to that restaurant anymore (from now on). B 왜요? 음식이 맛이 없어요? Why? Is the food not good?
Can be used with the present progressive form of verbs **–고 있다**. • 지금 공부하고 있어요. (○) (I) am studying now. • (일 이외의 다른 것을 하고 있다가) 자, 지금 일합시다. (×)	cannot be used with the present progressive form of verbs **–고 있다**. • 이제 공부하고 있어요. (×) • (일 이외의 다른 것을 하고 있다가) 자, 이제 일합시다. (○) (After doing something unrelated to one's work) Okay, let's get to work.

● 요즘 recently

요즘 refers to the period of time beginning a short time ago until the present.

A **요즘** 피곤하세요? Have you been tired recently?
B 네, 조금 피곤해요. Yes, (I've been) a little tired.

A **요즘** 어떤 헤어스타일이 유행이에요? What's been the popular hairstyle recently?
B 단발머리가 유행이에요. Bobbed hair is popular.

03 먼저 first / 아까 a while ago / 나중에 later / 이따가 in a little while

먼저 first

먼저 refers to something being first in temporal order.

A 나탈리아 씨, 점심 안 먹어요? — Natalie, aren't you gong to have lunch?
B 저는 지금 할 일이 있으니까 **먼저** 드세요. — Please eat first because I have something to take care of.

A 민우 씨는 갔어요? — Did Minu leave?
B 네, 약속이 있어서 **먼저** 갔어요. — Yes, he left (first) because he has to meet somebody.

아까 a while ago

아까 refers to a time just before the present that is within the same day; earlier.

A 댄 씨 봤어요? — Have you seen Dane?
B **아까** 도서관에 가는 거 봤어요. — I saw him going to the library a while ago.

A **아까** 커피숍에서 인사한 사람이 누구예요?
Who was that person who greeted (you/us) earlier at the coffee shop?
B 대학교 때 후배예요.
He/sHe's one of my younger classmates from undergraduate school.

이따가 In a little while	**나중에** Later
After a little time has passed.	After some time has passed and after one has finished doing some other task. The range of time can be within the same day or sometime in the future.
A 오늘 영화 보러 갈 거야? Are you going to go see a movie today? B 응, **이따가** 갈 거야. Yeah, in a little while. A 오늘 모임에 와요? Are you coming to the meeting today? B 네, **이따가** 만나요. Yes. See you in a little while. (They will meet later today after some time has passed.) A 언제 결혼할 거예요? When will you get married? B **이따가** 결혼할 거예요. (×)	A 여보세요? 댄 씨, 지금 전화할 수 있어요? Hello? Dane, can you talk now? B 미안해요. 지금 바쁘니까 **나중에** 전화할게요. Sorry. I'm busy right now, so I'll call you later. A 오늘 모임에 와요? Are you coming to the meeting today? B 아니요, 못 가요. 우리 **나중에** 만나요. No. I can't attend. Let's meet up later. (It won't be later today, but they will meet sometime in the future after some time has passed.)

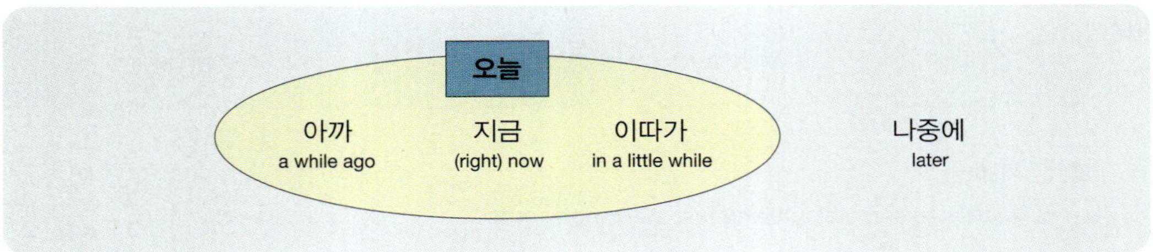

3. Frequency Adverbs

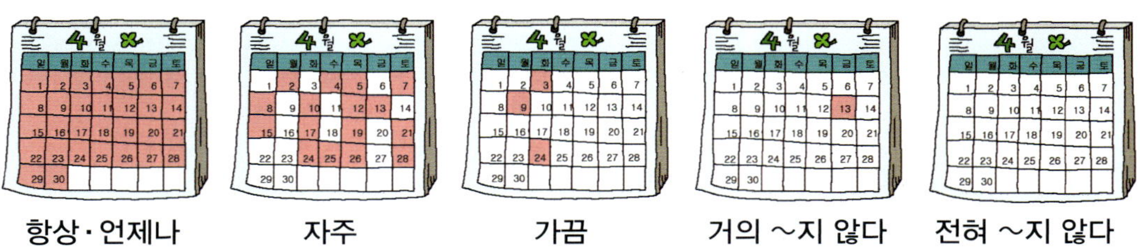

항상 · 언제나 always / 자주 often / 가끔 sometimes
거의 -지 않다 hardly / 전혀 -지 않다 never

늘 (항상 · 언제나), **자주**, and **가끔** are used in both positive and negative sentences, while **별로** and **전혀** are used only in negative sentences.

- 저는 매일 아침에 운동해요. **항상(언제나)** 운동해요.
  I exercise every day in the morning. I always exercise.
- 저는 일주일에 4번 운동해요. **자주** 운동해요.
  I exercise four times a week. I exercise often.
- 저는 일주일에 한 번 운동해요. **가끔** 운동해요.
  I exercise once a week. I sometimes exercise.
- 저는 한 달에 한 번 운동해요. **거의** 운동을 하지 않아요.
  I exercise once a month. I hardly (ever) exercise.
- 저는 운동을 싫어해요. **전혀** 운동을 하지 않아요.
  I don't like to exercise. I never exercise.

4. Connective Adverbs

그리고 and

그리고 is used when indicating that two sentences form a list or series, or that the two sentences are in temporal order. It means 'and' in English.

- 하영 씨는 날씬해요. **그리고** 예뻐요.
  Hayeong is thin. And sHe's pretty.
- 농구를 좋아해요. **그리고** 축구도 좋아해요.
  I like basketball. And I like soccer, too.
- 주말에 친구를 만났어요. **그리고** 같이 영화를 봤어요.
  I met a friend over the weekend. And we saw a movie together.

그렇지만 however

그렇지만 is used when the content of the first sentence is in contrast with that of the second sentence. It means 'however' or 'but' in English. Both **하지만** and **그러나** also have the same meaning, but **하지만** is used mainly in colloquial speech, while **그러나** is used mainly in the written, literary style.

- 요코 씨는 일본 사람이에요. **그렇지만** 재준 씨는 한국 사람이에요.
  Yoko is Japanese. However, Jaejun is Korean.
- 한국어는 영어와 다릅니다. **그러나** 배우기 어렵지 않습니다.
  Korean is different from English. However, it is not difficult to learn.
- 고기를 좋아해요. **하지만** 채소는 안 좋아해요.
  I like (to eat) meat. But I don't like vegetables.

그래서 so, that is why

그래서 is used when the first sentence is the reason or cause for the result described in the second sentence. It means '(and) so' or 'that is why' in English.

A 어디 아파요?
Where does it hurt?

B 어제 술을 많이 마셨어요. **그래서** 머리가 아파요.
I drank a lot of alcohol last night. So my head hurts.

A 왜 차가 안 가요?
Why isn't the car moving?

B 주말이에요. **그래서** 길이 막혀요.
It's the weekend and so there's a lot of traffic.

- 외국 사람입니다. **그래서** 한국말을 못합니다.
  I'm a foreigner, so that's why I can't speak Korean.

그러니까 therefore, for that reason

그러니까 is used when the first sentence is the inevitable or natural reason for the second sentence. It means 'therefore' in English. Normally, **그러니까** is followed by **–(으)세요**, **–(으)ㅂ시다**, **–아/어야 하다**, or **–(으)ㄹ 거다**.

- 비가 와요. **그러니까** 우산을 가져가세요.
  It's raining. Therefore (you should) take an umbrella with you.
- 이 영화는 재미없어요. **그러니까** 다른 영화를 봅시다.
  This movie's boring. So (for that reason) let's see a different one.
- 한국 대학교에 입학하고 싶어요. 그리고 한국 회사에 취직해서 한국에서 살고 싶어요. **그러니까** 한국말을 열심히 공부할 거예요.
  I want to enter a Korean university. And I want to get a job at a Korean company and live in Korea. Therefore (for those reasons), I plan to study Korean diligently.

A 여보, 우리 차가 있는데 왜 버스를 타요?
Dear, why are we taking the bus when we have a car?

B 자동차가 고장 났어요. **그러니까** 버스를 타야 해요.
The car broke down, so therefore we have to take the bus.

그러면 then, in that case

그러면 indicates that the first sentence is the premise or assumption behind the second sentence. It means 'then' or 'in that case' in English. In colloquial speech, the contracted form **그럼** is used often in place of **그러면**.

A 점심시간이에요. 배가 고파요.
It's lunchtime. I'm hungry.

B **그러면** (=**그럼**) 같이 식당에 가서 식사할까요?
In that case, shall we go to a restaurant and eat together?

A 한국말을 잘하고 싶어요.
I want to be able to speak Korean well.

B 그래요? **그러면** 한국 친구를 사귀세요.
Really? Then you should make some Korean friends.

• 나는 피곤할 때 목욕을 해요. **그러면** 기분이 좋아져요.
When I'm tired, I take a bath. Then I feel better.

06 그런데 however, by the way

그런데 indicates that the first sentence is background information about the second sentence. In this sense, it corresponds to 'however', 'by the way', or 'now' in English.

(1) It can be used when the first and second sentences are in contrast. In this sense, it means the same as **그렇지만**.

• 아버지는 키가 작아요. **그런데** 아들은 키가 커요.
The father is short. However, his son is tall.

(2) It can be used when the first sentence provides background or other information related to the situation described in the second sentence. In this sense it corresponds to '(and) yet' or 'and then (to one's surprise)' in English.

• 어제 명동에 갔어요. **그런데** 거기에서 영화배우를 봤어요.
I went to Myeongdong yesterday. And (to my surprise), I saw a movie star there.

(3) It can be used when the speaker broaches a new topic rather than continues to speak about the topic under discussion.

A 올해 나이가 어떻게 되세요? — How old are you this year?
B 네? 저, **그런데** 지금 몇 시예요? — Pardon? I, oh, by the way, what time is it now?

07 그래도 but (still), nevertheless

그래도 indicates that what is stated in the second sentence is true regardless of what is stated in the first. It means 'but' (still) or 'nevertheless' in English.

• 아까 밥을 많이 먹었어요. **그래도** 배가 고파요.
I ate so much a little while ago. But I'm still hungry.

• 5년 동안 한국에서 살았어요. **그래도** 아직 한국말을 잘 못해요.
I lived in Korea for five years. But I still can't speak Korean well.

• 그 여자는 나를 좋아하지 않아요. **그래도** 나는 그 여자를 좋아해요.
That girl doesn't like me. Nevertheless, I like her.

Answer Key

Getting Ready

01 이다 (to be)

(1) A 입니까 (= 예요) B 입니다 (= 예요)
(2) A 입니까 (= 이에요) B 입니다 (= 예요)
(3) A 입니까 (= 예요) B 입니다 (= 예요)
(4) 입니다 (= 이에요)

02 있다 (to exist/be, to have)

(1) 위 (2) 뒤 (3) 웨슬리 (4) 안
(5) 밑 (= 아래) (6) 댄 씨

03 Numbers

<Sino-Korean Numbers>
(1) 공일공 칠삼팔의 삼오공구 (2) 삼십사
(3) 백칠십오 (4) 육만 이천

<Native Korean Numbers>
(1) 한 마리 (2) 한 대, 두 대 (3) 두, 한 개
(4) 네 병, 두 잔 (5) 여덟 권, 일곱

04 Dates and Days of the Week

(1) 이천이십 년 유월 육일, 토
(2) 이천십오 년 십일월 십오일, 일
(3) 이천십칠 년 시월 십일, 화

05 Time

(1) 오전 일곱 시 삼십 분 (= 일곱 시 반)
(2) 오전 아홉 시 (3) 오후 한 시
(4) 오후 세 시 이십 분
(5) 오후 여섯 시 삼십 분 (= 여섯 시 반) (6) 여덟 시
(7) 열 시 (8) 열한 시

Unit 1. Tenses

01 Present Tense A/V-(스)ㅂ니다

(1) A 먹습니까 B 네, 먹습니다 (2) 기다립니다
(3) A 읽습니까 B 네, 읽습니다
(4) B 만납니다 (5) 씁니다
(6) A 삽니까 B 네, 삽니다

02 Present Tense A/V-아/어요

1 (1) A 학생이에요 B 네, 학생이에요
(2) A 의사예요 B 네, 의사예요
(3) A 책상이에요 B 네, 책상이에요
(4) A 사과예요 B 네, 사과예요

2 (1) A 봐요 B 봐요 (2) 전화해요
(3) A 읽어요 B 읽어요 (4) A 먹어요 B 먹어요
(5) 공부해요 (6) A 마셔요 B 마셔요

03 Past Tense A/V-았/었어요

(1) 만났어요 (2) 먹었어요 (3) 맛있었어요
(4) 갔어요 (5) 샀어요 (6) 쌌어요 (7) 아팠어요
(8) 불렀어요 (9) 청소했어요 (10) 봤어요
(11) 재미있었어요

04 Future Tense V-(으)ㄹ 거예요 ①

(1) 갈 거예요 (2) 놀 거예요 (3) 탈 거예요
(4) 공부할 거예요 (5) 먹을 거예요
(6) 부를 거예요 (7) 쉴 거예요

05 Progressive Tense V-고 있다 ①

(1) 세수하고 있어요 (2) 한국어를 배우고 있어요
(3) 밥을 먹고 있어요 (4) 반지를 찾고 있었어요

06 Past Perfect Tense A/V-았/었었어요

(1) 키가 작았었어요 (2) 머리가 길었었어요
(3) 고기를 안 먹었었어요 (4) 치마를 안 입었었어요

Unit 2. Negative Expressions

01 Word Negation

(1) 가 아니에요 (= 가 아닙니다)
(2) 가 없어요 (= 가 없습니다)
(3) 가 없어요 (= 가 없습니다)
(4) 몰라요 (= 모릅니다)

02 안 A/V-아/어요 (A/V-지 않아요)

(1) 안 봐요 (= 보지 않아요)
(2) 매일 운동 안 해요 (= 매일 운동하지 않아요)
(3) 안 깊어요 (= 깊지 않아요
(4) 안 친절해요 (= 친절하지 않아요)

03 못 V-아/어요 (V-지 못해요)

(1) 못했어요 (= 하지 못했어요)
(2) 못 가요 (= 가지 못해요)
(3) 못 봤어요 (= 보지 못했어요)

Unit 3. Particles

01 N이/가

1 (1) 티루엔이 (2) 유키가 (3) 부디가 (4) 댄이
2 (1) 가 (2) 이 (3) 가 (4) 이

02 N은/는

1 (1) 은 (2) 는 (3) 은 (4) 는 (5) 는 (6) 는
(7) 은 (8) 은 (9) 는 (10) 은
2 (1) 은 (2) 는 (3) 은 (4) 는 (5) 는

03 N을/를

(1) 를 (2) 를 (3) 커피를/차를 마셔요
(4) 빵을 사요

04 N와/과, N(이)랑, N하고

(1) 과 (= 이랑, = 하고) (2) 와 (= 랑, = 하고)
(3) 가족과 (= 가족이랑, = 가족하고) 여행을 할 거예요
(4) 재준 씨와 (= 재준 씨랑, = 재준 씨하고)

05 N의

(1) 제 (2) 부디 씨의 (3) 김 선생님의 남편이에요
(4) 우리 어머니예요

06 N에 ①

(1) 도서관에 가요 (2) 회사에 다녀요
(3) 공원에 있어요 (4) 탁자 위에 있어요

07 N에 ②

(1) 오전 11시에 만나요 (2) 2021년 5월 13일에 왔어요
(3) 목요일에 해요 (4) 겨울에 결혼해요

08 N에서

(1) 우체국에서 일해요 (2) 서울역에서 타요
(3) 백화점에서 쇼핑할 거예요
(4) 헬스클럽에서 운동했어요

09 N에서 N까지, N부터 N까지

(1) 에서, 까지 (2) 학교에서 집까지 (자전거로)
(3) 부터, 까지 (4) 10월 8일부터 (10월)10일까지

10 N에게/한테

(1) 에게 (= 한테) (2) 에
(3) 호앙 씨에게 (= 한테) (4) 에

11 N도

(1) 도 (2) 캐럴 씨도 예뻐요
(3) 만났어요, 도 만났어요
(4) 샀어요, 구두도 샀어요

12 N만

(1) 캐럴 씨만 미국 사람이에요
(2) 부모님에게만/부모님께만 썼어요
(3) 회사에서만 일해요

13 N밖에

(1) 밖에 (2) 밖에
(3) 한 명밖에 없어요 (4) 선풍기밖에 없어요

14 N(으)로

(1) B 자전거로 C 택시로 D 지하철로 (2) 걸어서
(3) 컴퓨터로, 펜으로 (4) 로

15 N(이)나 ①

(1) 이나 (2) 이나 (= 에서나) (3) 산이나 바다에

16 N(이)나 ②

(1) 한 시간이나 (2) 세 번이나 (3) 다섯 번이나
(4) 열 마리나 (5) 여섯 잔이나

17 N쯤

(1) 일곱 시쯤 일어났어요 (2) 두 시간쯤 걸려요
(3) 2주일쯤 여행했어요 (4) 30,000원쯤 해요

18 N처럼, N같이

(1) ⓔ (2) ⓑ (3) ⓐ (4) ⓒ (5) ⓓ (6) ⓕ

19 N보다

(1) 적비 씨의 가방이 운룡 씨의 가방보다 (더) 무거워요
(2) 소파가 의자보다 더 편해요
(3) 신발이 가방보다 더 싸요
(4) 중국이 호주보다 더 가까워요

20 N마다

(1) 방학마다 고향에 가요 (2) 나라마다
(3) 토요일마다 (4) 5분마다 지하철이 와요

Unit 4. Listing and Contrast

01 A/V-고

(1) 불고 (2) 멋있고 친절해요
(3) 운동하고, 데이트해요
(4) 요리, 하, 텔레비전, 봤어요

02 V-거나

(1) 외식을 하거나 (2) 쓰거나 (3) 물어보거나
(4) 영화를 보거나

03 A/V-지만

(1) 맵지만 맛있어요 (2) 학생이지만, 회사원이에요
(3) 바쁘지만, 한가해요 (4) 옷을 많이 입었지만 추워요

04 A/V-(으)ㄴ/는데 ①

(1) 맛있는데 비싸요 (2) 크지 않은데, 2개예요
(3) 결혼 안 했는데 (4) 먹었는데

Unit 5. Time Expressions

01 N 전에, V-기 전에

(1) ⓓ, 회의 전에 (= 회의하기 전에)
(2) ⓒ, 식사 전에 (= 식사하기 전에, = 밥을 먹기 전에)
(3) ⓑ, 방문 전에 (= 친구 집에 가기 전에)
(4) ⓐ, 자기 전에

02 N 후에, V-(으)ㄴ 후에

(1) ⓓ, 운동 후에 (= 운동한 후에, = 운동한 다음에)
(2) ⓐ, 이사 후에 (= 이사한 후에, = 이사한 다음에)
(3) ⓑ, 내린 후에 (= 내린 다음에)
(4) ⓒ, 우유를 산 후에 (= 우유를 산 다음에)

03 V-고 나서
(1) 일어나서 (2) 샤워하고 나서 (3) 먹고 나서
(4) 가서 (5) 가르치고 나서
(6) 보고 나서 (7) 끝나고 나서 (8) 운동하고 나서
(9) 가서

04 V-아/어서
(1) 만나서 (2) 가서 (3) A 사(서) B 만들어(서)
(4) 들어가서

05 N 때, A/V-(으)ㄹ 때
(1) 크리스마스 때
(2) 식사 때 (= 식사할 때 = 밥을 먹을 때)
(3) 없을 때 (4) 더울 때

06 V-(으)면서
(1) 커피를 마시면서 신문을 봐요 (= 신문을 보면서 커피를 마셔요)
(2) 노래를 하면서 샤워를 해요 (= 샤워를 하면서 노래를 해요)
(3) 아이스크림을 먹으면서 걸어요 (= 걸으면서 아이스크림을 먹어요)
(4) 친구를 기다리면서 책을 읽어요 (= 책을 읽으면서 친구를 기다려요

07 N 중, V-는 중
(1) ⓑ (2) ⓐ (3) ⓓ (4) ⓒ
(5) ⓖ (6) ⓗ (7) ⓔ (8) ⓕ

08 V-자마자
(1) ⓓ, 오자마자 (2) ⓒ, 나가자마자
(3) ⓑ, 시작하자마자 (4) ⓐ, 끊자마자

09 N 동안, V-는 동안
(1) 10분 동안 (2) 한 달 동안 (3) 요리하는 동안
(4) 자는 동안

10 V-(으)ㄴ 지
(1) 졸업한 지 (2) 결혼한 지 (3) 온 지
(4) 영어를 가르친 지 (5) 한국어를 배운 지
(6) 헬스클럽에 다닌 지 (7) 한국 여행을 한 지

Unit 6. Ability and Possibility

01 V-(으)ㄹ 수 있다/없다
(1) 고칠 수 있어요
(2) A 부를 수 있어요 B 부를 수 있어요, 출 수 있어요
(3) 걸을 수 없어요
(4) A 열 수 없어요 B 열 수 있어요

02 V-(으)ㄹ줄 알다/모르다
1 탈 줄 알아요
2 A 둘 줄 알아요 B 둘 줄 알아요, 둘 줄 몰라요
3 사용할 줄 몰라요.

Unit 7. Demands and Obligations, Permission and Prohibition

01 V-(으)세요
(1) ⓑ (2) ⓒ (3) ⓓ (4) ⓐ

02 V-지 마세요
(1) 햄버거를 먹지 마세요 (2) 담배를 피우지 마세요
(3) 커피를 마시지 마세요
(4) 컴퓨터게임을 하지 마세요

03 A/V-아/어야 되다/하다
(1) 공항에 가야 돼요 (= 공항에 가야 해요)
(2) 프랑스어를 잘해야 돼요 (= 프랑스어를 잘해야 해요)
(3) 운전해야 돼요 (= 운전해야 해요)
(4) 12시에 출발해야 돼요 (= 12시에 출발해야 해요)
(5) 병원에 가야 됐어요 (= 병원에 가야 했어요)

04 A/V-아/어도 되다
(1) 술을 마셔도 돼요 (2) 켜도 돼요
(3) 들어가도 돼요 (4) 써도 돼요

05 A/V-(으)면 안 되다
(1) 키우면 안 돼요 (2) 마시면 안 돼요
(3) 버리면 안 돼요 (4) 들어오면 안 돼요

06 A/V-지 않아도 되다 (안 A/V-아/어도 되다)
(1) 기다리지 않아도 돼요 (= 안 기다려도 돼요)
(2) 맞지 않아도 돼요 (= 안 맞아도 돼요)
(3) 책을 사지 않아도 돼요 (= 안 사도 돼요)
(4) 일찍 일어나지 않아도 돼요 (= 일찍 안 일어나도 돼요)

Unit 8. Expressions of Hope

01 V-고 싶다
(1) 제주도에서 말을 타고 싶어요
(2) 가수에게 사인을 받고 싶어요
(3) 휴대 전화를 사고 싶어요
(4) 좋아하는 가수를 만나고 싶어요
(5) 쇼핑을 하고 싶어요

02 A/V-았/었으면 좋겠다
1 (1) 애인이 생겼으면 좋겠어요
(2) 세계 여행을 했으면 좋겠어요
(3) 아파트로 이사했으면 좋겠어요
2 (1) 키가 컸으면 좋겠어요
(2) 주말이었으면 좋겠어요
(3) 운동을 잘했으면 좋겠어요

Unit 9. Reasons and Causes

01 A/V-아/어서 ②

(1) 맛있어서 (2) 많아서 (3) 와서 (4) 마셔서

02 A/V-(으)니까 ①

1 (1) 모르니까 (2) 고장 났으니까 (3) 일이 많으니까 (4) 깨끗하니까 (5) 가니까

2 (1) 없으니까 (2) 더우니까 (3) 나니까 (4) 도와주셔서 (5) 떠났으니까

03 N 때문에, A/V-기 때문에

(1) 휴일이기 때문에 (2) 내일은 약속이 있기 때문에 (3) 회사 일 때문에 (4) 향수 냄새 때문에

Unit 10. Making Requests and Assisting

01 V-아/어 주세요, V-아/어 주시겠어요?

(1) 문을 (좀) 열어 주시겠어요
(2) 천천히 이야기해 주세요
(3) 조용히 해 주세요 (4) 책을 (좀) 찾아 주시겠어요

02 V-아/어 줄게요, V-아/어 줄까요?

(1) 빌려줄게요 (= 빌려 드릴게요)
(2) 내려 줄까요 (= 내려 드릴까요)

Unit 11. Trying New Things and Experiences

01 V-아/어 보다

1 (1) 한복을 입어 보세요 (2) 비빔밥을 먹어 보세요 (3) 한라산에 올라가 보세요

2 (1) 안 가 봤어요 (= 가 보지 않았어요) (2) 가 봤어요 (3) 마셔 봤어요 (4) 구경해 보세요

02 V-(으)ㄴ 적이 있다/없다

(1) 탄 적이 없어요, 탄 적이 있어요
(2) 간 적이 없어요, 간 적이 있어요
(3) 잃어버린 적이 없어요, 잃어버린 적이 있어요

Unit 12. Asking Opinions and Making Suggestions

01 V-(으)ㄹ까요? ①

(1) 볼까요 (2) 봐요 (3) 만날까요 (4) 만나요 (5) 먹을까요 (6) 쇼핑할까요 (7) 이야기해요

02 V-(으)ㄹ까요? ②

(1) A 가져갈까요 B 가져가세요
(2) A 먹을까요 B 드세요
(3) A 갈까요 B 가세요
(4) A 볼까요 B 보지 마세요

03 V-(으)ㅂ시다

(1) 갑시다 (= 가요) (2) 여행합시다 (= 여행해요)
(3) 갑시다 (= 가요)
(4) 선탠도 합시다 (= 선탠도 해요)
(5) 가져갑시다 (= 가져가요)
(6) 먹읍시다 (= 먹어요)

04 V-(으)시겠어요?

(1) ⓓ (2) ⓐ (3) ⓔ (4) ⓑ

05 V-(으)ㄹ래요? ①

(1) 앉을래요 (= 앉으실래요) (2) 탈래요
(3) 쇼핑할래요 (4) 걸을래요
(5) 보지 않을래요 (= 안 볼래요)

Unit 13. Intentions and Plans

01 A/V-겠어요 ①

1 (1) 공부하겠어요 (2) 놀아 주겠어요 (3) 컴퓨터게임을 하지 않겠어요 (= 컴퓨터게임을 안 하겠어요)

2 (1) 눈이 오겠습니다 (2) 바람이 불겠습니다 (3) 흐리겠습니다

02 V-(으)ㄹ게요

(1) 살게요 (2) 보내 드릴게요
(3) 이야기하지 않을게요 (= 이야기 안 할게요)
(4) 늦게 자지 않을게요 (= 늦게 안 잘게요)

03 V-(으)ㄹ래요 ②

(1) 입을래요 (2) 먹을래요 (3) 배울래요
(4) 안 먹을래요 (= 먹지 않을래요)

Unit 14. Background Information and Explanations

01 A/V-(으)ㄴ/는데 ②

(1) 친구인데 (2) 고픈데 (3) 오는데 (4) 없는데

02 V-(으)니까 ②

(1) ⓓ, 지하철을 타 보니까 빠르고 편해요
(2) ⓐ, 한국에서 살아 보니까 한국 생활이 재미있어요
(3) ⓑ, 부산에 가 보니까 생선회가 싸고 맛있었어요.
(4 ⓔ, 동생의 구두를 신어 보니까 작았어요

Unit 15. Purpose and Intention

01 V-(으)러 가다/오다

(1) 만나러 (2) 데이트하러 (3) 씻으러

02 V-(으)려고

(1) 한국 사람과 이야기하려고 (2) 한국을 여행하려고
(3) 한국에서 살려고 (4) 한국 회사에 취직하려고
(5) 한국 드라마를 보려고

03 V-(으)려고 하다

(1) 쓰려고 해요 (2) 공부하려고 해요
(3) 들으려고 해요 (4) 주려고 해요
(5) 치려고 해요 (6) 찍으려고 해요
(7) 하려고 해요

04 N을/를 위해(서), V-기 위해(서)

(1) 건강을 위해서 (2) 당신을 위해서
(3) 취직하기 위해서 (4) 만나기 위해서

05 V-기로 하다

(1) 사기로 했어요 (2) 끊기로 했어요
(3) 배우기로 했어요 (4) 공부하기로 했어요
(5) 하지 않기로 했어요

Unit 16. Conditions and Suppositions

01 A/V-(으)면

(1) ⓑ, 먹으면 (2) ⓒ, 출발하면
(3) ⓓ, 오지 않으면 (4) ⓐ, 가면

02 V-(으)려면

(1) ⓓ (2) ⓒ (3) ⓑ (4) ⓐ

03 A/V-아/어도

(1) 먹어도 (2) 반대해도 (3) 보내도

Unit 17. Conjecture

01 A/V-겠어요 ②

(1) 피곤하겠어요 (2) 한국말을 잘하겠어요
(3) 바빴겠어요 (4) 기분이 좋겠어요
(5) 일본 요리를 잘하겠어요 (6) 배가 고프겠어요

02 A/V-(으)ㄹ 거예요 ②

(1) 올 거예요 (2) 문을 닫았을 거예요
(3) 알 거예요 (4) 갔을 거예요
(5) 바빴을 거예요 (6) 잤을 거예요
(7) 걸릴 거예요 (8) 예쁠 거예요

03 A/V-(으)ㄹ까요? ③

(1) 돈이 많을까요 (2) 막힐까요 (3) 도착했을까요
(4) 바쁘실까요 (5) 돌아오실까요

04 A/V-(으)ㄴ/는/(으)ㄹ 것 같다

(1) 가족인 것 같아요 (= 가족일 것 같아요)
(2) 안 한 것 같아요
(3) 맑은 것 같아요
(4) 먹을 것 같아요. ('쉴 것 같아요', '잘 것 같아요' 등 '-(으)ㄹ 것 같아요'를 사용해서 대답 가능)

Unit 18. Changes in Parts of Speech

01 관형형: -(으)ㄴ/-는/-(으)ㄹ N

1 (1) 맵고 뜨거운 음식을 먹고 싶어요
(2) 볼 영화는 해리포터예요

2 (1) 매운 (2) 맵지 않은 (3) 재미있는 (4) 뜨거운
(5) 갈

02 A/V-기

(1) 우표 모으기 (2) 요리하기
(3) 회사에 가기 (4) 배우기

03 A-게

(1) 행복하게 (2) 맛있게 (3) 재미있게 (4) 예쁘게

04 A-아/어하다

(1) 귀여워요 (2) 좋아해요
(3) 배고파해서 (4) 추워해서

Unit 19. Expressions of State

01 V-고 있다 ②

(1) 쓰고 있어요 (= 끼고 있어요) (2) 하고 있어요
(3) 매고 있어요 (= 하고 있어요)
(4) 입고 있어요 (5) 입고 있어요 (6) 메고 있어요
(7) 들고 있어요 (8) 신고 있어요 (9) 신고 있어요

02 V-아/어 있다

(1) 써 (2) 열려 (3) 놓여 (4) 켜져 (5) 찾고
(6) 떨어져 (7) 쓰고 (8) 마시고 (9) 부르고
(10) 서 (11) 앉아

03 A-아/어지다

(1) 건강해졌어요 (2) 커졌어요 (3) 예뻐졌어요
(4) 시원해졌어요 (5) 빨개졌어요
(6) 적어졌어요 (7) 넓어졌어요 (8) 많아졌어요
(9) 높아졌어요

04 V-게 되다

(1) 들어가게 되었어요, 만나게 되었어요
(2) 끊게 되었어요 (3) 먹게 되었어요
(4) 가게 되었어요 (5) 저축하게 되었어요

Unit 20. Confirming Information

01 A/V-(으)ㄴ/는지

(1) 누구인지 (2) 몇 살인지 (3) 언제 한국에 왔는지
(4) 어느 학교에 다니는지 알아요 (5) 좋아하는지
(6) 없는지

02 V-는 데 걸리다/들다

(1) B 만드는 데 A 먹는 데 (2) 외우는 데
(3) A 치료하는 데 B 치료하는 데, 들어요
(4) 자르는 데, 들어요

03 A/V-지요?

(1) 쇼핑했지요 (2) 세일을 하지요 (3) 많았지요
(4) 샀지요 (5) 줄 거지요

Unit 21. Discovery and Surprise

01 A-군요, V-는군요

(1) 막혔군요 (2) 예쁘군요 (3) 유행하는군요
(4) 점심시간이군요

02 A/V-네요

(1) 싸고 좋군요 (2) 아름답군요/아름답네요
(3) 왔군요/왔네요 (4) 아프군요

Unit 22. Additional Endings

01 A-(으)ㄴ가요?, V-나요?

(1) 피곤한가요 (2) 걸리나요
(3) 언제 왔나요 (= 오셨나요) (4) 결혼할 건가요

02 A/V-(으)ㄴ/는데요

(1) 대단한데요 (2) 먹었는데요
(3) 없는데요 (4) 부는데요

Unit 23. Quotations

01 Direct Quotations

(1) "전화할게요."라고/하고 말했어요
(2) "지수 씨 전화번호 알아요?"라고/하고 물어봤어요
(3) "생일 축하합니다."라고 썼어요
(4) "항상 감사하세요."라고 쓰여 있어요
(5) "정말 마음에 들어요."라고 (말)했어요/하고 (말)했어요

02 Indirect Quotations

(1) 요코 씨가 어제 쇼핑했다고 했어요.
(2) 란란 씨가 빨간색 가방은 자기(의) 것이라고 했어요.
(3) 민우 씨가 언제 고향에 가(느)냐고 물어봤어요.
(4) 마틴 씨가 허리가 아프면 수영을 하라고 했어요.

03 Indirect Quotation Contracted Forms

(1) 같이 영화를 보재요 (2) 좋아하내요
(3) 안 좋아한대요 (4) 보고 싶대요
(5) 예매했대요 (6) 쇼핑하러 가재요 (7) 살 거래요
(8) 사래요 (9) 커플 티를 입재요
(10) 멋있는 커플이 될 거래요

Unit 24. Irregular Conjugations

01 'ㅡ' 불규칙 (Irregular Conjugation)

(1) 꺼 (2) 바빠서 (3) 커요 (4) 예뻐요 (5) 아파도
(6) 기뻤어요 (7) 썼어요 (8) A 고파요 B 고프지 않아요 (9) 예쁘지만

02 'ㄹ' 불규칙 (Irregular Conjugation)

(1) 부니까 (2) 우는 (3) 파는데 (4) 드세요
(5) 삽니다 (6) 힘들지만 (7) 아는 (8) 살 때
(9) 긴

03 'ㅂ' 불규칙 (Irregular Conjugation)

(1) 가벼워요 (2) 어려운데 (3) 추우니까
(4) 좁아서 (5) 맵지만 (6) 쉽고 (7) 입으니까

04 'ㄷ' 불규칙 (Irregular Conjugation)

(1) 물어 (2) 들으세요 (3) A 걸었는데 B 걸어서
(4) A 닫아요 B 닫는데

05 '르' 불규칙 (Irregular Conjugation)

(1) 빨라서 (2) 달라요 (3) 서툴러서 (4) 눌렀는데

06 'ㅎ' 불규칙 (Irregular Conjugation)

(1) 노란 (2) 빨개요 (3) 하얘요 (4) 이런
(5) A 어떤 B 까만

07 'ㅅ' 불규칙 (Irregular Conjugation)

(1) 부었어요 (2) 저어서 (3) 나은 (4) 짓고
(5) 웃을 (6) 나아요 (7) 그으면서 (8) 씻어서
(9) 벗은 (10) 부으세요

한국어의 개요

1. 한국어의 문장 구조

한국어의 문장은 주어+서술어(혹은 동사)로 구성되거나 주어+목적어+서술어(혹은 동사)로 구성된다. 단어 뒤에는 조사가 오는데 조사는 그 단어가 문장에서 어떤 역할을 하는지 나타내 준다. 문장의 주어 뒤에는 '이'나 '가'가 오고, 문장의 목적어 뒤에는 '을'이나 '를'이 오며, '에'나 '에서'가 오면 문장의 부사어가 된다. (참고: 3. 조사)

문장의 서술어는 항상 문장 끝에 오지만 주어, 목적어, 부사어 등의 순서는 말하는 사람의 의도에 따라 자리가 바뀌기도 한다. 그러나 자리가 바뀌어도 단어 뒤에 나오는 조사에 의해 무엇이 주어이고 목적어인지 알 수 있다. 또한 문맥 안에서 주어를 분명히 알 수 있는 경우, 주어가 생략되기도 한다.

2. 동사와 형용사의 활용

한국어의 동사와 형용사는 시제, 높임 표현, 수동, 사동, speech style 등에 따라 활용을 한다는 특징이 있다. 동사와 형용사는 어간과 어미로 구성되는데 동사와 형용사의 기본형은 단어의 의미를 지니는 어간에 '다'가 붙으며 보통 '사전형'이라고도 한다. 따라서 사전을 찾으면 기본형인 '가다, 오다, 먹다, 입다' 등의 형태로 되어 있다. 활용을 할 때는 어간은 변하지 않고 '다'가 빠지며 '다'의 자리에 화자의 의도에 따라 다른 형태가 붙는다.

3. 문장의 연결

한국어에서 문장을 연결하는 방법은 두 가지가 있다. 접속부사(그리고, 그렇지만, 그런데)를 사용해서 연결하는 방법과 연결 어미를 사용하는 방법이 있다. 접속 부사로 연결할 때는 문장과 문장 사이에 접속 부사를 넣으면 되지만 연결 어미를 사용할 때는 어간에 연결 어미를 붙여 문장을 연결한다.

4. 문장의 종류

한국어 문장의 종류는 크게 평서문, 의문문, 명령문, 청유문 4가지로 나뉜다. 문장은 발화될 때 장소와 대상에 따라 격식체와 비격식체(반말 포함)로 나뉠 수 있다. 격식체 '-(스)ㅂ니다'는 군대나 뉴스, 발표, 회의, 강의와 같은 격식적이거나 공식적 상황에서 많이 쓰인다. 비격식체 '-아/어요'는 일상생활에서 많이 쓰이는 존댓말의 형태이다. 격식체에 비해 부드럽고 비공식적이고 가족이나 친구 사이 등 보통 친근한 사이에서 많이 사용된다. 격식체의 경우 평서문, 의문문, 명령문, 청유문의 형태가 다 다르지만 비격식체는 격식체와는 달리 서술문, 의문형, 명령형, 청유형이 따로 없고, 대화의 상황과 억양에 따라 구분하여 비격식체가 격식체에 비해 간단하고 쉽다. 비격식체 중의 반말 '-아/어'는 친한 친구나 선후배 사이, 가족 사이에서 주로 쓰이고, 모르는 사이나 친하지 않은 사이에서 쓰면 실례가 된다. 여기에서는 격식체와 비격식체의 문장 형태만 보기로 하겠다.

(1) 평서문: 어떤 것에 대해 설명하거나 질문에 답을 할 때 사용한다. (참고: 1. 시제 02 현재 시제)

① 격식체: 격식체의 평서문은 어간에 '-(스)ㅂ니다'를 붙인다.

② 비격식체: 비격식체의 평서문은 어간에 '-아/어요'를 붙인다.

(2) 의문문: 질문할 때 사용한다. (참고: 1. 시제 01 현재 시제)

① 격식체: 격식체의 의문문은 어간에 '-(스)ㅂ니까?'를 붙인다.

② 를 붙이는데 평서문과 형태는 같고 문장의 끝만 올리면 의문 형태가 된다.

(3) 명령문: 명령을 하거나 충고를 할 때 사용한다. (참고: 7. 명령과 의무, 허락과 금지 01 V-(으)세요)

① 격식체: 격식체의 명령문은 '-(으)십시오'를 어간에 붙여 만든다.

② 비격식체: 비격식체의 명령문은 다른 문장 형태와 같이 어미 뒤에 '-아/어요'를 붙여도 되지만, '-(으)세요'가 '-아/어요'보다 좀 더 공손한 느낌을 주므로 '-(으)세요'를 사용하는 것이 좋다.

(4) 청유문: 제안을 하거나 어떤 제안에 동의할 때 사용한다. (참고: 12. 의견 묻기와 제안하기 03 V-(으)ㅂ시다)

① 격식체: 격식체의 청유문은 어간에 '-(으)ㅂ시다'를 붙여 만든다. '-(으)ㅂ시다'는 상대방이 말하는 사람보다 아래거나 비슷한 나이나 위치일 때 사용할 수 있고, 윗사람에게는 사용할 수 없다. 윗사람에게 사용하면 예의에 어긋난 표현이 된다.

② 비격식체: 비격식체의 청유문은 비격식체의 다른 문장 형태와 마찬가지로 어간에 '-아/어요'를 붙여서 만든다.

5. 높임 표현

한국은 유교적인 사고방식의 영향으로 나이, 가족 관계, 사회적인 지위, 사회적 거리(친분 관계)에 따라 상대를 높이기도 하고 낮추기도 한다.

(1) 문장의 주어를 높이는 방법: 문장에 나오는 사람이 화자보다 나이가 많을 때, 가족 중에서 웃어른일 때, 사회적 지위가 높은 사람일 때 높임말을 사용한다. 형용사나 동사 어간에 높임을 나타내는 '-(으)시-'를 붙여서 사용한다. 동사의 어간이 모음으로 끝난 경우 '-시-'를 붙이고, 자음으로 끝날 경우는 '-으시-'를 붙인다.

(2) 말을 듣는 상대를 높이는 방법: 말을 듣는 사람이 말하는 사람보다 나이가 많거나 사회적 지위가 높은 경우, 또 상대와 나이가 같거나 어려도 친분이 없는 경우에는 높임말을 쓴다. 종결어미에 따라 높임의 정도가 표현되는데 격식체, 비격식체가 그 형태이다.

(참고: 한국어의 개요 4. 문장의 종류)

(3) 그 밖의 높임법

① 몇몇 동사는 동사의 어간에 '-(으)시-'를 붙이지 않고 다른 형태의 동사로 바꿔서 높임을 표현한다.

② 높임의 의미를 가지고 있는 명사를 사용한다.

③ 사람을 가리키는 명사 뒤에 높임을 나타내는 조사를 붙인다.

④ 명사 뒤에 '-님'을 붙여서 사람을 나타내는 명사를 높인다.

⑤ 말을 듣는 상대나 행위를 받는 대상을 높일 경우 다음의 단어를 사용한다.

⑥ 말하는 사람이 듣는 상대를 높이지 않고 말하는 자신을 낮추어 상대를 높이는 방법도 있다.

(4) 높임법 사용 시 주의점

① 한국어에서는 누구에 대해 이야기하거나 그 사람을 부를 때 '당신', '너', '그', '그녀', '그들' 등의 표현을 쓰지 않고 이름이나 호칭을 여러 번 반복해서 쓴다.

② 나보다 나이가 많거나 사회적 지위가 높은 상대, 또는 모르는 사람의 이름이나 나이를 물을 때는 "성함이 어떻게 되세요?", "연세가 어떻게 되세요?" 등의 표현을 사용한다.

③ 윗사람의 나이를 말할 때 '살'을 쓰지 않는 경우가 많다.

④ '주다'의 높임말 '드리다'와 '주시다'

행동의 주체가 행동을 받는 상대보다 나이가 어릴 때는 '드리다'를 사용하고, 행동의 주체가 행동을 받는 상대보다 나이가 많을 때는 '주시다'를 사용한다.

준비합시다

01 이다

명사 뒤에 붙어 그 명사가 문장의 서술어가 되게 한다. 문장에서 주어와 술어가 동일함을 나타내거나 사물을 지정하는 뜻을 나타낸다. 격식체의 경우 서술형은 '입니다'이고 의문형은 '입니까?'이다. 비격식체의 서술형과 의문형은 '예요/이에요'로 형태가 같다. '예요/이에요.'는 서술형, 끝을 올린 '예요?/이에요?'는 의문형이다. 앞 명사가 모음으로 끝날 때는 '예요', 자음으로 끝날 때는 '이에요'를 쓴다. 부정형은 '아니다'이다. (참고: 2. 부정 표현 01 어휘 부정)

02 있다

1 존재나 사물이 위치하는 곳을 나타낸다. 영어로는 'be located in/on'의 뜻이다. 'N이/가 N(place)에 있다'의 형태로 쓰이는데, 이때 'N(place)에 N이/가 있다'처럼 주어와 장소가 바뀌어도 상관이 없다. 반대말은 '없다'이다. 'N에 있다'가 위치를 나타낼 때 이와 함께 사용하는 위치 명사로 다음과 같은 것들이 있다. ➡ 앞, 뒤, 위, 아래(=밑), 옆(오른쪽, 왼쪽), 가운데, 사이, 안, 밖

2 '있다'는 'N이/가 있다'로 쓰여 소유의 뜻을 나타내기도 한다. 영어로는 'have'의 뜻이다. 반대말은 '없다'이다. (참고: 2. 부정 표현 01 어휘 부정)

03 수

〈한자 숫자〉

한국어에서 수를 나타낼 때는 두 가지 방식이 있다. 하나는 한자 숫자이고 하나는 한국 고유 숫자이다. 그중 한자 숫자는 전화번호나 버스번호, 키, 몸무게, 방 호수, 연도, 월, 시간의 분, 초, 물건의 가격 등을 표시할 때 사용한다.

Check It Out!

① 한국어에서 숫자는 천(thousand) 단위가 아니라 만(ten thousands) 단위로 끊어서 읽는다. 그래서 354,790은 35/4970(35만 4970 → 삼십오만 사천구백칠십)으로 읽고, 6,354,790은 635/4790(635만 4790 → 육백삼십오만 사천칠백구십)으로 읽는다.

② 숫자가 1(일)로 시작할 때는 '일'을 생략하고 읽는다.

③ '16', '26', '36'…… '96'은 [심뉵], [이심뉵], [삼심뉵]…… [구심뉵]으로 발음한다.

④ '0'은 '공'이나 '영'으로 읽는데 전화번호나 휴대전화 앞 번호는 주로 '공'으로 읽는다.

⑤ 전화번호를 읽을 때는 두 가지 방법이 있다. 7804-3577 → 칠팔공사의[에] 삼오칠칠, 칠천팔백사 국의[에] 삼천오백칠십칠 번, 이때 '의'는 [의]라고 발음하지 않고 [에]로 발음한다.

〈한국 고유 숫자〉

한국 고유 숫자는 물건이나 사람을 셀 때 단위를 나타내는 명사와 함께 사용하는데 한국 고유 숫자 뒤에 '명, 마리, 개, 살, 병, 잔……' 같은 단위 명사를 붙여 사용한다. 이때 숫자 뒤에 단위 명사가 오면 '하나 → 한', '둘 → 두', '셋 → 세', '넷 → 네', '스물 → 스무'로 바뀌어 '학생 한 명, 개 두 마리, 커피 세 잔, 콜라 네 병, 사과 스무 개……' 같은 형태가 된다.

04 날짜와 요일

Check It Out!

① 6월과 10월은 '육월', '십월'이라고 하지 않고 '유월', '시월'이라고 읽고 쓴다.

② 연도를 물을 때는 '몇 년'이라 하고 월을 물을 때는 '몇 월'이라고 한다. 그렇지만 날짜를 물을 때는 '몇일'이라고 적지 않고 '며칠'이라고 적는다.

05 시간

- 시간은 '한 시, 두 시, 세 시, 네 시, 다섯 시, 여섯 시, 일곱 시, 여덟 시, 아홉 시, 열 시, 열한 시, 열두 시'와 같이 한국 고유 숫자로 읽고, 분은 '일 분, 이 분, 십 분……'과 같이 한자 숫자로 읽는다. 동작이 행해진 시간을 말할 때는 시간 뒤에 조사 '에'를 쓴다. (일곱 시에 일어나요.)

• A.M.은 '오전', P.M.은 '오후'의 뜻이지만, 한국에서는 보통 '오전'이라고 하면 '아침 시간'을, '오후'라고 하면 '낮 시간'을 이야기한다. 그리고 한국에서는 보통 '새벽', '아침', '점심', '저녁', '밤' 등으로 시간을 좀 더 세분화해서 말한다.

Unit 1. 시제

01 현재 시제 A/V-(스)ㅂ니다

한국어의 현재 시제는 격식체의 경우 어간에 '-(스)ㅂ니다'를 붙여 사용하는데, 격식체는 군대에서나 뉴스, 발표, 회의, 강의 같은 격식적이거나 공식적인 상황에서 많이 쓰인다.

02 현재 시제 A/V-아/어요

비격식체는 격식체에 비해 일상생활에서 많이 쓰이는 존댓말의 형태이다. 격식체에 비해 부드럽고 비공식적이고 가족이나, 친구 사이 등 보통 친근한 사이에서 많이 사용된다. 비격식체는 서술형과 의문형이 같다. 문장의 끝을 내리면 서술형이 되고, 끝을 올리면 의문형이 된다.

Check It Out!

〈현재 시제 형태의 특징〉

① 한국어의 현재 시제 형태는 현재뿐만 아니라 진행형, 그리고 분명히 일어날 미래 사건에도 사용할 수 있다.

② 보편적인 진리나 습관적으로 반복되는 사실도 현재 시제로 표현한다.

03 과거 시제 A/V-았/었어요

형용사나 동사 어간에 '-았/었-'을 붙여 과거형으로 만든다. 앞 어간의 마지막 모음이 'ㅏ, ㅗ'이면 '-았어요'를, 그 외의 모음일 경우에는 '-었어요'를 붙인다. '하다'로 끝나는 동사나 형용사는 '-였어요'가 붙어 '하+였어요'가 되고 이것이 줄어들어 '했어요'가 된다. 격식체일 경우는 '-았/었습니다', '했습니다'이다.

Check It Out!

'주다'는 '주었어요', '줬어요'로도 쓰이고 '보다'도 '보았어요', '봤어요'로도 다 쓰이지만 '오다'는 '오았어요'로 쓰이지 않고 '왔어요'로만 쓰인다.

04 미래 시제 V-(으)ㄹ 거예요 ①

미래의 계획이나 예정을 나타낼 때 사용하며 영어로는 'will, is going to'의 뜻이다. 동사 어간에 '-(으)ㄹ거예요'를 붙이는데 모음이나 'ㄹ'로 끝나면 '-ㄹ 거예요'를, 자음으로 끝나면 '-을 거예요'를 붙인다.

05 진행 시제 V-고 있다 ①

어떤 동작이 진행되고 있음을 나타내는 표현이며 영어로는 '-ing'에 해당한다. 동사 어간에 '-고 있다'를 붙인다. 과거의 어느 때에 동작이 진행되고 있었음을 나타낼 때는 동사 어간 뒤에 '-고 있었다'를 사용한다.

Check It Out!

단순히 과거에 했던 동작을 나타낼 때는 단순 과거 '-았/었어요'를 쓴다.

06 대과거 A/V-았/었었어요

과거에 일어난 일이나 상황이 그 후에 계속되지 않고 현재와 다를 때나 말하는 시점보다 아주 긴 시간 전의 일이어서 현재와 단절되어 있음을 표현할 때 사용한다. 영어로는 'did/had (in the past)'에 해당한다. 동사나 형용사 어간의 모음이 'ㅏ, ㅗ'로 끝나면 '-았었어요', 그 외의 모음으로 끝나면 '-었었어요'가 오며, '하다'로 끝난 동사는 '했었어요'로 바뀐다.

What's the Difference?

• -았/었어요: 단순한 사건이나 행동이 과거에 일어났음을 나타내거나 과거에 끝난 행위나 상태가 유지됨을 나타낸다.
• -았/었었어요: 현재와 이어지지 않는 과거의 사건을 나타낸다.

Unit 2. 부정 표현

01 어휘 부정

한국어에서 부정문은 그 문장을 부정 형태로 만드는 경우가 있고, 어휘로 부정을 하는 경우가 있다. 어휘를 사용해서 부정문을 만드는 경우에, '이다'는 '아니다'를, '있다'는 '없다'를, '알다'는 '모르다'를 쓴다. 이 중 '아니다'는 '이/가 아니다'의 형태로 쓰이는데, 구어체에서는 '이/가'가 생략되기도 한다. '아니다'의 경우 'N1이/가 아니라 N2이다'의 표현으로 쓰이기도 한다.

02 안 A/V-아/어요 (A/V-지 않아요)

• 동사나 형용사에 붙어 행위나 상태를 부정한다. 영어로는 'not'에 해당한다. 동사 앞에 '안'을 붙이거나 동사 어간 끝에 '-지 않아요'를 붙인다.
• '하다'로 끝나는 동사의 경우 '명사+하다'의 구성이므로 동사 앞에 '안'을 써서 'Noun 안 하다'의 형태로 쓴다. 그렇지만 형용사는 '안+형용사'의 형태로 쓴다. 다만, 동사 '좋아하다', '싫어하다'의 경우는 'N+하다'의 형태가 아닌 하나의 동사이므로 '안 좋아하다/좋아하지 않다', '안 싫어하다/싫어하지 않다'의 형태로 쓴다.
• '안'이나 '-지 않다'는 서술문과 의문문에는 쓰이지만 명령문이나 청유문에는 쓰일 수 없다.

03 못 V-아/어요 (V-지 못해요)

주어의 능력이 없거나 주어의 의지나 바람은 있지만 외부의 어떤 이유 때문에 의지대로 되지 않음을 나타내는 표현이다. 영어로는 'cannot'에 해당한다. 동사 앞에 '못'을 붙이거나 동사 어간 끝에 '-지 못해요'를 붙인다. 그러나 'Noun+하다'의 형태는 명사 뒤에 '못'이 와서 'Noun+못하다'의 형태로 쓴다.

What's the Difference?

• '안' (-지 않다): ① 동사, 형용사와 모두 결합한다. ② 능력이나 외부 조건에 상관없이 하지 않음을 나타낸다.

• '못' (-지 못하다): ① 동사와 결합하고 형용사와는 보통 결합하지 않는다. ② 능력이 안 되거나 가능하지 않을 때 사용한다.

Unit 3. 조사

01 N이/가

1 문장의 주어 다음에 와서 '이/가'가 붙은 말이 문장의 주어임을 나타낸다. 모음으로 끝나는 단어 뒤에는 '가'가, 자음으로 끝나는 단어 다음에는 '이'가 온다.

2 '이/가' 앞에 오는 말을 특별히 선택하여 지적한다는 뜻을 나타낸다.

3 문장의 새 정보를 나타내는 데 쓰인다. 즉 새로운 화제를 도입할 때 쓴다.

Check It Out!

'나, 저, 누구'와 '가'가 결합할 때, '나+가 → 내가', '저+가 → 제가', '누구+가 → 누가'가 된다.

02 N은/는

1 '은/는' 앞에 오는 말이 그 문장에서 이야기하려고 하는 주제, 설명의 대상임을 나타낸다. '~에 대해서 말하면'과 같은 뜻이다. 단어가 모음으로 끝나면 '는'이, 자음으로 끝나면 '은'이 온다.

2 앞에서 말한 것을 다시 이야기하거나 대화하는 사람이 이미 알고 있는 것을 이야기할 때 쓴다. 즉, 구정보를 나타내는 데 쓴다. (참고: 3. 조사 01 N이/가)

3 두 개를 대조하거나 비교할 때 쓰는데, 주어의 자리뿐 아니라 목적어나 기타 문장의 다른 자리에도 쓰일 수 있다.

03 N을/를

명사 뒤에 붙어 그 명사가 문장의 목적어임을 나타내 준다. 명사가 모음으로 끝나면 '를', 자음으로 끝나면 '을'을 붙인다. 목적격 조사를 필요로 하는 동사로는 보통 '먹다, 마시다, 좋아하다, 읽다, 보다, 만나다, 사다, 가르치다, 배우다, 쓰다' 등이 있다. 구어에서는 목적격 조사 '을/를'을 생략하고 말하기도 한다.

Check It Out!

① N+하다 → N하다: '공부를 하다, 수영을 하다, 운동을 하다, 산책을 하다 …….' 등은 조사 '을/를'을 생략하면 '공부하다, 수영하다, 운동하다, 산책하다……' 같이 하나의 동사가 된다. 그러나 '좋아하다' '싫어하다'는 '좋아-' '싫어-'가 명사가 아니기 때문에 '좋아하다' '싫어하다' 자체가 하나의 동사이다.

② 뭐 해요?: 의문 대명사 '무엇'이 줄어 '무어'가 되고 이것이 또 줄어 '뭐'가 된다. 그래서 '무엇을 해요?'가 '뭐를 해요?'가 되고, 이것이 다시 '뭘 해요?'로 되고, 이것은 다시 '뭐 해요?'가 된다. '뭐 해요?'는 회화체에서 많이 사용한다.

04 N와/과, N(이)랑, N하고

1 여러 가지 사물이나 사람을 나열하는 의미를 나타내며 영어로는 'and'에 해당한다. '와/과'는 주로 글이나 발표, 연설 등에서 사용되고, '(이)랑'과 '하고'는 일상적인 대화에서 사용된다. 모음으로 끝나는 명사에는 '와', '랑'을 사용하고 자음으로 끝나는 명사에는 '과', '이랑'을 사용한다. '하고'는 받침의 유무와 관계없이 쓰인다.

2 행위를 함께 하는 대상임을 나타내며 영어로는 'with'에 해당한다. 행위를 함께 하는 대상을 나타낼 때는 주로 '같이', '함께' 등과 자주 쓰인다.

Check It Out!

① 열거의 기능으로 쓰일 때 '(이)랑'과 '하고'는 마지막에 연결되는 명사 뒤에 쓰이기도 하지만 '와/과'는 마지막에 연결되는 명사 뒤에는 쓸 수 없다.

② '와/과', '(이)랑', '하고'는 동일하게 열거의 기능을 가지고 있지만 이들을 섞어서 사용하지 않는다.

05 N의

앞 단어가 뒤 단어의 소유가 됨을 나타내는 말로 영어로는 'of' 혹은 'Noun's'의 의미이다. '의'가 소유의 의미일 경우 '의'의 발음은 [의]와 [에] 둘 다 가능한데 보통 [에]로 발음을 많이 한다. 구어에서는 조사 '의'가 생략되는 경우가 많다. 사람을 나타내는 명사 '나, 저, 너'의 경우에는 '나의 → 내', '저의 → 제', '너의 → 네'로 축약되며 '의'가 보통 생략되지 않는다. 소유자와 소유물 사이에 '의'를 넣어 표시한다.

Check It Out!

한국에서는 자신이 소속감을 갖는 단체(집, 가족, 회사, 나라, 학교)에 대해서는 '나'보다는 '우리/저희'라는 말을 쓴다. 또한 가족 구성원에 대해서도 '제, 내' 대신에 '우리'라는 말을 많이 쓴다. 그러나 '동생'의 경우는 '우리 동생(our younger brother/sister)'보다는 '내 동생' 혹은 '제 동생'을 많이 쓴다. 상대방을 높여서 표현할 때는 '우리'의 낮춤말인 '저희'를 사용하여 '저희 어머니, 저희 아버지' 등으로 말한다. 그러나 '나라'를 이야기할 때는 '저희 나라'라고 쓰지 않고 '우리나라'라고 쓴다.

06 N에 ①

1 주로 '가다', '오다', '다니다', '돌아가다', '도착하다', '올라가다', '내려가다' 등의 동사와 결합하여 행동이 진행되는 방향을 나타낸다. 영어로는 'to'에 해당한다.

2 '있다', '없다'와 결합하여 사람이 존재하는 곳이나 사물이 위치하는 곳을 나타내는데 영어로는 'in' 혹은 'on'에 해당한다. (참고: 준비합시다 02 있다)

07 N에 ②

• 시간을 나타내는 명사와 결합하여 어떤 행동이나 일, 상태가 일어나는 시간이나 때를 나타내며 영어로는 'at' 혹은 'on'에 해당한다. 조사 '는', '도'와 결합하여 '에는', '에도'로 사용되기도 한다.

• 시간을 나타내는 단어 중 그제(그저께), 어제(어저께), 오늘, 내일, 모레, 언제 등에는 '에'를 쓰지 않는다.

Check It Out!

시간을 나타낼 때 시간 표현이 여러 번 겹쳐질 경우에는 마지막에 한 번만 '에'를 사용한다.

08 N에서

명사 뒤에 '에서'를 붙여서 어떤 행위나 동작이 이루어지고 있는 장소를 나타낸다. 영어로는 'at' 혹은 'in'에 해당한다.

Check It Out!

'살다' 동사 앞에는 조사 '에'와 '에서'를 둘 다 쓸 수 있는데 조사 '에'와 '에서'가 '살다' 동사와 함께 쓰이면 의미 차이가 거의 없어진다.

What's the Difference?

- 에: 사람이나 사물의 동작이나 상태가 나타나는 지점을 가리키므로 주로 이동, 위치나 존재를 나타내는 동사와 함께 쓰인다.
- 에서: 어떤 행위나 동작이 이루어지고 있는 장소임을 나타내므로 여러 가지 동사와 함께 쓰인다.

09 N에서 N까지, N부터 N까지

어떤 일이나 행위가 일어나는 장소나 시간의 범위를 표현하며 영어로는 'from ~ to/until ~'에 해당한다. 장소를 나타낼 때는 보통 'N에서 N까지'를 쓰고 시간의 범위를 나타낼 때는 'N부터 N까지'를 쓴다. 때로 이 둘을 구분 없이 쓰기도 한다.

10 N에게/한테

- 사람이나 동물을 나타내는 명사에 붙어서 그 명사가 어떤 행동의 영향을 받는 대상임을 나타낸다. '에게'보다 '한테'가 더 구어적 표현이다. 선행 명사가 사람이나 동물인 경우에는 '에게/한테'를 쓰고, 사람이나 동물이 아닌 경우(식물, 물건, 장소 등)에는 '에'를 쓴다. 모든 동사에 '에게/한테' 조사를 쓸 수 있는 것은 아니고, 제한된 동사에 사용하는데 '에게/한테'를 사용하는 동사로는 '주다, 선물하다, 던지다, 보내다, 부치다, 쓰다, 전화하다, 묻다, 가르치다, 말하다, 팔다, 가다, 오다' 등이 있다.

Check It Out!

① 친구나 동생같이 아랫사람에게 무엇인가를 줄 때는 '에게 주다'라고 한다. 그러나 '할아버지나 할머니, 아버지, 어머니, 선생님, 사장님'과 같이 높여야 할 대상에게 줄 경우에는 '에게/한테'를 '께'로 바꾸고 '주다'를 '드리다'로 바꾸어 말한다. (참고 한국어의 개요 5. 높임표현)

② 다른 사람에게서 무엇인가를 받거나 배울 때는 '에게서 받다/배우다' '한테서 받다/배우다'라고 한다. 이때 '서'를 생략하고 '에게 받다/배우다' '한테 받다/배우다'라고 쓰기도 한다. 높임의 대상에게서 받거나 배울 때는 '에게서', '한테서' 대신 '께'를 사용한다.

11 N도

- 주어나 목적어 기능을 하는 명사 뒤에서 쓰여 대상을 나열하거나 그 앞의 대상에 더해짐을 나타낸다. 영어로 'also' 혹은 'too'의 뜻이다.
- '도'가 주어 다음에 올 때는 조사 "은/는", "이/가"가 생략됩니다.
  마찬가지로 '도'가 목적어 다음에 올 때 역시 조사 '을/를'이 생략됩니다.
- '도'는 주격 조사, 목적격 조사 외에 다른 조사와 같이 쓰일 때는 '도' 앞의 조사를 생략하지 않는다.

12 N만

- 다른 것은 배제하고 유독 그것만 선택함을 나타낸다. 영어로는 'only, just'에 해당한다. 숫자 뒤에 붙을 경우 그 수량을 최소로 제한한다는 의미도 가진다. 다른 것을 배제하거나 선택하고자 하는 단어 뒤에 '만'을 붙여 사용한다.
- 조사 '만'은 문장에서 조사 '이/가', '은/는', '을/를' 등과 대치해서 쓸 수 있고 같이 쓸 수도 있다 이들 조사와 같이 쓸 경우 '만' 뒤에 '이', '은', '을'이 와서 '만이', '만은', '만을'의 형태가 된다. 그러나 '이/가', '은/는', '을/를' 이외의 조사 경우에는 '만'이 뒤에 와서 '에서만', '에게만', '까지만' 등의 형태가 된다.

13 N밖에

- 다른 가능성이 없고 그것이 유일하게 선택할 수 있는 경우임을 나타낸다. 영어로는 'only' 혹은 'nothing but'에 해당한다. '밖에' 앞에 오는 단어가 매우 적거나 작다는 느낌을 준다. 뒤에 반드시 부정 형태가 온다.
- 조사 '밖에' 뒤에는 항상 부정문이 오지만 '아니다'가 올 수 없고, '명령형', '청유형'도 올 수 없다.

What's the Difference?

조사 '밖에'는 조사 '만'과 비슷한 의미를 가지지만 '만'이 긍정문과 부정문이 모두 쓰이는 반면, '밖에'는 부정문과 쓰인다.

14 N(으)로

1 (어떤 장소 쪽으로의) 방향을 나타내는 조사이다. 영어로는 'to' 혹은 'toward'의 뜻이다. 앞의 명사가 모음이나 'ㄹ'로 끝나면 '로'를 쓰고, 그 외의 자음으로 끝나면 '으로'를 쓴다.

2 '이동 수단', '수단', '도구', '재료'를 나타낼 때도 사용한다. 영어로는 'by' 혹은 'with/using'의 뜻이다.

Check It Out!

이동의 수단이 명사가 아닌 동사일 때는 '-아/어서'를 사용하여 '걸어서, 뛰어서, 달려서, 운전해서, 수영해서 ……' 등으로 쓴다.

What's the Difference?

① '차로 왔어요'와 '운전해서 왔어요'는 어떻게 다를까?
: '차로 왔어요'는 차를 타고 왔는데, 그 차를 주어가 운전할 수도 있고 다른 사람이 운전할 수도 있는 경우 다 된다. 그렇지만 '운전해서 왔어요'는 반드시 주어가 운전을 해서 오는 경우이다.

② '○○(으)로 가다'와 '○○에 가다'는 어떻게 다를까?
: '○○(으)로 가다'는 방향성에 초점을 두어 그 방향을 향해서 가는 것을 나타낸다. '○○에 가다'는 목표점에 초점을 둔다. 그래서 이때는 방향성은 없고 오직 목적지만을 나타낸다.

15 N(이)나 ①

- 둘 이상의 나열된 명사 중에서 하나를 선택한다는 의미이다. 앞의 명사가 모음으로 끝나면 '나'를 쓰고 자음으로 끝나면 '이나'를 쓴다.
- '(이)나'는 주격 조사 뒤에서는 주격 조사를 '이/가'를 생략하고 '(이)나'를 쓰고, 목적격 조사 뒤에서도 목적격 조사 '을/를'을 생략하고 '(이)나'를 쓴다.

• '(이)나'를 조사 '에, 에서, 에게'와 같이 쓰는 경우에는 앞 단어에 '(이)나'를 쓰고 뒤 단어에 '에, 에서, 에게'를 쓰기도 하고, 앞에서 조사에 '(이)나'를 붙여 '에나, 에서나, 에게나'를 쓰기도 한다. 그러나 '(이)나'를 한 번 사용하는 것이 더 자연스럽다.

16 N(이)나 ②

수량이 기대하는 것보다 상당히 많거나 혹은 보통 사람들이 생각하는 일반적인 수준을 넘었음을 나타낸다. 영어로는 'as many as' 혹은 'no less than'에 해당한다. 모음으로 끝나는 단어 다음에는 '나'가 오고, 자음으로 끝나는 단어 다음에는 '이나'가 온다.

What's the Difference?

조사 '밖에'가 수량이 기대한 것보다 적거나 일반적인 기준에 미치지 못함을 나타내는 반면, 조사 '(이)나'는 수량이 기대한 것보다 많거나 일반적인 기준을 넘음을 나타낸다. 같은 수량에 대해 사람에 따라 그것이 기대보다 적다고 느낄 수도 있고, 많다고도 느낄 수 있는데 이때 '밖에'와 '(이)나'를 사용해서 표현할 수 있다.

17 N쯤

시간, 양(quantity), 숫자 뒤에 쓰여서 대략적인 것을 나타낸다. 영어로는 'about, around'에 해당한다.

Check It Out!

대략적인 가격을 말할 때 'N쯤이다'보다는 'N쯤 하다'로 많이 쓴다.

18 N처럼, N같이

어떤 모양이나 행동이 앞의 명사와 같거나 비슷함을 나타내며 'N같이'로 바꿔 쓸 수 있다. 영어로는 'like' 혹은 'as ~ as'에 해당한다.

Check It Out!

'처럼/같이'는 보통 동물이나 자연물에 비유해서 특징을 표현하기도 한다. 그래서 무서운 사람을 '호랑이처럼 무섭다', 귀여운 사람을 '토끼처럼 귀엽다', 느린 사람이나 행동을 '거북이처럼 느리다', 마음이 넓은 사람을 '바다처럼 마음이 넓다' 등으로 비유해서 말한다.

19 N보다

'보다' 앞에 오는 말이 비교의 기준이 되는 대상임을 나타내며 영어로는 'more ~ than' 혹은 '~er than' 에 해당한다. 명사 뒤에 '보다'를 붙여서 'N이/가 N보다 -하다'의 형태로 쓰는데 주어와 '보다'의 위치를 바꿔서 'N보다 N가 -하다'의 형태로도 쓸 수 있다. 보통 '더', '덜' 등의 부사와 함께 쓰이는데 이들은 생략이 가능하다.

20 N마다

1 시간을 나타내는 말에 붙어서 일정한 기간에 비슷한 행동이나 상황이 반복됨을 나타낸다. 영어로는 'every' 혹은 'once every'에 해당한다.

2 하나도 빠짐없이 모두를 나타낸다. 영어로는 'every' 혹은 'all'의 뜻이다. 명사 다음에 '마다'를 붙인다.

Check It Out!

① '날마다, 일주일마다, 달마다, 해마다'는 '매일, 매주, 매월/매달, 매년'으로 바꾸어 쓸 수 있다.

② '집'은 '집마다'라고 하지 않고 '집집마다'로 말한다.

Unit 4. 나열과 대조

01 A/V-고

1 두 가지 이상의 행동이나 상태, 사실을 나열하는 표현이며 영어로는 'and'에 해당한다. 동사나 형용사 어간 뒤에 '-고'를 붙인다.

2 선행절의 행동을 하고 후행절의 행동을 한다는 의미를 나타내며 영어로는 'and (then)'에 해당한다. 시제는 앞 문장에 표시하지 않고 뒷 문장에 표시한다. (참고 5. 시간을 나타내는 표현 03 V-고 나서)

Check It Out!

동일 주어로 두 가지 이상의 사실을 나열할 때는 'N도 Vst고 N도 V'의 형태로 쓰인다.

02 V-거나

동사나 형용사 뒤에 붙어 앞이나 뒤의 것 중에서 하나를 선택함을 나타낸다. 영어로는 'or'의 뜻이다. 보통 두 내용이 연결되지만 세 가지 이상의 내용을 연결하여 사용할 수도 있다. 동사나 형용사 어간 뒤에 '-거나'를 붙여 쓴다. 명사 다음에는 '이나'가 온다. (참고: 3. 조사 15 N(이)나 ①)

03 A/V-지만

선행절의 내용과 반대되는 내용을 후행절에서 이어서 말할 때 사용한다. 영어로는 'but'에 해당한다. 동사와 형용사의 어간 뒤에 '-지만'을 붙인다. 과거의 경우 '-았/었지만'을 붙인다.

04 A/V-(으)ㄴ/는데 ①

선행절의 내용과 반대되거나 대조되는 상황이나 결과가 뒤에 이어질 때 사용하며 영어로는 'but'에 해당한다. 형용사 현재일 때 어간이 모음으로 끝나면 '-ㄴ데', 자음으로 끝나면 '-은데'와 결합한다. 동사 현재, 동사 과거형과 '있다/없다'는 모두 '-는데'와 결합한다.

Unit 5. 시간을 나타내는 표현

01 N 전에, V-기 전에

'일정한 시간 전'이나 '어떤 행동 이전에'라는 뜻으로 영어로는 'before', 'ago'가 이에 해당한다. 'Time 전에', 'Noun 전에', 'V-기 전에'로 사용한다. 'Noun 전에'는 주로 '하다'가 붙는 명사와 쓰인다. 그래서 같은 뜻의 동사에 '-기 전에'를 붙여 써도 괜찮다(식사 전에, 식사하기 전에). 그렇지만 '하다'가 붙지 않는 동사는 '-기 전에'만 쓸 수 있다.

What's the Difference?

'1시 전에'와 '1시간 전에'는 어떻게 다를까?

• 1시 전에 오세요. (12시 50분에 와도 좋고, 12시나 11시에 와도 좋다는 뜻. 다만 1시가 되기 전까지 오라는 뜻)

• 1시간 전에 오세요. (약속 시간이 3시라면 1시간 전인 2시에 오라는 뜻)

02 N 후에, V-(으)ㄴ 후에

'일정한 시간 다음'이나 '어떤 행동의 다음'이라는 뜻으로 영어로는 'after', 'later'가 이에 해당한다. 'time 후에', 'N 후에', 'V-(으)ㄴ 후에'로 사용한다. 동사의 어간이 모음으로 끝날 때는 '-ㄴ 후에' 'ㄹ'로 끝날 때는 'ㄹ'을 삭제하고 '-ㄴ 후에', 동사의 어간이 'ㄹ' 이외의 자음으로 끝날 때는 '-은 후에'를 쓴다. '-(으)ㄴ 후에'는 '-(으)ㄴ 다음에'로 바꿔 쓸 수 있다.

What's the Difference?

'1시 후에'와 '1시간 후에'는 어떻게 다를까?

- 1시 후에 오세요. (1시 10분에 와도 좋고, 2시나 3시 혹은 그 이후에 와도 좋다는 뜻. 다만 1시가 넘은 다음에 오라는 뜻)
- 1시간 후에 오세요. (약속 시간이 3시라면 1시간 후인 4시에 오라는 뜻)

03 V-고 나서

- 하나의 행동이 끝나고 그 다음의 행동이 이어진다는 뜻으로 영어의 'do (something) after', 'upon finishing'에 해당한다. '-고 나서'는 "일을 하고 나서 쉬세요."를 "일을 하고 쉬세요."처럼 '나서'를 생략한 '-고'의 형태로 사용하기도 한다. 그렇지만 '-고 나서'가 '-고'보다 앞 행위가 끝났음을 분명하게 드러내 준다.
- '-고 나서'는 시간적인 순서를 나타내기 때문에 동사와만 쓸 수 있다. 그리고 선행절의 주어와 후행절의 주어가 같은 경우 '가다, 오다, 들어가다, 들어오다, 나가다, 나오다, 올라가다, 내려가다' 등의 이동 동사와 '일어나다, 앉다, 눕다, 만나다' 등의 동사에는 '-고', '-고 나서'를 쓰지 않고 '-아/어서'를 사용한다.

04 V-아/어서 ①

- 시간의 선후 관계를 나타내는 연결 어미로 앞의 행위가 일어난 상태에서 뒤의 행위가 일어남을 나타낸다. 이때 앞의 행위와 뒤의 행위는 아주 밀접한 관계에 있어서 앞의 행위가 일어나지 않으면 뒤의 행위도 일어날 수 없다. 영어로는 'and' 혹은 '(in order) to'의 뜻이다. '-아/어서'에서 '서'를 생략한 형태로 쓰이기도 한다. 어떤 동사의 경우(가다, 오다, 서다)에는 '서'를 생략하지 않고 사용한다. 어간이 'ㅏ' 또는 'ㅗ'로 끝나면 '-아서'를 쓰고, 그 외의 모음으로 끝나면 '-어서'를 붙이고, '하다' 동사일 경우에는 '해서'가 된다.
- 과거나 현재, 미래일 때 시제는 앞의 동사에는 쓰지 않고, 뒤의 동사에만 쓴다.

What's the Difference?

① 시간의 선후 관계를 나타내는 연결 어미 '-아/어서'와 비슷한 것으로 '-고'가 있다. '-아/어서'가 주로 앞의 행위와 뒤의 행위가 밀접한 관계에 있을 때 사용되는 반면, '-고'는 앞의 행위와 뒤의 행위가 연관성 없이 시간적인 선후 관계만을 나타낼 때 사용된다.

② 착용 동사(입다, 신다, 쓰다, 들다......)와 함께 쓸 때는 '-아/어서' 대신에 '-고'를 쓴다.

05 N 때, A/V-(으)ㄹ 때

동작이나 상태가 진행되는 때나 진행되는 동안을 나타낸다. 영어로는 'when' 혹은 'during'의 뜻이다. 명사로 끝날 때는 '때'를 쓰고, 동사의 어간이 모음이나 'ㄹ'로 끝나면 '-ㄹ 때', 자음으로 끝나면 '-을 때'를 쓴다.

Check It Out!

오전, 오후, 아침, 요일에는 '때'가 붙지 않는다.

What's the Difference?

'크리스마스에'와 '크리스마스 때'는 어떻게 다를까?

: 일부 명사(저녁, 점심, 방학……)는 'N 때'와 'N에'를 같은 의미로 쓰기도 한다. 그러나 크리스마스, 추석, 명절 …… 같은 일부 명사는 뜻이 달라지는데 'N에'는 그날 당일을 말하고 'N 때'는 그 날을 전후한 즈음을 말한다. 즉, '크리스마스에'는 크리스마스 날인 12월 25일에를 의미하지만, '크리스마스 때'는 크리스마스인 12월 25일을 전후하여 전날이나 다음 날 즉 그 즈음을 포함하여 말하는 것이다.

06 V-(으)면서

- 앞의 동사와 뒤의 동사의 행위나 상태가 동시에 일어나는 것을 나타낸다. 영어로는 'while'의 뜻이다. 동사의 어간이 모음이나 'ㄹ'로 끝나면 '-면서', 그 외 자음으로 끝나면 '-으면서'를 붙인다.
- 선행절의 주어와 후행절의 주어는 같다. 즉 같은 사람이어야 한다.
- 선행절의 동사와 후행절 동사의 주어가 다를 때에는 '-는 동안'을 쓴다.
- '-(으)면서' 앞에 오는 동사에는 과거, 미래 시제는 붙지 않는다. 항상 현재로 쓴다.

07 N 중, V-는 중

동작의 내용을 나타내는 명사와 사용하여 지금 어떤 행위를 하는 도중에 있음을 뜻한다. 영어로는 'in the process/middle of' 혹은 'currently doing'의 뜻이다. 명사 다음에는 '중' 동사 다음에는 '-는 중'을 쓴다.

Check It Out!

'-는 중이다'와 '-고 있다'는 비슷하게 사용한다. 그렇지만 '-고 있다'는 주어 제약이 없는 반면 '-는 중이다'는 자연물 주어는 오지 못한다.

08 V-자마자

- 어떤 사건이나 행동이 끝나고 바로 뒤의 행동이 일어남을 뜻한다. 동사의 어간 뒤에 '-자마자'를 붙인다. 영어로는 'as soon as' 혹은 'right after'의 뜻이다.
- 선행절의 주어와 후행절의 주어는 같아도 되고 달라도 된다.
- 선행절의 동사에는 시제를 표시하지 않고, 후행절의 동사에 표시한다.

09 N 동안, V-는 동안

- 어느 한 때부터 어느 한 때까지나 어느 행동을 시작해서 그 행동이 끝날 때까지 시간의 길이를 나타낸다. 영어로는 'during' 혹은 'while'의 뜻이다. 명사 다음에는 '동안' 동사 다음에는 '-는 동안'이 온다.
- 'V-는 동안'의 형태로 쓰일 경우 앞 동사의 주어와 뒤 동사의 주어는 같아도 되고 달라도 된다.

What's the Difference?

'-(으)면서'와 '-는 동안'은 어떻게 다를까?

: -(으)면서'는 한 사람이 두 개 이상의 동작을 동시에 할 때 쓴다. 그러나 '-는 동안(에)'는 선행절의 주어와 후행절의 주어가 다를 때에도 사용할 수 있다. 즉 선행절의 주어가 어떤 행동을 하는 시간에 후행절의 주어도 어떤 행동을 할 때도 사용할 수 있다.

- -(으)면서: 선행절과 후행절의 주어가 같아야 한다.
- -는 동안에: 선행절의 주어와 후행절의 주어가 달라도 된다.

10 V-(으)ㄴ 지

이것은 사건의 발생 시점으로부터 시간이 얼마나 지났는지를 나타낸다. 영어로는 'since'에 해당한다. '-(으)ㄴ 지 ~ 되다', '-(으)ㄴ 지 ~ 넘다', '-(으)ㄴ 지 ~ 안 되다' 등으로 사용된다. 동사의 어간이 모음이나 'ㄹ'로 끝날 때는 '-ㄴ 지'를, 자음으로 끝날 때는 '-은 지'를 붙인다.

Unit 6. 능력과 가능

01 V-(으)ㄹ 수 있다/없다

능력이나 가능성을 나타낸다. 능력이나 가능성이 있을 때는 '-(으)ㄹ 수 있다'를, 능력이나 가능성이 없을 때는 '-(으)ㄹ 수 없다'를 쓴다. 영어로는 'can'의 뜻이다. 동사의 어간이 모음이나 'ㄹ'로 끝날 때는 '-ㄹ 수 있다/없다'를 쓰고, 자음으로 끝날 때는 '-을 수 있다/없다'를 쓴다.

Check It Out!

'-(으)ㄹ 수 있다/없다'에 보조사 '-가'를 붙여 '-(으)ㄹ 수가 있다/없다'로 쓰면 '-(으) 수 있다/없다'보다 뜻이 강조된다.

02 V-(으)ㄹ줄 알다/모르다

- 이것은 어떤 행위의 방법을 아는지 모르는지, 또는 능력이 있는지 없는지를 나타낸다. 동사의 어간이 모음이나 'ㄹ'로 끝날 때는 '-ㄹ 줄 알다/모르다'를 쓰고, 자음으로 끝날 때는 '-을 줄 알다/모르다'를 쓴다. 영어로는 'don't know how to'의 뜻이다.

What's the Difference?

- -(으)ㄹ 줄 알다/모르다: 어떤 행위의 방법을 아는지 모르는지, 또는 능력이 있는지 없는지를 나타낸다.
- -(으)ㄹ 수 있다/없다: 어떤 일을 할 수 있는 능력뿐만 아니라 그 일을 할 수 있는 상황인지 아닌지를 나타낼 때도 사용한다.

Unit 7. 명령과 의무, 허락과 금지

01 V-(으)세요

- 듣는 사람에게 어떤 일을 할 것을 공손하게 부탁하거나 요청, 지시 혹은 명령할 때 사용하며 영어로는 'please (do)'에 해당한다. 이러한 상황에서 '-아/어요'로 표현할 수도 있지만 '-(으)세요'가 '-아/어요'보다 좀 더 공손한 느낌을 준다. 어간이 모음으로 끝나면 '-세요'를, 자음으로 끝나면 '-으세요'를 붙인다. 그러나 몇몇 단어의 경우 특별한 형태로 바뀐다. 격식체는 '-(으)십시오'를 사용한다.
- 명령을 나타내는 '-(으)세요'는 '이다'와 '형용사'에는 쓸 수 없고 동사에만 쓸 수 있다.

  그러나 몇몇 '하다'가 붙는 형용사에는 관용적으로 '-으세요'가 붙어서 사용되기도 한다.

02 V-지 마세요

- '-지 마세요'는 듣는 사람에게 어떤 행동을 하지 않도록 요청, 설득, 지시, 혹은 명령할 때 사용한다. 이것은 '-(으)세요'의 부정형으로, 영어로는 'Please, do not~'에 해당한다. 격식체는 '-지 마십시오'이다. 동사의 어간에 '-지 마세요'를 붙여 사용한다.
- '-지 마세요'는 '이다'와 '형용사'에는 쓸 수 없고 동사에만 쓸 수 있다.

03 A/V-아/어야 되다/하다

어떤 일을 꼭 할 의무나 필요가 있거나 반드시 어떤 조건이 필요하다는 것을 나타낸다. 영어로는 'must' 혹은 'have (to)'이다. 어간의 모음이 'ㅏ, ㅗ'로 끝나면 '-아야 되다/하다', 그 외 모음으로 끝나면 '-어야 되다/하다'가 오며, '하다'로 끝난 동사는 '해야 되다/하다'로 바뀐다. 과거형은 '-아/어야 됐어요/했어요'이다.

Check It Out!

'-아/어야 되다/하다'의 부정 형태는 할 필요가 없다는 의미의 '-지 않아도 되다'와 어떤 행동에 대한 금지를 나타내는 표현인 '-(으)면 안 되다'가 있다.

04 A/V-아/어도 되다

어떤 행동이나 상태에 대한 허락이나 허용을 나타낸다. 영어로는 'someone may do (something), be allowed to'에 해당한다. 어간의 모음이 'ㅏ, ㅗ'로 끝나면 '-아도 되다', 그 외의 모음으로 끝나면 '-어도 되다'가 오며, '하다'로 끝난 동사는 '해도 되다'로 바뀐다. '-아/어도 되다' 대신 '-아/어도 괜찮다', '-아/어도 좋다'로도 쓸 수 있다.

05 A/V-(으)면 안 되다

듣는 사람의 특정 행동을 금지하거나 제한함을 나타낸다. 그리고 사회 관습적으로 혹은 상식적으로 어떤 행동이나 상태가 금지되어 있거나 용납되지 않음을 나타내기도 한다. 영어로는 'someone may not do (something), not be allowed to'에 해당한다. 어간이 모음이나 'ㄹ'로 끝나면 '-면 안 되다'를, 'ㄹ' 이외의 자음으로 끝나면 '-으면 안 되다'를 쓴다.

Check It Out!

'-(으)면 안 되다'를 이중 부정하여 '-지 않으면 안 되다'로 말하는 경우가 있는데, 이것은 어떤 행동을 반드시 해야 한다는 뜻을 강조해서 표현하는 것이다.

06 A/V-지 않아도 되다 (안 A/V-아/어도 되다)

어떤 상태나 행동을 꼭 할 필요가 없음을 나타낸다. 어떤 행동에 대한 의무를 나타내는 '-아/어야 되다/하다'의 부정 형태이다. 영어로는 'does not have to'에 해당한다. 어간 뒤에 '-지 않아도 되다'를 붙이거나 '안 -아/어도 되다'로 표현한다. (참고 16. 조건과 가정 03 A/V-아/어도)

Unit 8. 소망 표현

01 V-고 싶다

말하는 사람이 원하거나 바라는 내용을 나타낸다. 영어로는 'want to'에 해당한다. 동사의 어간에 '-고 싶다'를 붙여서 사용한다. 주어가 1, 2인칭일 경우 '-고 싶다'를 3인칭일 경우에는 '-고 싶어 하다'를 쓴다. (참고 Check It Out!).

Check It Out!

① 주어가 3인칭일 때는 '-고 싶어 하다'를 쓴다. (참고 18. 품사 변화 04 A-아/어하다)

② '-고 싶다'는 형용사와 결합할 수 없으나 형용사 뒤에 '-아/어지다'가 붙어 동사가 되면 '-고 싶다'를 쓸 수 있다. (참고 19. 상태를 나타내는 표현 03 A-아/어지다)

③ '-고 싶다'는 조사 '을/를'이나 '이/가'와 모두 결합할 수 있다.

02 A/V-았/었으면 좋겠다

아직 이루어지지 않은 일에 대한 자신의 소망이나 바람을 나타낸다. 또, 현재 상황과 반대되는 상황을 바라는 마음을 가정해서 이야기할 때도 사용한다. 영어로는 'hope/want'에 해당한다. 어간의 모음이 'ㅏ, ㅗ'로 끝나면 '-았으면 좋겠다', 그 외의 모음으로 끝나면 '-었으면 좋겠다'가 오며, '하다'로 끝난 동사와 형용사는 '-했으면 좋겠다'로 바뀐다. '-았/었으면 좋겠다' 이외에 '-았/었으면 하다'도 사용되는데, '-았/었으면 좋겠다'가 소망과 바람을 더욱 강하게 표현한다.

Check It Out!

'-았/었으면 좋겠다'와 같은 뜻으로 '-(으)면 좋겠다'도 사용되는데 '-았/었으면 좋겠다'는 바람이 아직 이루어지지 않은 상태에서 이미 이루어진 상황을 가정하여 서술하기 때문에 동사를 강조하는 느낌이 있다.

Unit 9. 이유와 원인

01 A/V-아/어서 ②

- '-아/어서'의 앞에 오는 내용이 후행절의 이유나 원인을 나타내는 표현으로 영어로는 'because (of)', 'on account of' 그리고 'so... that...' 등에 해당한다. 어간의 모음이 'ㅏ, ㅗ'로 끝나면 '아서', 그 외의 모음으로 끝나면 '어서'가 오며, '하다'로 끝난 동사는 '해서'로 바뀐다. '이다'의 경우 '이어서'가 되지만 대화에서는 '이라서'로 많이 쓰인다.
- '-아/어서' 는 명령문이나 청유문에는 쓸 수 없다.
- '-아/어서' 앞에는 '-았/었-' 이나 '-겠-' 등의 시제가 올 수 없다.

02 A/V-(으)니까 ①

이유나 원인을 나타내는 표현으로 영어로는 'so' 혹은 'because'에 해당한다. 어간이 모음이나 'ㄹ'로 끝나면 '-니까'를, 자음으로 끝나면 '-으니까'를 붙인다.

What's the Difference?

- -아/어서: ① 명령문이나 청유문에는 쓸 수 없다. ② '-았/었' 이나 '-겠' 등의 시제가 올 수 없다. ③ 주로 일반적인 이유를 말할 때 쓰인다. ④ '반갑다', '고맙다', '감사하다', '미안하다' 등과 함께 쓰이는 인사말에 쓸 수 있다.
- -(으)니까: ① '-(으)세요', '(으)ㄹ까요?', '(으)ㅂ시다' 등 명령문이나 청유문이 올 수 있다. ② '-았/었-' 이나 '-겠-' 등의 시제가 올 수 있다. ③ 주관적인 이유를 말하거나 어떤 근거를 제시해서 이유를 밝힐 때 또, 상대방도 알고 있는 내용을 말할 때 주로 쓰인다. ④ '반갑다', '고맙다', '감사하다', '미안하다' 등과 함께 쓰이는 인사말과 쓸 수 없다.

03 N 때문에, A/V-기 때문에

- 후행절의 이유나 원인을 나타내는 표현으로 영어로는 'because'에 해당한다. '-기 때문에'는 확실한 이유를 표현할 때 쓰이며 '-아/어서'나 '-(으)니까'와 비교했을 때 문어체에서 주로 쓰인다. 앞에 명사가 올 경우 '때문에'와 결합하고 동사나 형용사가 올 경우 '-기 때문에'와 결합한다.
- '-기 때문에'는 명령문이나 청유문에는 쓸 수 없다.

What's the Difference?

- N 때문에: 아기 때문에 밥을 못 먹어요. (아기가 잠을 안 자고 계속 우는 등의 이유로 (내가) 밥을 못 먹어요.)
- 학생 때문에 선생님이 화가 나셨어요. (학생이 거짓말을 했어요. 그래서 선생님이 화가 나셨어요.)

Unit 10. 요청하기와 도움 주기

01 V-아/어 주세요, V-아/어 주시겠어요?

다른 사람에게 어떤 행동을 해 줄 것을 요청함을 나타내며 영어로는 'please/would you'에 해당한다. '-아/어 주시겠어요?'가 '-아/어 주세요'보다 상대방을 좀 더 배려하는 공손한 느낌의 표현이다. 도움의 행위를 받는 대상이 윗사람이나 공손하게 대해야 할 사람인 경우 '-아/어 드리세요'를 사용한다. 어간의 모음이 'ㅏ, ㅗ'로 끝나면 '-아 주세요/주시겠어요?', 그 외의 모음으로 끝나면 '-어 주세요/주시겠어요?'가 오며, '하다'로 끝난 동사는 '-해 주세요/주시겠어요'로 바뀐다.

Check It Out!

'-아/어 주다, 드리다'는 문장의 주어나 화자가 청자 또는 행위를 받는 대상에게 도움이 되는 행동을 할 때 사용하는데 도움을 이미 준 상태에서는 '-아/어 줬어요'나 '-아/어 드렸어요'가 쓰인다.

02 V-아/어 줄게요, V-아/어 줄까요?

다른 사람에게 도움을 주려고 할 때의 표현이며 영어로는 'shall I/let me/I will'에 해당한다. 행위를 받는 대상이 윗사람인 경우 '-아/어 드릴게요'나 '-아/어 드릴까요?'를 사용한다. 어간의 모음이 'ㅏ, ㅗ'로 끝나면

'-아 줄게요/줄까요?', 그 외의 모음으로 끝나면 '-어 줄게요/줄까요?'가 오며, '하다'로 끝난 동사는 '해 줄게요/줄까요?'로 바뀐다.

What's the Difference?

- -(으)세요: 단순히 명령하거나 듣는 사람을 위해서 어떤 행동을 할 것을 요구한다.
- -아/어 주세요: 말하는 사람을 위해 어떤 행동을 할 것을 요청한다.

Unit 11. 시도와 경험

01 V-아/어 보다

어떤 행동을 시도하거나 경험함을 나타내는 표현으로 영어로는 'try'에 해당한다. 어간의 모음이 'ㅏ, ㅗ'로 끝나면 '-아 보다', 그 외의 모음으로 끝나면 '-어 보다'를 쓰며, '하다'로 끝난 동사는 '해 보다'로 바뀐다. 보통 현재 시제로 쓰이면 '시도'를, 과거 시제로 쓰이면 '경험'을 나타낸다.

Check It Out!

'-아/어 보다'는 경험의 뜻을 나타낼 때는 동사 '보다'와는 결합하지 않는다.

02 V-(으)ㄴ 적이 있다/없다

- 과거에 어떤 행동을 경험한 일이 있고 없음을 나타내는 표현으로 영어로는 'have done/had'에 해당한다. 경험이 있을 때는'-(으)ㄴ 적이 있다'를 쓰고, 경험한 일이 없으면 '-(으)ㄴ 적이 없다'를 쓴다. 어간이 모음으로 끝나면 '-ㄴ적이 있다/없다'를, 어간이 자음으로 끝나면 '-은 적이 있다/없다'를 붙인다. '-(으)ㄴ 일이 있다/없다'도 같은 뜻으로 쓰이나 주로 '-(으)ㄴ 적이 있다/없다'가 많이 쓰인다.
- '-(으)ㄴ 적이 있다'는 '-아/어 보다'와 결합하여 '-아/어 본 적이 있다'의 형태로도 많이 쓰이는데 그 의미는 어떤 시도를 해 본 경험을 나타낸다.

Check It Out!

'-(으)ㄴ 적이 있다'는 항상 반복되거나 일반적인 일에는 쓰지 않는다.

Unit 12. 의견 묻기와 제안하기

01 V-(으)ㄹ까요? ①

말하는 사람이 듣는 사람에게 어떤 것을 같이 할 것을 제안하거나 의향을 물을 때 사용한다. 주어로는 '우리'가 오는데 보통 생략이 많이 된다. 영어로는 'Shall we~? Why don't we~?'가 해당한다. 대답은 청유 형태인 '-(으)ㅂ시다'나 '-아/어요'가 온다. (참고 12. 의견 묻기와 제안하기 03 V-(으)ㅂ시다) 어간이 모음이나 'ㄹ'로 끝나면 '-ㄹ까요?', 자음으로 끝나면 '-을까요?'가 온다.

02 V-(으)ㄹ까요? ②

듣는 사람에게 말하는 사람의 의견을 제시하거나 혹은 듣는 사람의 의견을 물어볼 때 사용하는데 주어는 '제가'나 '내가'가 되며 생략할 수 있다. 영어로는 'Shall I~?, Do you want me to do ~?'에 해당한다. 대답은 명령 형태인 '-(으)세요'나 '-(으)지 마세요'가 온다. 어간이 모음이나 'ㄹ'로 끝나면 '-ㄹ까요?', 'ㄹ' 이외의 자음으로 끝나면 '-을까요?'가 온다.

03 V-(으)ㅂ시다

어떤 일을 같이 하자고 제안하거나 제의할 때 사용하는데 영어로는 'let's' 혹은 'shall we'에 해당한다. '-아/어요'로도 말할 수 있다. 어간이 모음이나 'ㄹ'로 끝나면 '-ㅂ시다', 자음으로 끝나면 '-읍시다'를 붙인다. 한편, 어떤 것을 하지 말자고 제안할 때는 '-지 맙시다' 혹은 '-지 마요'로 말한다.

Check It Out!

'-(으)ㅂ시다'는 공식적인 자리에서 여러 사람에게 요청 · 권유할 때 사용하거나 상대방이 말하는 사람보다 나이나 지위가 손아래이거나 비슷한 경우에 사용할 수 있고, 윗사람에게는 사용할 수 없다. 윗사람에게 사용하면 예의에 어긋난 표현이 된다. 윗사람에게는 '같이 -(으)세요' 정도가 적당하다.

04 V-(으)시겠어요?

정중하게 상대방에게 권하거나 상대방의 의향이나 의도를 물어보는 데 사용한다. 영어로는 'Would you (mind/like to)...?' 혹은 'Why not...?'에 해당한다. '-(으)ㄹ래요?/-(으)실래요?'보다 상당히 격식적이고 정중한 느낌을 준다. 동사의 어간이 모음으로 끝나면 '-시겠어요?', 자음으로 끝나면 '-으시겠어요?'를 붙인다.

05 V-(으)ㄹ래요? ①

듣는 사람의 의견이나 의도를 물어보거나 가볍게 부탁할 때 사용한다. 구어에서 많이 쓰이는 말로 친근한 사이에서 많이 사용하며 '-으시겠어요?'보다 정중한 느낌을 주지는 않는다. 영어로는 'Want to...?' 혹은 'How about...?'에 해당한다. '-(으)ㄹ래요?'로 질문을 한 경우 '-(으)ㄹ래요', '-(으)ㄹ게요'로 대답할 수 있으며 '-(으)ㄹ래요?' 대신 '-지 않을래요? (안 -(으)ㄹ래요?)'로도 질문할 수 있는데, 부정 형태이지만 '-(으)ㄹ래요?'와 뜻은 같다. 친근하지만 좀 더 공손하게 말을 하고 싶으면 '-(으)실래요?'로 하면 좋다. 동사의 어간이 모음이나 'ㄹ'로 끝나면 '-ㄹ래요?', 'ㄹ' 이외의 자음으로 끝나면 '-을래요?'를 붙인다.

Unit 13. 의지와 계획

01 A/V-겠어요 ①

1 동사 뒤에 붙어서 말하는 사람이 어떤 것을 할 것이라는 의지나 의도를 나타낸다. 영어로는 '(I) will/am going to' 혹은 '(I) plan to'에 해당한다. 동사 어간에 '-겠어요'를 붙여 사용하며 부정 형태는 '-지 않겠어요' 나 '안 -겠어요'가 된다. '-겠어요'가 의도나 의지를 나타날 때 주어로 3인칭이 올 수 없다.

2 어떠한 일이 곧 일어날 것이라는 정보를 줄 때 사용한다. 영어로는 'should' 혹은 'will'에 해당한다.

Check It Out!

① 아래와 같은 상황에서 관용적으로 '-겠-'이 쓰인다.
: 처음 뵙겠습니다. 이민우입니다. / 잘 먹겠습니다. / 어머니, 학교 다녀오겠습니다.

② 말하는 사람의 생각을 단정적으로 말하지 않고 부드럽고 공손하게 말할 때 쓴다.

02 V-(으)ㄹ게요

- 말하는 사람이 자신의 결심이나 다짐, 의지를 상대방에게 약속하듯 이야기할 때 혹은 상대방과 어떤 것을 약속할 때 사용한다. 또한 말하는 사람이 무엇을 하겠다는 것을 말하기도 한다. 영어로는 'will'에 해당한다. 구어에서 쓰며 비교적 친한 사이에서 많이 쓴다. 동사의 어간이 모음이나 'ㄹ'로 끝나면 '-ㄹ게요', 자음으로 끝나면 '-을게요'를 붙인다.
- 주어의 의지를 나타내는 동사와만 쓸 수 있다.
- 일인칭 주어만 가능하다.
- 질문에는 쓰지 않는다.

What's the Difference?

- -(으)ㄹ게요: 듣는 사람과 관계가 있어서 상대방을 고려한 주어의 의지와 생각을 말한다.
- -(으)ㄹ 거예요: 듣는 사람과 상관없는 일방적인 주어의 생각이나 의지, 계획을 말한다.

03 V-(으)ㄹ래요 ②

- 말하는 사람이 어떤 일을 하겠다는 의지, 의향, 의사가 있음을 나타낸다. 구어에서 많이 쓰이는 말로 친근한 사이에서 많이 사용하며 정중한 느낌을 주지는 않는다. 영어로는 'be going to' 혹은 'will'에 해당한다. 의문형으로 쓰면 상대방의 의향을 물어보는 것이다. (참고 12. 의견 묻기와 제안하기 05 V-(으)ㄹ래요? ①) 동사의 어간이 모음이나 'ㄹ'로 끝나면 '-ㄹ래요', 'ㄹ' 이외의 자음으로 끝나면 '-을래요'를 붙인다.

  1 동사와만 쓸 수 있다.

  2 일인칭 주어만 가능하다.

Unit 14. 배경과 설명

01 A/V-(으)ㄴ/는데 ②

후행절에 대한 배경이나 상황을 나타내거나, 후행절의 소개에 대한 내용을 선행절에서 제시할 때 사용한다. 영어로는 'so/therefore' and 'and' 에 해당한다. 형용사와 결합할 때 어간이 모음으로 끝나는 경우는 '-ㄴ데', 어간이 자음으로 끝나는 경우는 '-은데'와 결합한다. 동사의 경우에는 '-는데'와 결합한다.

02 V-(으)니까 ②

- 선행절의 행위를 한 결과 후행절의 사실을 발견하게 됨을 나타낸다. 영어로는 'when' 혹은 '(do) only to discover'에 해당한다. 어간이 모음으로 끝나면 '-니까'를, 어간이 자음으로 끝나면 '-으니까'를 쓴다. 발견의 '-(으)니까'는 동사하고만 결합한다.
- 결과(발견)를 나타내는 '-(으)니까' 앞에는 '-았-'이나 '-겠-' 등이 올 수 없다.

Unit 15. 목적과 의도

01 V-(으)러 가다/오다

- 앞의 행동을 이룰 목적으로 뒤의 장소에 가거나 오는 것을 나타낸다. 영어로는 '(in order) to'의 뜻이다. 동사가 모음이나 'ㄹ'로 끝날 때는 '-러 가다/오다'를, 'ㄹ' 이외의 자음으로 끝날 때는 '-(으)러 가다/오다'를 쓴다.
- '-(으)러'는 항상 뒤에 '가다, 오다, 다니다' 같은 이동 동사와 사용한다.
- 앞 문장의 동사로는 '가다, 오다, 올라가다, 내려가다, 들어가다, 나가다, 여행하다, 이사하다' 같이 이동을 나타내는 동사를 쓸 수 없다.

02 V-(으)려고

- 말하는 사람의 의도나 계획을 나타낸다. 선행절의 행동을 할 의도를 가지고 후행절의 행동을 한다는 뜻이다. 영어로는 '(in order) to' 혹은 'so that'의 뜻이다. 동사의 어간이 모음이나 'ㄹ'로 끝날 때는 '-려고'를, 자음으로 끝날 때는 '-으려고'를 쓴다.

What's the Difference?

- -(으)러: ① '가다, 오다, 다니다, 올라가다, 나가다' 같은 이동동사와 사용한다. ② -(으)러 다음에 오는 동사에는 현재, 과거, 미래 시제를 다 사용할 수 있다. ③ -(으)ㅂ시다, -(으)세요'와 같이 쓸 수 있다.
- -(으)려고: ① 모든 동사와 사용할 수 있다. ② 뒤에 오는 동사에는 현재, 과거와 사용할 수 있지만, 의미상으로 볼 때 미래와 사용하면 어색한 문장이 된다. ③ -(으)ㅂ시다, -(으)세요'와 어울리지 않는다.

03 V-(으)려고 하다

주어가 어떤 일을 하고자 하는 의도나 계획이 있으나 아직 행위로 옮기지 않은 상태를 나타낸다. 영어로는 'plan to' 혹은 'intend to'의 뜻이다. 동사의 어간이 모음이나 'ㄹ'로 끝날 때는 '-려고 하다', 자음으로 끝날 때는 '-으려고 하다'를 쓴다. 한편 '-(으)려고 했다'는 '-(으)려고 하다'의 과거형인데 어떤 일을 계획했지만 그 계획이 실현되지 않았을 때 사용한다.

04 N을/를 위해(서), V-기 위해(서)

- 앞의 행위를 목적으로 뒤의 동작을 할 때 사용한다. 명사의 경우에는 '을/를 위해서'라고 쓴다. '위해서'는 '위하여서'의 준말인데 '서'를 빼고 '위해'라고 쓰기도 한다. 영어로는 'for the sake of' 혹은 '(in order) to'의 뜻이다. 동사일 경우에는 어간에 '-기 위해서'를 붙여

사용한다.

- '-기 위해서'는 형용사와 쓸 수 없다. 그러나 형용사에 '-아/어지다'가 붙어 동사가 되면 '-기 위해서'와 쓸 수 있다.

What's the Difference?

- -(으)려고: '-아/어야 해요', '-(으)ㅂ시다', '-(으)세요', '-(으)ㄹ까요?' 와 사용할 수 없다.
- -기 위해서: '-아/어야 해요', '-(으)ㅂ시다', '-(으)세요', '-(으)ㄹ까요?' 와 사용할 수 있다.

05 V-기로 하다

1 다른 사람과 약속한 것을 나타낸다. 동사의 어간에 '-기로 했다'를 붙여 사용한다.

2 자신과의 약속 즉, 결심, 결정을 나타낼 때 쓰인다. 동사의 어간에 '-기로 했다'를 붙여 사용한다.

Check It Out!

'-기로 하다'는 주로 '-기로 했어요/했습니다' 같은 과거형으로 쓰이지만 현재형인 '-기로 해요'로 쓰이는 경우가 있다. 이때는 대화에서 어떤 내용을 약속하자는 뜻일 경우이다.

Unit 16. 조건과 가정

01 A/V-(으)면

- 뒤의 내용이 사실적이고 일상적이고 반복적인 것에 대한 조건을 말할 때나, 불확실하거나 이루어지지 않은 사실을 가정할 때 쓴다. 영어로는 'if', 'when'의 뜻이다. 가정을 나타낼 때는 '혹시', '만일' 과 같은 부사와 쓸 수 있다. 동사의 어간이 모음이나 'ㄹ'로 끝나면 '-면', 자음으로 끝나면 '-으면'을 붙인다.
- '-(으)면' 앞에는 과거의 내용을 쓸 수 없다. 그리고 어떤 행동이 한 번 일어나는 경우일 때는 '-(으)ㄹ 때'를 쓴다.

Check It Out!

선행절의 주어가 후행절의 주어와 다를 때 선행절의 주어에는 '은/는' 대신 '이/가'를 쓴다.

02 V-(으)려면

'-(으)려고 하면'의 준말이다. 동사와 함께 사용하며 앞 문장의 동작을 할 생각이나 의도가 있으면 뒤 문장의 동작이 전제되어야 함을 나타낸다. 그러므로 보통 뒤에 '-아/어야 해요/돼요', '-(으)면 돼요', '-(으)세요', '이/가 필요해요', '-는 게 좋아요' 같은 문법 형태가 많이 쓰인다. 영어로는 'if you want to' 혹은 'if your intention is to'의 뜻이다. 동사의 어간이 모음이나 'ㄹ'로 끝나면 '-려면', 자음으로 끝나면 '-으려면'을 사용한다.

03 A/V-아/어도

- 선행절의 행동이나 상태와 관계없이 후행절의 내용이 나타냄을 뜻한다. 영어로는 'even if' 혹은 'regardless whether'의 뜻이다. 어간의 모음이 'ㅏ, ㅗ'로 끝나면 '-아도', 나머지 모음으로 끝나면 '-어도'를 붙이며 '하다'로 끝난 동사는 '해도'로 바뀐다.

Check It Out!

'-아/어도' 앞에 '어떻게 해도'의 뜻인 '아무리'를 써서 강조를 하기도 한다.

Unit 17. 추측

01 A/V-겠어요 ②

말할 때의 상황이나 상태를 보고 추측하는 표현으로 영어로는 'looks like', 'sounds' 혹은 'appears'에 해당한다. 동사와 형용사의 어간에 '-겠어요'을 붙여서 활용한다. 과거 추측의 경우 '-겠-' 앞에 '-았/었-'을 결합하여 '-았/었겠어요'가 된다.

02 A/V-(으)ㄹ 거예요 ②

- 근거가 되는 것을 보거나 듣거나 경험한 것을 바탕으로 말하는 사람의 추측을 나타내는 표현이다. 영어로는 'think' 혹은 'will'에 해당한다. 형용사와 동사의 어간이 모음이나 'ㄹ'로 끝나면 '-ㄹ 거예요', 자음으로 끝나면 '-을 거예요'를 붙인다. 과거 추측의 경우 '-(으)ㄹ 거예요' 앞에 '-았/었-'을 결합하여 '-았/었을 거예요'를 쓴다.
- 추측을 나타내는 '-을 거예요'는 의문문으로 쓸 수 없다. 의문문으로 나타낼 때는 '-(으)ㄹ까요?'를 사용한다.

03 A/V-(으)ㄹ까요? ③

아직 일어나지 않은 상태나 행동에 대해 추측하며 질문할 때 쓰는 표현이다. 영어로는 'I wonder if...?' 혹은 'Do you think...?'에 해당한다. 대답으로는 '-(으)ㄹ 거예요', '-(으)ㄴ/는 것 같아요'를 많이 쓴다. 형용사와 동사의 어간이 모음이나 'ㄹ'로 끝나면 '-ㄹ까요?', 자음으로 끝나면 '-을까요?'를 붙인다. 과거 추측의 경우, '-(으)ㄹ까요?' 앞에 '-았/었-'을 결합한 형태인 '-았/었을까요?' 쓴다.

04 A/V-(으)ㄴ/는/(으)ㄹ 것 같다

1 여러 상황으로 미루어 과거에 일어났다고 추측하거나 아직 일어나지 않은 상태나 행동에 대해 추측할 때 쓰는 표현이다. 영어로는 'looks/sounds like' 혹은 'appears that'에 해당한다. 형용사 현재와 동사 과거는 '-(으)ㄴ', 동사 현재는 '-는', 동사 미래는 '-(으)ㄹ'과 각각 결합한다.

2 화자의 생각이나 의견을 완곡하게 말하는 표현으로 강하거나 단정적으로 말하지 않고 부드럽고 공손하게 표현할 때 사용한다.

Check It Out!

- '-(으)ㄴ 것 같다'는 '-(으)ㄹ 것 같다'보다 좀 더 직접적이고 확실한 근거가 있을 때 사용하고 '-(으)ㄹ 것 같다'는 간접적이고 막연한 추측일 때 사용한다.
- 오늘 날씨가 더운 것 같아요. (사람들이 더워하는 모습을 보거나 자신이 밖의 더위를 경험하고 나서 말하는 추측)
- 오늘 날씨가 더울 것 같아요. (어제 날씨가 더웠으니 오늘도 더울 것 같다든지 하는 막연한 추측)

What's the Difference?

- -겠어요: 근거나 이유 없이 그 상황에서의 직관적이고 순간적인 추측
- -(으)ㄹ 거예요: 근거가 있는 추측으로 화자만 추측에 대한 정보를 가지고 있을 때 사용한다.
- -(으)ㄴ/는/(으)ㄹ 것 같다: 직관적이고 주관적인 추측으로 근거나 이유가 있을 때와 없을 때 모두 사용 가능하다. 어떤 것을 단정적으로 말하지 않고 완곡하게 말할 때 사용한다.

Unit 18. 품사 변화

01 관형형 -(으)ㄴ/-는/-(으)ㄹ N

동사나 형용사에 붙어 명사를 꾸며 주는 역할을 한다. 영어로는 'that' 혹은 'who'에 해당한다. 형용사 현재와 동사 과거에는 '-(으)ㄴ', 동사 현재에는 '-는', 동사 미래에는 '-(으)ㄹ'이 각각 온다. 부정형 현재의 경우 형용사는 '-지 않은'과 결합하고 동사의 경우 '-지 않는'과 결합한다.

Check It Out!

형용사를 두 개 이상 연결할 때는 마지막에 나오는 형용사만 관형형으로 바꾼다.

02 A/V-기

동사와 형용사 뒤에 붙어 명사로 만드는 역할을 한다. 영어로는 '-ing'에 해당한다. 문장 안에서 주어나 목적어 등 다양한 문장성분으로 쓰일 수 있다. 동사나 형용사 어간에 '-기'를 붙여서 명사형으로 만든다.

Check It Out!

'-기'는 몇몇 조사와 결합하여 문장에서 주어, 목적어, 부사어 등으로 쓰인다.

03 A-게

뒤에 나오는 행위에 대한 목적이나 기준, 정도, 방식, 생각 등을 나타내며 문장에서 부사의 기능을 한다. 영어로는 'in a ~ manner' 혹은 '-ly'에 해당한다. 형용사 어간에 '-게'를 붙여서 부사로 만든다.

Check It Out!

① 일반적으로 형용사의 부사형은 어간에 '-게'를 붙여 만드는데, '많다'와 '이르다'는 '많게', '이르게'보다는 '많이'와 '일찍'을 주로 쓴다.

② 부사로 만들 때 '-게' 형태와 또 다른 형태 두 가지를 다 사용하는 것도 있다.

04 A-아/어하다

- 일부 형용사 뒤에 붙어 그 형용사를 동사로 만드는 역할을 하는데 화자의 심리나 느낌이 행동이나 겉모습으로 표현된다. 영어로는 'appears (to be)' 혹은 'seems'에 해당한다. 어간의 모음이 'ㅏ, ㅗ'로 끝나면 '-아하다', 그 외의 모음으로 끝나면 '-어하다'가 오며, '하다'로 끝난 동사는 '-해하다'로 바뀐다.
- 형용사 어간에 '-지 마세요'가 붙는 경우 '-아/어하지 마세요'의 형태가 된다.

Check It Out!

'예쁘다', '귀엽다'에 '-아/어하다'를 결합한 형태인 '예뻐하다', '귀여워하다'는 아끼고 좋아한다는 의미이다.

Unit 19. 상태를 나타내는 표현

01 V-고 있다 ②

'입다, 신다, 쓰다, 끼다, 벗다' 등의 착용동사에 붙어 그러한 행동이 끝난 결과가 현재 계속되고 있는 상태임을 나타낸다. 영어로는 'is ~ing'에 해당한다. 같은 의미로 완료 상태를 나타내는 과거형 '-았/었어요'를 사용하기도 한다.

02 V-아/어 있다

동작이 끝난 후에 그 상태가 계속되고 있음을 나타낸다. 영어로는 'is ~ed/~ing'의 뜻이다. '열리다, 닫히다, 켜지다, 꺼지다, 떨어지다, 놓이다' 등의 피동사와 결합되어 사용되는 경우가 많다.

Check It Out!

① '입다, 신다, 쓰다 ……'와 같은 착용동사일 경우에는 '입어 있다, 신어 있다, 써 있다 ……'라고 하지 않고 이때는 '-고 있다'를 사용해서 '입고 있다, 신고 있다, 쓰고 있다'라고 한다. ② '-아/어 있다'는 목적어가 필요 없는 동사와만 쓴다.

What's the Difference?

- -고 있다: 지금 동작이 진행되고 있음을 나타낸다.
- -아/어 있다: 동작이 끝난 후에 그 상태가 계속됨을 나타낸다.

03 A-아/어지다

시간이 지나면서 어떤 상태로 변화함을 나타낸다. 영어로는 'become' 혹은 'turn'의 뜻이다. 어간이 'ㅏ, ㅗ'로 끝날 때는 '-아지다'를, 그 외의 모음으로 끝날 때는 '-어지다'를, '하다'로 끝날 때는 '해지다'를 붙인다.

Check It Out!

① 항상 형용사와 함께 쓴다. 동사와는 같이 사용하지 않는다.

② 과거의 어떤 행동 결과 변화된 현재의 상태를 나타낼 때는 과거형 '-아/어졌어요' 를 쓰고, 일반적으로 어떤 행동을 할 경우 변화된다는 뜻일 때는 현재형 '-아/어져요'를 쓴다.

04 V-게 되다

어떤 상태에서 다른 상태로 변화하거나 주어의 의지와 관계없이 다른 사람의 행위나 환경에 의해서 어떤 상황이 되었음을 나타낸다. 동사 어간에 '-게 되다'를 붙여 사용한다. 영어로 'became', 'came to (be/do)', 'has been decided'의 뜻이다.

Unit 20. 정보 확인

01 A/V-(으)ㄴ/는지

• 어떤 정보를 필요로 하는 문장과 뒤의 동사를 결합할 때 사용하는 연결 어미이다. 영어로 'who/what/where/when/how/whether+CLAUSE'라고 표현한다. 이때 뒤에는 주로 '알다, 모르다, 궁금하다, 질문하다, 조사하다, 알아보다, 생각나다, 말하다, 가르치다 ……' 등의 동사가 온다.
• 형용사 현재일 때 어간이 모음이나 'ㄹ'로 끝나면 '-ㄴ지' 자음으로 끝나면 '-은지'를 쓴다. 동사 현재일 때는 동사 어간에 '-는지'를 붙인다. 형용사나 동사의 과거일 경우에는 '-았/었는지'를 동사 미래의 경우에는 '-(으)ㄹ 건지'를 붙인다.

Check It Out!

'-는지'는 다음과 같은 여러 형태로 쓰인다.
① 의문사+V-(으)ㄴ/는지'의 형태
② 'V1-(으)ㄴ/는지 V2-(으)ㄴ/는지'의 형태
③ V1-(으)ㄴ/는지 안 V1-(으)ㄴ/는지'의 형태

02 V-는 데 걸리다/들다

동사 뒤에 붙어 어떤 일을 할 때 돈, 시간, 노력이 쓰이는 것을 나타낼 때 사용한다. 영어로는 'takes/requires/costs ... to (do)'의 뜻이다. 동사의 어간에 '-는 데 들다/걸리다'를 붙여 사용한다. 소요 시간을 나타낼 때는 '-는 데 걸리다' 소요 비용을 나타낼 때는 '-는 데 들다'를 사용한다.

03 A/V-지요?

화자가 알고 있는 사실을 청자에게 다시 물어서 확인하거나 동의를 구하기 위해 물어볼 때 사용하는 표현이다. 영어로는 'Isn't/Aren't……?' 혹은 'Don't/Doesn't……?'의 뜻이다. 형용사, 동사 현재일 때는 '-지요?' 형용사, 동사 과거일 때는 '-았/었지요?' 동사 미래일 때는 '-(으)ㄹ 거지요?'를 쓴다. 구어체에서 '-지요?'를 줄여 '-죠?'라고 말하기도 한다.

Unit 21. 사실 발견과 감탄

01 A-군요/-V는군요

자신이 직접 경험하거나 다른 사람에게서 들어 새롭게 알게 된 사실에 대해 그 상황에서 감탄이나 놀라움을 표현할 때 사용한다. 영어로는 'I see (that)', 'indeed', 'how' 혹은 'simply an exclamation point'에 해당한다. 형용사와 결합할 때는 '-군요'가 오고, 동사와 결합할 때는 '-는군요'가 오며 명사와 결합할 때는 '-(이)군요'가 온다. 과거의 경우에는 '-았/었군요'와 결합한다.

Check It Out!

'-군요'의 반말 형태로는 형용사일 경우, '-구나/-군'을 쓰고 동사일 경우, '-는구나/-는군'를 쓴다. 또, 명사일 경우는 '-(이)구나/(이)군'과 결합한다.

02 A/V-네요

• 자신이 직접 경험한 것을 통해 새롭게 알게 된 사실에 대해 감탄이나 놀람을 나타내거나 다른 사람의 이야기를 듣고 동의할 때 나타내는 표현이다. 형용사, 동사 어간에 '-네요'가 결합한다. 영어로는 'certainly', 'wow', 혹은 'My(!)'에 해당한다.

What's the Difference?

• -군요: ① 주로 책이나 글 등 문어체에서 사용한다. ② 자신이 직접 경험하거나 다른 사람에게서 들어 새롭게 알게 된 사실에 대해 감탄이나 놀라움을 표현할 때 사용한다.
• -네요: ① 주로 일상 대화에서 많이 쓰인다. ② 나의 직접 경험을 통하여 새롭게 알게 된 사실이 아닌 경우에는 쓸 수 없다.

Unit 22. 다른 종결 표현

01 A-(으)ㄴ가요?, V-나요?

상대방에게 친절하고 부드럽게 질문할 때 쓰는 표현이다. 영어로는 'Is/Were there...?', 'Is/Was it...?', 'Are/Were you...?' 혹은 'Do/Did you...?'에 해당한다. 형용사의 경우, 형용사의 어간이 모음으로 끝나면 '-ㄴ가요?', 자음으로 끝나면 '-은가요?'와 결합하고, 동사의 경우 동사 어간에 '-나요?' 를 결합한다.

02 A/V-(으)ㄴ/는데요

1 대화에서 상대방의 말에 대해 동의하지 않거나 반대되는 생각을 나타낼 때 사용한다. 영어로는 'well (in my case)'에 해당한다. 형용사의 경우, 어간이 모음으로 끝나면 '-ㄴ데요', 자음으로 끝나면 '-은데요'와 결합하고, 동사의 경우 '-는데요' 와 결합한다.
2 어떤 상황에서 상대방의 반응을 기다리거나 기대하며 말할 때 사용한다. 영어로는 '...and?' 혹은 '...but?'에 해당한다.
3 어떤 장면을 보면서 알게 되거나 느낀 사실에 대해 다소 놀랍거나 의외라는 뜻으로 감탄하듯이 말할 때 사용한다. 영어로는 '(I'm surprised to learn that...) is so...'에 해당한다.

Unit 23. 인용문

01 직접 인용

• 직접 인용은 글이나 생각 혹은 누군가의 말을 따옴표 (quotation mark " ") 안에 넣어 그대로 인용하는 것을 말한다. 따옴표 다음에는 '하고/라고 동사'가 온다. 질문을 할 때는 "무엇을 말했어요?, 무엇을 썼어요?"와 같이 '무엇을'이라고 하지 않고 '뭐라고'라고 한다. 즉, "카일리 씨가 뭐라고 말했어요?"와 같이 쓴다. '하고/라고' 다음에는 '이야기하다, 물어보다, 말하다, 생각하다, 쓰다' 등이 오는데 이와 같은 동사 대신 '하다' 나 '그러다'로 쓸 수 있다.

Check It Out!

① 따옴표 안의 말이 '하다'로 끝났을 때 뒤에는 '하고 했어요'를 쓰지 않는다. 또한 '하고' 다음에 오는 동사도 '하다'를 피하는 것이 좋다. 이는 '하다'가 여러 번 중복되면 어색하게 들리기 때문이다.

② 인용되는 문장 다음에 오는 '하고'와 '라고'는 같이 쓰이지만 약간의 뉘앙스 차이가 있다. '하고'가 붙은 인용 문장은 '라고'의 경우와는 달리 억양이나 표정, 감정까지 그대로 인용되는 느낌이 있다. 따라서 의성어나 동화 · 옛날이야기와 같이 생생한 느낌을 전달해야 하는 경우 '하고'가 쓰인다. 일상적인 대화나 글에서는 대체로 '라고'가 많이 쓰인다.

02 간접 인용

- 간접 인용은 글이나 생각 혹은 누군가의 말을 따옴표(quotation mark " ") 없이 인용하는 것으로, 따옴표 안의 문장의 종류, 시제, 품사 등에 따라 형태가 달라진다. 따라서 직접 인용보다 형태가 많고 복잡하다. 인용하고자 하는 문장의 형태를 바꾼 후 '-고'를 붙이고 '말하다, 물어보다, 전하다, 듣다' 등의 동사를 쓴다. 이때 이들 동사는 '하다'나 '그러다'로 대신할 수 있다.
- 청유형과 명령형의 간접 인용문의 부정형은 각각 '-지 말자고 하다', '-지 말라고 하다'가 된다.
- 1인칭의 '나/내' 혹은 '저/제'는 인용문에서 '자기'로 바뀐다.

Check It Out!

인용되기 전의 원래 문장이 '주세요' 혹은 '-아/어 주세요'로 끝나면 간접 인용문은 '달라고 하다', '-아/어 달라고 하다'나 '주라고 하다', '-아/어 주라고 하다'가 된다. 말하는 사람이 자신에게 해 줄 것을 부탁하는 경우에는 '달라고 하다'나 '-아/어 달라고 하다'가 되고 말하는 사람이 듣는 사람에게 제3자를 도와줄 것을 부탁하는 경우 '주라고 하다'나 '-아/어 주라고 하다'가 된다.

03 간접 인용 준말

간접 인용은 줄어든 형태로도 많이 쓰이는데, 보통 구어에서 많이 사용한다.

Unit 24. 불규칙용언

01 'ㅡ' 불규칙

어간이 'ㅡ'로 끝나는 동사나 형용사는 모음 '-아/어'로 시작하는 어미가 올 때 예외 없이 'ㅡ'가 탈락한다. 'ㅡ'가 탈락하고 나면 'ㅡ' 앞의 모음이 무엇이냐에 따라 뒤에 오는 모음도 달라진다. 즉, 'ㅡ' 앞의 모음이 'ㅏ, ㅗ'이면 'ㅏ'가 오고, 그 외의 모음은 'ㅓ'가 연결된다. 그리고 어간이 한 음절인 경우 'ㅡ'가 탈락하고 'ㅓ'가 온다.

02 'ㄹ' 불규칙

- 어간이 'ㄹ'로 끝나는 동사나 형용사는 예외 없이 'ㄴ, ㅂ, ㅅ' 앞에서 'ㄹ'이 탈락한다. 'ㄹ'로 끝나는 동사와 형용사는 '-으'로 시작하는 어미와 결합할 때 'ㄹ'이 받침으로 있지만 'ㄹ'은 자음보다는 모음으로 취급되어 '-으'가 오지 않는다.
- 'ㄹ'로 끝나는 형용사나 동사 다음에 '-(으)ㄹ 때, -(으)ㄹ게요, -(으)ㄹ래요?' 등과 같이 '-(으)ㄹ'이 올 때, '-(으)ㄹ'이 없어지고 어미가 결합한다.

03 'ㅂ' 불규칙

- 'ㅂ'으로 어간이 끝나는 일부 동사와 형용사가 모음으로 시작하는 어미를 만나면 'ㅂ'이 '오'나 '우'로 바뀐다. '아/어'가 올 때 '오'로 바뀌는 동사는 '돕다, 곱다' 두 개만 있고 다른 단어는 모두 '우'로 바뀐다.
- 어간이 'ㅂ'으로 끝나지만 '좁다, 입다, 씹다, 잡다' 등은 규칙 활용을 한다.

04 'ㄷ' 불규칙

- 어간이 'ㄷ'으로 끝나는 일부 동사 다음에 모음으로 시작하는 어미가 올 경우 'ㄷ'이 'ㄹ'로 바뀐다.
- 어간이 'ㄷ'으로 끝나지만 '닫다, 받다, 믿다'는 규칙이다.

05 'ㄹ' 불규칙

어간이 '르'로 끝나는 대부분의 동사와 형용사 다음에 모음 '아/어'로 시작하는 어미가 오면 '르'의 'ㅡ'가 탈락하고 'ㄹ'이 붙어 'ㄹ ㄹ'이 된다.

06 'ㅎ' 불규칙

- 어간이 'ㅎ'으로 끝나는 형용사가 뒤에 모음으로 시작하는 어미 앞에서 'ㅎ'이 탈락하는 현상이다.

1 'ㅎ' 형용사의 어간이 뒤에 '-으'로 시작하는 어미가 오면 'ㅎ'이 탈락한다.

2 'ㅎ' 형용사의 어간 뒤에 '-아/어'로 시작하는 어미가 오면 'ㅎ'은 없어지고 어간에 'ㅣ'가 덧붙는다. '좋다, 많다, 낳다, 놓다, 넣다' 등은 어간이 'ㅎ'으로 끝나지만 규칙 활용을 한다.

Check It Out!

'이렇다, 그렇다, 저렇다, 어떻다' 다음에 '-아/어'로 시작하는 어미가 오면 '이레, 그레, 저레, 어떼'가 되지 않고 '이래, 그래, 저래, 어때'처럼 활용한다.

07 'ㅅ' 불규칙

- 어간이 'ㅅ'으로 끝나는 일부 동사와 형용사 다음에 모음으로 시작하는 어미가 올 경우 'ㅅ'이 탈락한다.
- 어간이 'ㅅ'로 끝나지만 '벗다, 웃다, 씻다' 등은 규칙이다.

Check It Out!

한국어에서 모음이 겹쳐질 때는 대부분 축약을 한다. (배우+어요 → 배워요) 그러나 'ㅅ' 불규칙의 경우 'ㅅ' 이 탈락하고 나면 모음이 겹쳐지는데 이 경우에는 모음 축약되지 않는다.

Grammar Index